YEAR OF THE LORD'S FAVOUR

YEAR OF THE LORD'S FAVOUR

A Homiliary for the Roman Liturgy

VOLUME 2
The Temporal Cycle: Advent and Christmastide, Lent and Eastertide

Aidan Nichols, OP

GRACEWING

First published in England in 2012
by
Gracewing
2 Southern Avenue
Leominster
Herefordshire HR6 0QF
United Kingdom
www.gracewing.co.uk

ISBN 978 085244 792 5

Typeset by Gracewing

Cover design by Bernardita Peña Hurtado

CONTENTS

INTRODUCTION TO VOLUME 2

This Homiliary provides a comprehensive guide to doctrinally based preaching for the entire Church year, presented in the Dominican tradition: a preaching of Scripture which takes doctrine as guide to the clarification of the Bible's main themes. Doctrine is necessary to preachers because in its absence the Scriptural claims and themes do not easily hang together.

The homilies presented here are in the Dominican tradition of doctrinal preaching: a preaching of Scripture which takes doctrine as guide to the clarification of the Bible's main lines. Without doctrine, we should find it more difficult to see the biblical wood for the profusion of the Scriptural trees. Doctrine is necessary to preachers because in its absence the Scriptural claims and themes do not hang together. They do not of their own accord organize themselves into a religion a person can live by: a coherent vision of truth, and a picture of human excellence that is imitable because it makes sense as a whole. Where doctrine is not permitted to serve this purpose, we can be sure that some other scheme of thought will be brought in to do the job instead. That is when theology becomes ideology, rather than a service to the Word of God in the message of the Church.

The grace the Word imparts always has a reference to the Mystical Body which mediates all the grace that is given by Christ as the Head. So, precisely as a fruit of grace, preaching is necessarily related to ecclesial awareness. Doctrine ensures that preaching does not fall short of its true dimensions—expressing the biblical revelation, the faith of the Church. This second volume furnishes texts for the Privileged Seasons—Advent, Christmastide, Lent and Eastertide.

ADVENT

THE FIRST WEEK OF ADVENT

First Sunday of Advent (Year A)

Christians are not the only people who have ever celebrated Advent, the time when we make ourselves sit up and listen out for the coming, the *adventus*, of our God. In the pagan world the Church converted, they knew about Advent — in some sense. They spoke of the *adventus*, the *parousia*, as the day each year when the god entered his temple in the form of a statue or image, to dwell there on his feast. The god's presence wasn't tangible, after all, without his image. When the day came, amid great festivity and rejoicing, earth and sky, men and the gods, all seemed to belong together in a great unity.

By contrast, as Christians we recall not the coming of God to be present in a cultic image, but his coming to us *as man*. We recall his coming not into a temple of stones but into the living temple of our human flesh. And we recall that coming in order to prepare for Christmas, the feast day of Christ, when we shall adore the Child of Bethlehem, the incarnated or humanized divine Word, as the Lord of all.

We don't, however, recall Christ's coming simply as an extraordinary thing that happened a very long time ago. In the Liturgy we can't remember Christ in that sort of way because the worship of the Church, simply by its celebration, actually involves us in a relation with him. The Church only prays *as Church* by sharing in the prayer of Christ before the Father as he makes it right now. It is his prayer before it is hers, just as it is hers before it is ours. In Advent, as in other seasons, the chief actor in the Liturgy is our great High Priest himself, living in the Father's glory, the Christ who is now hidden to history, hidden to the cosmos, yet more powerful than ever before since he is living totally in God and for us.

In the Advent season, we put ourselves into the shoes of the ancient prophets waiting for God's salvation to dawn. But more profoundly, in the certainty of the Lord who has already appeared on earth we are preparing ourselves for a future meeting with him.

We use the ancient prophecies to form our sense of expectation for him, but in the Advent Liturgy he is really bringing us closer to the threshold of his *second* coming, his conclusive coming. Every year that passes brings the human race closer to that final coming after which God will be all in all.

So Advent is the Lord of the Church giving us a practice-run, a dress-rehearsal, for the end of time. And what are we asked to do with the here-and-now by way of preparation for the End? That extraordinary priest Angelus Silesius who tramped the roads of seventeenth century Germany like a vagabond but wrote poetry so beautiful people called him the 'Cherubinic Wanderer', had an answer. It is to let Christ be born not in Mary (that has already happened) but in our own lives. 'Christ may be born in Bethlehem a thousand times, but if he is not born in you, you are for ever lost'. St Bernard had said the same thing centuries before. 'Christ must be born in you; you must become Bethlehem of Judah'. He will be born in us if we accept that we need him.

My novice-master, Father Geoffrey Preston, used to say, 'When God visits, he doesn't just say, "Hello"'. Geoffrey meant: he comes to transform us, not without suffering, into the fullness of joy of his own ever-blessed life.

First Sunday of Advent (Year B)

Advent begins with the words of Jesus to his disciples, 'Stay awake'. This command does not seem at all self-explanatory. Is it rather odd that the Church troubled to register it, pass it down and, through the centuries, have it read out at the start of this significant season? The evangelist Mark evidently didn't think so, because in his Gospel he makes these words the last words of any consequence Jesus utters before his Passion.

What do they mean? We can rule out of court one interpretation straight away. There is no reason to think our Lord had a Puritan distaste for staying in bed. This is not a tirade against heavy sleepers. On the whole, sleep is highly regarded in the Bible and in Christian tradition. Dreams play a large part in the biblical narrative and often in the lives of the saints too. They are possible carriers of divine influence: a sub-conscious part of you might accept something a conscious part is resisting. The idea of Purgatory is, among other things, the notion of a healing sleep. The Roman Canon calls the souls in Purgatory those who 'sleep the sleep of peace'. And in everyday life, the Office of Compline sees the ability to go to sleep without tension or anxiety as a gift of God. And so on. 'Stay awake' is not, then, the opposite of 'Go to sleep'.

Another translation of the text of the New Testament here might be 'Keep alert, stay keen-minded'. Various religious traditions— Zen, for example—are concerned with teaching people how to discipline themselves to attend more to the realities around them. The spiritual person is the person who takes things in, and is alert to the implications of their actions. If we walk around with our heads full of a confused blur of half-formulated thoughts and semi-articulated emotions, we are likely to miss out on a lot, exteriorly and interiorly too.

But in this case the keeping awake, the vigilance, would be a general ethical quality which the Lord was encouraging us to develop. It would be like saying: Be just, be kind, be forgiving. Certainly, that sort of general moral precept has its place in the teaching of Jesus. Without morality there is no human life worthy of the name. We should all be beasts, not to say rats. And yet the centre of his preaching was never morality for its own sake. He proclaimed not some thing but some one. He proclaimed that the Father in his altogether amazing love and mercy was drawing close to mankind; that he was about to send his Spirit on all flesh; and that he himself, Jesus, the beloved Son, would play a crucial role in bringing this about. His message is, then, centrally about someone (if I may repeat myself here). It is about getting ready for an encounter. So: 'Stay awake' means 'Get ready for him'. He is coming, so don't get drowsy or you may miss his visitation. And this is in fact what Advent is all about. He is at the gates, he has nearly made it. Open your heart and he will gain entrance there.

Now the timing of just when God is going to take possession of human history as a whole is not our personal affair. The Second Coming is not our responsibility. But at least we can get our own house into order. We can offer our own will, our own mind, our own body, as a place for God to enter. The risen Christ says in the Apocalypse, 'Behold, I stand at the door and knock. If any man hears my voice and opens to me, I shall go in and sup with him and he with me'. In Advent, more than at any other time in the year, we consciously listen out for that knock, the knock of someone. Christ our hope and joy, our peace, righteousness and sanctification is coming, and with him he brings the Father and the Holy Spirit.

The First Sunday of Advent (Year C)

'Your liberation is near at hand': words of Jesus to his disciples somewhere about the time of his death. To all appearances, this is one of the great unfulfilled prophecies. What reason is there to think that people after the year 30 AD or thereabouts became more 'liberated' in any obvious sense we could give that word? What reason is there to think, come to that, that people ever will be 'liberated' in any total sense? Unless we are very naïve, or have been reading the doctrinaire philosophies of history Western Europe produced between the Age of Enlightenment and the First World War, we probably share an intuitive sense that human life is a bit of a mess, as much a burden as a privilege, and is always going to be like that, one way or another. The three main ways the word 'liberation' has been taken tend to confirm this.

The first way of taking the word 'liberation' is liberation from death, from mortality. No matter what you achieve, or what kind of person you become, death will one day smother you and your works, and most likely even the memory of you will disappear. We shall fall from the tree of life like withered leaves in the November air. To give this proposition real assent is an oppressive thought. Not surprisingly, poets, philosophers and the common man have expressed the desire to be freed from death and corruption. We can call this a desire for physical liberation.

A second way of seeing liberation would be as liberation from guilt, from the shadow of moral blame. Leaving aside the case of those who get all worked up about things they couldn't help, there is such a thing as rational guilt. I look at the occasional misery I cause others and I say, I have done that which I ought not to have done, and I have failed to do that which I might and should have done, and, so I am tempted to add in the spirit of Thomas

Cranmer's Prayer Book, 'there is no health in [me]'. We identify the behaviour patterns by which we diminish others and feel trapped by them. Perhaps they go back into adolescence, child-hood, babyhood, even pre-natal life in the womb. How can I be freed from my past, which in a certain sense means from myself? We can call this a desire for moral liberation.

Thirdly, we can see liberation in political and social terms. States are not infrequently instruments of organized oppression, but let's not blame them for everything. Civil society is itself often an instrument of unorganized oppression: racial, religious, sexual, cultural, economic, disabilities do not always yield to public policies or legal arrangements. People construct blueprints for a better future but revolutions have a habit of generating new kinds of oppression. Someone called the French Revolution the simulta-neous incarnation of freedom and terror. The virtues of a counter-order when in opposition tend to become its vices when in power. The desire to escape this law of history can be called the desire for political and social liberation.

Some scholars, studying the Gospels, conclude that the libera-tion Jesus was talking about included all these dimensions — physical liberation, moral liberation, political and social liberation, because, after all, each and every one of them was part and parcel of Israel's Messianic hope. Jesus, they say, held his life's mission to be the instrument for bringing into the present the Age to Come when all these shackles would be swept away. But liberation was not at hand. The confrontation with the powers-that-be and with his own destiny that was involved in his decision to 'go up to Jerusalem' did not in fact change the world. His expectations were built on sand.

This scheme wholly fails to do justice to his originality. He did not simply take Old Testament ideas and apply them as they stood. He gave a creative turn to everything he touched. The Jews were expecting a mighty Messiah, he spoke about a suffering Messiah. The Jews said God was the Father of Israel; he spoke of the *Abba*, the 'dear Father', of a multitude of brethren. And so likewise here. The Jews hoped for physical, moral and political liberation; he spoke of a liberation to be brought about in his sacrificial Death which would transform root-and-branch the relation between God and ourselves. Deeper than mortality or morality or matters of State, God and man were to enjoy a new intimacy, a new friendship, a new communion. This is the fundamental claim of the apostolic writers: 'neither death, nor life, no prince, nothing that exists, nothing still to come, not any power, or height or depth, nor any created thing, can ever come between us and the love of God made visible in Christ Jesus our Lord'. These are words of the apostle Paul.

In the humanity of the incarnate Word, God took hold of this world in a new way. He had an instrument which enabled him to be with us for the first time as he truly wants to be. In the Incarnation, he provided for the existence of a human being whose spirit was the perfect medium for the Holy Spirit and whose Sacrifice set the Holy Spirit free into this world, to furnish people with a share in the uncreated life and love of God himself.

Does this mean, then, that Christianity has nothing to say about those other kinds of liberation: physical, moral, political? It means that these dimensions are not to be mentioned first. In the first place, we must respond to the Gospel in its own terms, in terms of its own unique offer: the gift of grace, of communion with the Holy Trinity, a new mode of being for us that needs for its expression a language which is not just a series of metaphors for something that might happen to physical nature, to morality, or to political society.

But in the second place, our redemption does indeed have implications for all these vital dimensions of human living. It does mean, in biology, deathless life; it does mean in morals forgiveness and newness of life; it does mean in politics brotherhood and sisterhood, a new quality of common life with particular attention to those who have suffered most, the poor and unfortunate.

The shared term here is the word 'life'. As our Lord had occasion to remark in controversy with the Sadducees, God is the God of the living. What we can call the 'pro-life' battle, which goes beyond the question of abortion, though certainly the aborted are the most unfortunate of all, is still being fought by the Church, yet in principle the battle is already won, for the Spirit of the Father and the Son has been poured out to renew the face of the earth. In the helpful comparison often drawn: the Allies invaded Occupied France on D-Day. Blood, tears and sweat separated D-Day from

V-Day, the day of victory and peace. But in retrospect it was on D-Day that the War was won. Just so the cosmic battle between Life and the enemies of life was won on the Cross of Christ.

In Advent we remember the birth of the Child whose life and death won that victory and we look forward in hope to the completion of his reign.

The First Monday of Advent

The distinctive feeling of the season of Advent is subdued joy, because we are awaiting the blessed hope of the coming of our King: expecting it liturgically at Christmas, expecting it in full reality at the Parousia.

But what would a King be without a Kingdom? This is what the readings of this first feria of Advent ask us to ponder.

Blessed John Henry Newman, thanks to his Anglican Evangelical background, was soaked in Scripture. He came to the Catholic Church because he saw in her the realization of the promise of Scripture: there would be a universal Kingdom to which many would come, 'from North and South, East and West', as today's Gospel says, to claim their citizenship thanks to their faith in Jesus Christ.

We have today, in contrast with biblical times or Newman's own, something of a tendency to remove from the Church these vast dimensions and cut her down to sociological size. People emphasise the parochial church or the national church, and think less of the universal Church of all peoples, cultures, and epochs. Yet when we were baptized, we were not just admitted into a local society. We were admitted into a world-wide communion, and indeed into the whole Church of the First-born which knows no limitation of either time or space.

If we forget that and think of the Church as only Father X's parish, or the diocese of Y, or the contents of this year's *Catholic Directory for England and Wales* is it surprising that, when disappointments or scandals come (as Scripture tells us, come they must), we are tempted to fall away?

But no, we can't separate the Church from the Kingdom of which she is the initial realization. She is one of the mysteries we give thanks for each time we recite the Creed. Here is the City set on a hill to which all the nations are coming, because it makes present on earth the divine Kingdom of truth and holiness.

Without his kingdom, what would a king be?

The First Tuesday of Advent

'Blessed are the eyes that see what you see', our Lord tells the disciples, and in the form in which St Matthew preserves this saying he adds, 'and the ears that hear what you hear'. St Thomas Aquinas says that sight and hearing are the senses that are pre-eminently helpful for knowing, for understanding. In today's Gospel, sight and hearing are declared blessed because when they see and hear Jesus they give access to the ultimate understanding for which our human faculties were made.

Sight and hearing: if they really are ways to understanding, then they must in some sense be equipment for our supernatural destiny when we shall see God as he is, and hear the voice of the One who sits upon the Throne say, 'I am the Alpha and the Omega, the Beginning and the End'.

How? Well, it's already happening, says Jesus, as you—the disciples—watch a young Jewish prophet outlining his teaching. So this simple human scene—a conversation between people—is actually a theophany, a manifestation of God.

The discretion of the Incarnation makes some people think Jesus' claims are feeble. The reticence of the Incarnation allows them to overlook the way human salvation lies within it. The poet Stefan George wrote:

> I know of lofts above each house,
> full of running wheat, ever newly heaped—
> and no one takes it.
> I know of cellars under every yard
> where the noble wine languishes and seeps away
> into the sand—
> and no one drinks it.
> I know of tons of pure gold, scattered in the dust:
> people brush it with their ragged hems,
> and no one sees it.

The First Wednesday of Advent

'This is our God and we have waited for him that he may save us.'
These words from Isaiah sum up well the distinctive feeling of
Advent, that feeling of subdued joy—because we are waiting for
the vindication of our God. We're waiting liturgically, deploying
signs and symbols, for the vindication of the hope of Israel which
happens at Christmas when Emmanuel, God-with-us, is born to
us at his coming in humility and we can see how right Israel was
in her expectation of a Saviour. But we're also waiting *in all reality*
for the vindication of the hope of the Church, when God will fulfil
all of his promises, including, and above all, those made in his Son,
the Child born at Bethlehem, which he will do at the Parousia, the
Coming in Glory.

The prophet says that what we are waiting for 'will take away
the reproach of his people'. Whatever that meant for Israel, at any
rate for us, for the Church, it means, surely, the reproach levelled
by unbelievers that our lives of faith are groundless and unjusti-
fied.

St Thomas tells that that, negatively, any objection to the faith
can always be met and countered, since there cannot be two
conflicting truths, a truth of faith and a truth of reason. But he
doesn't think that, positively, we can prove the truth of our faith,
actually demonstrate it—even though we can put forward considerations that may persuade people that what the faith teaches is
congruent with human nature, with the human heart. In a very
real sense, then, our faith remains unverified—until the Advent
hope is realized and our God reigns.

That is not the least of our reasons for 'subdued joy' this Advent.

The First Thursday of Advent

I suppose the reason today's readings have been put with each
other is that both of them include the word 'rock'—and not just
the word, which could refer to quite different things like Rock
music and Brighton Rock, but the word as standing for the same
thing: namely, God in his complete reliability. For Isaiah, the Lord
is the everlasting Rock and in the teaching of Jesus the rock on
which we must build is the Gospel of the Kingdom—to be

identified, in the last analysis, with the Bearer of the Good News of the Kingdom, Jesus himself. As we say in the Creed he is 'God from God', the divine substance communicated in human form and therefore, in the language of Isaiah, basic, primordial Rock.

In our spiritual lives it matters that we throw ourselves on this Rock for support. In fact that could almost be a definition of the spiritual life: having recourse to that Rock not just for survival (though that's more than some people can manage) but to draw strength from it for living courageously, sacrificially, and joyfully.

This is why it is not a good idea to look for Saviour substitutes, whether in gurus or spiritual guides or in other mortals on whom we become excessively reliant. That undermines what should be our primary orientation. On the other hand, in his Providence God can send us people who act as mediations of his own Rockiness. What we should ask of our leaders, or those who are influential in our lives, is not that they be God-substitutes but that they communicate to us something of God's own strength and reliability and so encourage us to pass beyond them to him.

The First Friday of Advent

It's fairly obvious why today's Gospel—the cure of the Two Blind Men—was chosen to be one of the first Advent readings even though there's nothing specially 'Advent-ish' about it. It goes very well with the great set piece from the prophet Isaiah we heard a moment earlier: one of those wonderful oracles about the peaceable Kingdom which have made Isaiah a favourite book among Bible—readers of all ages—not least George Frederick Handel in *Messiah*: the way I first encountered this passage in my not very Bible-reading Anglican family setting.

> And the eyes of the blind shall be opened,
> and the ears of the deaf unstopp-ed.

All in the tenor part.

It could be, couldn't it, sheer Utopianism. It could just be the description of a never-never land where everyone gets better and no one gets hurt and they all lived happily ever afterwards.

That is why we need today's Gospel where Jesus opens the eyes of two blind men. The poverty of the evangelist's language, so

different from the rich, almost Baroque, quality of Isaiah, underlines the realism of it. The doctrinally undeveloped attitude of the
two men—they have no high title of adoration to offer Jesus, only
the words 'Son of David'—underscores the intellectual poverty of
the scene. This is basic stuff, but the great thing about it is: it
happened. We are given a glimpse of the future, and it works.
Divine energies *are* in motion to bring the creative plan to fulfillment. The world will go out with a bang not a whimper, and the
bang of the total flowering of nature under the impact of supernatural grace will give the Big Bang of modern astronomy a run for
its money. How do we know? Two men rubbing their eyes in (I
almost said...) disbelief.

The First Saturday of Advent

'When Jesus saw the crowds, he had compassion for them, because
they were harassed and helpless, like sheep without a shepherd.'
It's one of the sayings of the Gospel tradition that registers the
merciful love of Christ for his own people, the consecrated nation.
In this spirit, he sends out his twelve closest collaborators, the inner
group of disciples, on mission to the House of Israel. He wagers
their futures, as he was wagering his own, seeing them as the new
'twelve patriarchs' of the tribes of Israel, destined to give the people
a new beginning, just as the great heroes of the past, the sons of
Jacob, had done before. And the result, sad to say, was a flop. The
Twelve do not convert Israel. Jesus will weep over the Jerusalem
that rejects him.

When God involves himself in our world and becomes incarnate
in human terms, empirically speaking his life is a failure and a
spectacular failure at that. This sounds like nonsense. How can
Divinity which, among other things, is Omnipotence, possibly be
said to fail? God is indeed omnipotent but in relation to his rational
creation his almightiness is exercised in the mode proper to his
saving love. His power realizes what his saving love intends. It
does not compel assent when the 'Yes' of rational creatures is
withheld. So if God is to show himself in our world precisely in
his love, he must be open to possibilities of defeat. In a world
affected through and through by original sin, it is morally inevita-

ble that he will be defeated at least at first. Boundlessly exigent, if also ennobling, love such as God's is: this puts limitless demands on us and we want to blot it out. That drama is already presented in the Passion Narrative of St Matthew, the First Gospel, though it will not be analysed until the Fourth Gospel, St John.

And then we remember: the upshot of the Passion of Christ is the Resurrection. It is God's refusal to take the human 'No' for a final answer, and the throwing open to human beings of the vision of God.

The Second Sunday of Advent (Year A)

And so the Gospel begins with John the Baptizer appearing in the wilderness. We know, perhaps more from Lent than from Advent, the significance of that desert location.

The desert is a lonely place. It brings home to us our essential solitude as spirits. That is not meant to deny, of course, that we are also social animals. Still, there is a depth to each of us which no one can plumb, not even ourselves. We shall encounter that 'true wilderness' in the moment of our dying, which not by chance will be the loneliest time of our lives.

The desert is also a place of self-stripping. In the desert there are few illusions. The masks we show each other, the roles we have in ordinary society, begin to slip away. Not there is anything wrong, necessarily, with masks and roles, inasmuch as we have to get on with life in society. And yet, with one exception—the role we are called on to play in the drama of salvation—they are not reliable clues to who ultimately we are.

For the Bible, the revelation of our ultimate identity—what Scripture calls our 'true name'—happens beyond this world, in the Kingdom of the Father, when we shall know as we are known: known from the beginning by our Creator who imagined us into existence in the first place. There alone shall we grasp fully our *raison d'être*, the part we had and have to play in the total drama of the world.

And because the One from whom we come, to whom we go, is very Goodness—Goodness Himself, the true wilderness must also be a place where we see our vices and virtues for what they are, and see, therefore, the distance between what we are now and what we are meant to be. The desert is, then, a place of moral self-knowledge as well.

It is in this solitude, self-stripping, and moral self-knowledge that the Word of God can enter our lives as it came to John the Baptist, and came *so as to act*. The Word of God is alive and active. It churns up souls. It converts rapists and murderers. It sends missionaries to Korea or Karakorum. It makes people found leper colonies or set up clinics for drug addicts. It causes them to challenge evil rulers, write poetry like Dante, paint icons like Rublev.

Christian doctrine tells us more about the power of the word of God. It tells us about the origin of this power, about its aim and its character. It tells us that the power of the Gospel word is really the power of the self-surrendering love of the Holy Trinity, which entered the world in the Incarnation of the Son with a view to the Cross, from which its fruitfulness poured forth Pentecostally, when from the Holy Spirit the Church was born with her preaching, her sacraments, her saints.

The Second Sunday of Advent (Year B)

Though John the Baptist said he was unworthy even to loosen the thongs of Jesus' sandals, Jesus himself acknowledged John as the greatest among the saints who had gone before him under the Old Covenant. Why? In our Lord's own words, John was the 'Bride-groom's friend'. By his deep spirit of penitence and his self-renouncing love, John so attuned himself to the Word of God that he could be the means for the Lord's human appropriation of his mission, for his setting out on his public ministry. He showed Christ to Israel. That was John's entirely Providential role. And so he helped the Bridegroom to bring home his Bride: that is, to bring our humanity home to God.

The desert experience—one, surely, of solitude and radical openness to God—led John to no merely human work. It led to his helping make possible the divine work of the Redeemer.

In Advent we should be thinking about our own roles in the drama of salvation: the great world-drama which takes history from creation via the Incarnation to its final goal in the Parousia, the new heavens and the new earth where righteousness dwells. How well do we know what God has disclosed of the plot, in Scripture, as mirrored in the Church's tradition and teaching? How closely do we inter-relate the roles we play in life to the role of the main protagonist in the great world-drama, Jesus Christ? How conscious are we of the missions of our fellow actors and actresses, the contributions those we meet have to make? How alert are we to the prompting of the producer of this play, who is the Holy Spirit?

That is the way we ask ourselves, at this time of year, in the words of St Peter in today's epistle: 'what sort of persons we ought to be in lives of holiness and godliness, waiting for and hastening the coming of the day of the Lord'.

The Second Sunday of Advent (Year C)

What a contrast between on the one hand the magnificent rolling titles of the people of power listed in today's Gospel—emperor, governor, tetrarch, pontiff—and on the other the simplicity of the reference to John the Baptist, in the wilderness! Our religion does not begin in palaces, with potentates, or in universities, with academics, but in the desert.

What is significant about that? It's significant that the environment where our faith took its rise was the sort where people tend to feel most exposed, vulnerable, on the knife-edge of existence. Many people cannot stand being alone; they have to be accompanied, even if only by a disembodied voice from a radio set or over the Internet. And this is strange, because there's nothing necessarily boring about being alone, at least for reasonable stretches of time. Each of us carries about an interior world which is alive with memories, impressions, feelings, attitudes, arguments, dispositions towards other people, and all the rest. What at any given moment each of us is doing in the outer world is likely to be duller than that inner world with all its inheritance from our personal past as well as the power of thought to range across time and space. So why is it that we shudder at the idea of a summer in the Sahara, or a crash-out in the Kalahari? Is it because we have a shrewd suspicion that, in a place like that, a desert place, a John the Baptist sort of place, we would have to come to terms with our life in a way we wouldn't much care for?

This is very much a John the Baptist kind of proposal, because he was evidently a person who made others uncomfortable. John the Baptist belongs with what the German philosopher Hegel called the 'practitioners of the negative'. In biblical language, his job was to 'preach a baptism of repentance for the forgiveness of sins'. Plainly, that was meant to have some positive consequences. But it was still primarily a negative undertaking. John's task was to place his finger on people's weak spots and keep it there till they noticed. It's not just a question of identifying our bad deeds, our obviously blameworthy deeds. It's also a matter of our good, apparently praiseworthy deeds, since these too can have an uninspiring background. St Augustine notes how often pride steals in to ruin even good deeds.

There must be some labour of the negative before we can be ready for the ultra-positive, the Gospel of the Kingdom. We have to go in for a bit of deconstruction, to clear away the rubble of complacency and self-deception. Otherwise we shall not have a path clear in our lives for the Incarnate One to come and enter where he is needed, and wanted, by those who should be waiting for him, yearning for him, rather than reassuring themselves that they are alright as they are.

The Second Monday of Advent

The most famous modern philosopher to have lived here in Cambridge was, I suppose, Wittgenstein, one of whose more memorable remarks was when he said the human body is the best picture we have of the human soul. If you want to look at a soul, look at a face. It is a truth icon-painters recognize.

And clearly our Lord's attitude in today's Gospel was congruent with this: expressing spirit by way of matter. It's a Gospel when at one and the same time he heals physically and forgives divinely. He treats the physical healing as the best way to picture the divine forgiveness. To see the divine forgiveness in action he invites us to look at the paralysed man walking.

Here divine revelation makes—or ought to make—a big differ-ence to the way we look at things. If we didn't know about revelation, we would probably say that physical healing is very real and concrete whereas spiritual healing is vague and elusive. On the contrary! For the Bible and the Church, the action of divine forgiveness by which we are re-made in justification as the friends of God is a new creation: much more real, much more wonderful,

than just patching up our bodies here and there. For this transformation, physical healing is a metaphor—not a metaphor written
out on a page but a metaphor written into someone's body.

And it is a highly appropriate metaphor. We are, after all, to
enjoy divine friendship body and soul, and not just in the soul only.
This is what the doctrine of the resurrection of the flesh tells us. In
the Apostles' Creed, not till we have affirmed out faith in that
resurrection do we add 'and [I believe in] the life everlasting',
affirming in that way the upshot of the entire process we celebrate
in Advent.

The Second Tuesday of Advent

The parable of the sheep that went astray is a familiar Gospel text
which tells us about the foundation of the pastoral ministry in the
Church.

First, as it stands, in its literal sense (as we say), this Gospel
licenses the often spectacularly inefficient use of energy that we
call pastoral care. The possible breakdown of Mrs Jones' marriage,
or the problem about little Freddie suddenly exhibiting religious
scruples, may take up inordinate amounts of the time of a pastoral
priest who, in principle, has huge swathes of countryside or town
as his responsibility. Such a priest may sometimes wonder what
he is achieving. Yet it is the Saviour's way: these individuals are
lost sheep or at any rate sheep who for the time being are
bewildered, at a loss.

But secondly, the parable can also be taken more widely, in its
spiritual sense, which is how the Fathers of the Church tended to
take it. This produces an equally important message, but one that
is very different to the first, seemingly opposed to it, yet actually,
I think, complementary. The one sheep the man went in search of
is the human race which, by contrast with the holy angels, has lost
its way in history. In a 'house of writers' such as Blackfriars
Cambridge was founded to be, that licences those who stand back
from pastoral care (except for hearing Confessions) and take a long
view—a long view of what will bring humankind back to God:
intellectually, morally, culturally, spiritually, sociologically, aes-

thetically. That too can be called pastoral mission if only we could see it.

The Second Wednesday of Advent

Today's Gospel is so short it's hardly more than a tag. It could well be an inscription added by an artist to an image of the Sacred Heart. But it's important for Advent. It helps to focus what it is in Advent we're waiting for.

The Jewish hope had many strands. Texts from the Old Testament about the future point in different directions. Only from after the first Christmas, looking back, do the pieces fall into place. We are waiting for the disclosure of the heart of God as a human heart.

We get that in the Incarnation. But Advent is also looking forward to the Parousia, the Second Coming. Is this Gospel also relevant to that stupendous event?

Very much so! The Parousia is the revelation that the heart of God disclosed in a human heart will be from then on the heart of the world.

The Second Thursday of Advent

Today's Gospel is a riddling one. First of all, how was John the Baptist the greatest man who ever lived—greater than Moses or Plato or Alexander, or, looking ahead, Michelangelo or Shakespeare or Einstein. A list like that makes us realize we have to ask, 'Greater in what respect?'. And surely our Lord means, greater in his function, his mission, to prepare the way for Emmanuel. Often, people don't like being thought of in terms of their function, but call it their 'mission' and it looks rather different. However, it pertains to humility to accept that we are partially defined by our functions, what others need us for.

But in any case, the praise is qualified: John the Baptist is the greatest of those outside the Kingdom, whereas the least inside the Kingdom is greater than he. Here is another riddle, and it's bound up with a further teaser which follows, when Jesus speaks of the Kingdom as 'suffering violence' from the time of John until the present.

Exegetes are not agreed about the meaning of these statements, but I venture the suggestion that the Kingdom is Jesus himself, as in the second century the great Greek-speaking theologian Origen will call him. He is *autobasileia*, which we can translate, 'The Kingdom in person'. And Jesus was certainly threatened from all sides during his ministry just as John had been. He never ceased to provoke opposition since, being in his own person a new relation between God and the world, he necessarily changed everything, shook everything up.

But then what about people being 'in the Kingdom', so as to be, for example, the 'least in the Kingdom'? There we can get some help from not the Greek East but the Latin West, from St Thomas. As soon as our Lord's humanity was, at his Incarnation, anointed with the Holy Spirit, he became the Head of a new humanity, and as that Head he brought with him his Body—all those who are to be his members. To be a member of Jesus Christ, to be so identified with him that, on occasion, at any rate, we can be his hand or his voice—his living instrument—that is a function we have as Christians which exceeds even the function of John the Baptist, the Forerunner.

And here all fears about being defined in terms of function fall away, since we realize this function is an absolutely huge privilege, and a sign of the call to glory.

The Second Friday of Advent

One way in which the Catholic Church appears rather clearly as the Church of the Word incarnate is the way she attracts a crossfire of mutually contradictory criticisms—the same crossfire, in fact, which Jesus notes in today's Gospel.

This crossfire was a feature of much human reaction to his mission, the mission which joined him to his cousin, the Forerunner, John the Baptist. John's prophetic severity attracted opposition—wasn't this, people grumbled, a negative Puritanism, rather than true religion? Our Lord's anticipation of the joys of his Father's Kingdom similarly aroused animosity—wasn't this a careless hedonism, rather than real religion?

So too the Church today is simultaneously accused of rigorism and laxism: both of having a moral code that is too demanding to practice, and also of irresponsibly encouraging people to indulge themselves in piety when the real ethical task of meeting the world's practical everyday needs still remains to be carried out.

This suggests that the Church has it about right. The truth in which she is grounded is the truth of the crucified and ascended Lord in whom, on the one hand, sacrifice, and, on the other, joy are at last united. So too in our lives discipline and delight go hand in hand.

It is because the world cannot find the synthesis between sacrifice and joy, or discipline and delight, without submitting to the Church, to the waters of Baptism, that the world criticizes by turn first the one thing and then the other. Not for nothing did G. K. Chesterton describe orthodoxy as a wild adventure where we career down the high road of truth, leaving the various heresies — in our time, these are especially the moral heresies — falling to left and right on either side.

So is everything in our garden lovely, then? Far from it. Ours is a mass Church with vast numbers of nominal members and large numbers of peripherally engaged members who have not yet internalized this combination of qualities — sacrifice and joy. That is why it is never a waste of time preaching to the converted — especially oneself.

The Second Saturday of Advent

'Poor girl', says Sherlock Holmes to Eugenia Ronder in 'The Adventure of the Veiled Lodger', 'the ways of fate are indeed hard to understand. If there is not some compensation hereafter then the world is a cruel jest'. 'The world is a cruel jest': many have thought so from the ancients to Thomas Hardy and beyond. Even in the heart of Scripture, in the Book of Ecclesiastes, we find this same profoundly pessimistic conclusion expressed. You might think it something of a scandal to have such a book in the Canon of the Bible. But it was necessary to have the painful question, 'Is the world a cruel jest?' posed starkly: necessary if the gradually unfolding answer of revelation to that question were to be perceived in all its power.

The first reading of today's Mass, from the Book of Sirach, a contemporary of the author of Ecclesiastes, is an important part of that 'gradually unfolding answer'. The traditional belief that the prophet Elijah had been snatched up to heaven arouses in the writer a sense of exultation, and if we analyse what that exultation involves we find two elements that are relevant to the hope of heaven.

First, there is a question of vindication. In this world, people suffer many injustices owing to the malice or negligence of their fellow creatures. Heaven is justice; it is redress; it is vindication.

Secondly, though, there are in this world many causes of frustration or dissatisfaction which can't be laid at anyone's door. The ways things are by no one's particular fault can still create limits that cramp the soul and depress it. Relevant here is the second element in Sirach's exultation which is his sense of joy. Joy is the delight of the mind in the stable possession of something manifestly good. Usually, it is the mind that possesses the good, unless the good in question is a pound of Belgian chocolates, though the body can and should resonate, tingle, in response to the joy-filled mind—and it does.

Elijah's heaven was not only vindication. It was also a marvellous glorying in seeing the plan of God of which he had formed part. His heaven was, therefore, also joy. Jewish belief in Elijah's bodily ascension points ahead to Christ's Resurrection and, through Christ, to the general resurrection which is history's end. There vindication will be made for all who suffer unjustly now, and, more widely, the body will exult after its own fashion in the glory of the soul.

THE THIRD WEEK OF ADVENT

The Third Sunday of Advent (Year A)

The texts of today's Liturgy, Gaudete Sunday, are so beautiful and eloquent that it seems almost an impertinence to say more about them. But every Sunday the preacher at Mass has a canonical mandate to fulfil.

The Isaiah passage we read was among the prophet's most celebrated prose-poems. When the Israelites return to their holy city, the desert will virtually flower under their feet, so marvellous will it be. And he invokes for us what it will be like to see Jerusalem again, after a generation in a pagan land. It will be like the blind seeing, the deaf hearing, the lame leaping for joy. It is fairly clear that Isaiah is talking about something happening inside people — happening to their minds, wills, emotions. You wouldn't take him literally any more than if Wordsworth wrote a poem about how his heart leapt up at the sunrise you would ask him if he really thought the sun travelled round the earth.

But then in the Gospel, we have our Lord going about actually doing all these things that are only metaphors in the prophets. The blind are actually seeing, the lame gambolling around. What he is doing is to turn the verbal metaphors of Isaiah into metaphors of a different kind: metaphors not written on parchment but in living human flesh. The people he healed became walking, talking, living metaphors. They were still, however, images in that, like the prophet's literary metaphors, they essentially pointed beyond themselves. Their physical healing was an indicator of something far bigger than physical healing, the far greater transformation we call 'salvation'.

In the Church's history there have been two principal ways of understanding what 'salvation' is. One of them belongs to our Western tradition here in the Latin church, and it sees salvation as essentially a matter of being healed from your sins. Salvation is liberation because it frees us from our guilt and makes it possible for us no longer to be dominated by our faults and failings, the distorted drives and flawed bits of ourselves that trip us up and make life awful for us and for others.

Plainly, that understanding of salvation is always going to be relevant, so long as there are fallen human beings on this planet. And indeed, the influence of this essentially moral view of salvation has been extended in recent decades in the movement called 'liberation theology', where the effects of sin are seen as accumulating in the shape of social forces that confirm the tendency to evil of human nature after the Fall.

The Western tradition of salvation thinking is much concerned with the dignity of man. Not only does God confer forgiveness and new resources for godly living through the agency of the Word made man. God does this in a way that requires us to make salvation our own by the contribution of our ethical efforts.

The second chief way in which people have understood the transformation we call salvation is more typical of Eastern Christianity and especially of the Greek church. There salvation is seen as liberation not so much from sin, first and foremost, as from corruptibility and death. You can be healed as much as you like from your sins, be living a beautiful, benevolent, creative life, but that will not save you from the inevitability of death, from tending to fall back into nothingness. Salvation is the antidote to death. It is eternal life, stronger than biological death, and a life we can, through faith, begin to experience here and now. In Christ, biological death is not a dying out of life but a dying into a more intense life.

Plainly, that understanding of salvation too is going to remain pertinent so long as there are mortal human beings on this planet. It's not that the Greek tradition is uninterested in morality, in developing the virtues in a Christian way. But it sees those virtues as signs of the deathless life taking hold of us, and through us, of the cosmos at large.

There is also a third way of seeing salvation, I think, which is not so obvious as these two, though it should be because it is suggested by the Advent Liturgy itself. This third way pops up here and there in descriptions of the other two, but it is more common in devotional writings, in mysticism, and in sacred art. Salvation lies not only in being delivered from sin and mortality. It also lies, and perhaps most characteristically lies, in being freed

from anonymity, from facelessness, from isolation, from being
unrelated to others. In modern Western society which is likely to
become, through the spread of technology, modern global society,
we tend to fear absolute loneliness more than we do either sin or
death. In this perspective, what saves us in Christianity is seeing
a face. The glory of God, wrote St Paul, has shone on us in the face
of Jesus Christ, and by 'glory' he meant God's indescribable
goodness, mercy, love. The first Christians glimpsed in the features
of a face, the face of Jesus, how much the Father loved them: that
they were not isolated, anonymous, outside personal dialogue and
encounter. For the face of Christ is the face of God. In the Gospels,
in the Liturgy, in the images of the Saviour in the Church's
iconography, we have seen a face, an unearthly face, a face that
expresses a love that is both human and more than human, since
it manifests the One through whom all things were made.

The Christian life consists in allowing the light of that face to
transform us. In Advent we are praying that this transformation
will really happen to us. 'Let your face shine on us', the Psalmist
cries, 'and we shall be saved'.

The Third Sunday of Advent (Year B)

When we open our New Testaments we find that the Church has
given a title of her own to each of the Gospels: 'The Gospel of our
Lord Jesus Christ according to Matthew [or Mark, Luke, or John]'.
It's the same when we encounter the Scriptures where, supremely,
the Church wishes them to be read — in her worship, at the Liturgy.
Not 'A Reading from St John's Gospel', but 'A Reading from the
Holy Gospel [of our Lord Jesus Christ, that means] according to
John'. No matter whom a Gospel is according to, its good news is
always the good news of Jesus himself: the good news about him
and the good news that he personally is. In any Gospel he comes
first and last, just as, according to the maxim, 'Christianity is
Christ', and no Christian life that lacks a personal relation with
him merits the name.

This is true, and yet in any Gospel we come upon Jesus in the
space opened for us by various other characters who play a part
in his story. One long-established method of meditating on the

Gospels is to put ourselves in the place of those he meets and converses with. If we approach the New Testament in that way we find that these characters fall into two categories.

In the first place, there are those who figure as triggers or stimuli for the reader's response. The paralysed man by the Pool of Siloam, say, or the blind beggar in Jericho: the evangelists present these characters as figures who exemplify in some way the human need for the Saviour. Other characters, however, belong to the very structure of the Gospel. They are irreplaceable features of it, with a permanent place in the origination of the Church. When it comes to our Lady, say, or St Peter, the evangelists have a message to present about them in their own right. Of course it is part and parcel of the message about Christ, but not because these figures are simply representative of those who need him. They are not just interchangeable with anybody else.

The subject of today's Gospel is one of these. St John the Baptist holds a permanent place in the Gospel (this is why we can concentrate on him for two successive Sundays of Advent), and he does so owing to his task of preparing the world for Christ's coming in all its imminence, its immediacy. In John, prophecy spoke against with its old accents—turn, turn back to God—but with a new urgency because now the Lord is personally at hand. In biblical language, John's role is to bind so that Jesus may loose. He has to say with conviction and efficacy that all lie under the power of sin which can strike at whom and through whom it will, even children of Abraham. Without that, it is impossible to understand what our Lord's offer of free forgiveness for mankind could be about.

In the old Roman *Confiteor*, Latin Catholics confessed their sins before God and the saints naming especially John the Baptist as they did so. While in one way that derived from a general desire to include in one's confession the mightiest patrons around the throne of God, there was also a special fittingness in naming St John in that context. We need his intercession so as to have the courage to say frankly that we did such and such owing to our own fault, our own most grievous fault.

As today's Gospel tells the story, St John is above all a witness. In the first place, he is a prosecution witness in the case against

humanity. He testifies to the universality of the need for forgiveness: this is what the baptism of water he practised at the Jordan
was about. But in the second place, and more fundamentally,
especially in the Fourth Gospel, he is also a defence witness in the
case on behalf of Christ. He says and declares and does not deny
(this was technical legal language in the period) what it was he
saw in Jesus. He identifies him before the world in a formula that
sums him up: 'This is the Lamb of God'.

The greatest of the icons of St John the Baptist is not, I think, a
Byzantine image but a Western one, in fact a Germanic one. It is
the portrayal by Matthias Grünewald commissioned in 1512 by
the Anthonite monks of Isenheim in Alsace. There John stands by
the side of Jesus, pointing him out with a deliberately elongated
finger. Who and what John is in the Church lies in that finger.
Normally, we see the soul most clearly in the human face, and yet
the whole of the body shares in the dignity of ensoulment, so a
gesture with a finger can be a spiritual act. In the painting,
however, the Jesus to whom John points is not the Jesus of the
public ministry. It is Jesus on the Cross. Though John was dead,
executed, by the time of the Lord's Crucifixion, this is symbolically
correct. The Lamb of God who takes away the sins of the world
can only be the Word made flesh who bore away our sins into
nothingness by his suffering and descent into Hell. In the simple
words of Mrs Alexander's children's hymn: 'There was no other
good enough/ to pay the price of sin./ He only could unlock the
gate/ of heaven, and let us in'.

This witness is why John the Baptist is great and glorious and
the patron of Advent *par excellence*.

The Third Sunday of Advent (Year C)

Today is Gaudete Sunday, literally 'Be Joyful Sunday'. When
Advent was a pre-Christmas fast, a fast of forty days like Lent, this
Sunday was a break when you went on a spree. The jollifications
were not just pleasurable relief, however. They were meant to
symbolize a deeper kind of happiness found in joy and peace,
exultation and praise.

It isn't necessarily all that easy to say what kind of happiness we should expect from our religion. Religion doesn't make one more popular, better paid, or better looking. It doesn't stop your dear ones from dying or your friends from giving you up as a bad job. In itself, we might think, it solves nothing, and leaves the world exactly as it was before. At best it provides a context in which to locate things that happen—but this is likely to induce resignation rather than a feeling of being over the moon. Yet the apostle tells, 'Rejoice always!'

I would suggest that happiness through rejoicing is found in Christianity in two primary ways. The first primary way stems from the personal presence in our lives of Jesus Christ, the God-man, the Saviour. The presence of Christ brings joy because the life of God is the most complete bliss and joy imaginable, and Jesus was filled with it at his Resurrection.

This presence is secret, mystical, discovered only in prayer, in the intimacy of communion, in the inmost heart—which is the only way you could expect to find the presence of the God-man in a post-Ascension world. There is not likely to be much joy in the practice of religion unless we cultivate this side of things, which means reading and re-reading the Gospels, studying how he is portrayed in sacred art, and above all by starting to pray. No amount of information about someone can substitute for getting involved in a conversation with them, and here the first and decisive step is to use their name. Calling on the Holy Name, or what the Orthodox call the Prayer of the Name (or the Jesus Prayer), is absolutely essential here.

The second kind of joy-filled happiness relevant to our religion is reserved for the future. Christ may be in our midst, but the world will know just as much pain and fear this Christmas as in the days when John the Baptist began his preaching. But we look forward, as Christians, to a time when human life and relationships and the whole of creation will be perfected, to a time of universal healing, reconciliation and peace. The joy to come is essentially a shared joy, an extension of the bliss of Christ to all mankind. As the hymn ascribed to St Bernard puts it, 'I know not, ah I know not/ what social joys are there...' This is a joy which cannot be had unless it is shared. It is as much hope for my neighbour as it is hope for myself, and it carries implications about how I am to live vis-à-vis my neighbour here and now if I am to live congruently with that social orientation.

Without personal mysticism our religion would be just a moralism, worthy but humourless and ultimately exhausting; but without the hope for a redeemed world, mysticism, personal devotion to Christ, could become self-indulgent.

These then are the two joys of Gaudete Sunday: joy in God here and now and the joy that comes from his disclosure that every tear will be wiped away under the sun that knows no setting, Christ the sun of justice. of whose Kingdom we say in the Creed: it 'will know no end'.

The Third Monday of Advent

The late Cardinal John Carmel Heenan of Westminster once got into hot water with the forward-thinking thanks to an answer he gave on television. Malcolm Muggeridge invited him to sum up in one word the essence of Catholicism, and without a moment's hesitation he replied, 'Authority'. 'Post-Tridentine authoritarianism', it was declared. Yet today's Gospel shows that some kind of concern with authority is perfectly evangelical. Back to that in a moment.

In any case, we all want to know what authorizes people in saying or doing things. What authorizes an expert in making a disputed statement? How in some conflictual political situation is the State authorized to act? Closer to our own domestic world, postmen who call at the front door with a registered package need an authorized signature before they can leave it. So there's nothing unusual about wanting to know the authority behind the moral and spiritual beliefs that are the single most important thing in our lives.

Not unusual, and yet the way the authority reaches us may be surprising. In today's Old Testament lection, from the Book of Numbers, it is a pagan prophet—not a Jew, then, a member of the People of the Promise—who is inspired to utter true prophecy about the future of Israel. And in today's Gospel, Jesus himself avoids stating, in fact, the grounds of his authority though he accepts the pertinence of the question.

Why was he so elusive on the point? In the mind of the evangelist, the answer to this question has to do with the discretion with which our Lord advanced his claim to be consubstantial with the Father. His Jewish hearers were devoted, and rightly so, to monotheism, to faith in one God. Only gradually could they be brought to understand the internal differentiatedness of that one God, and so come to faith in the Holy Trinity.

There is also something else here. There is an authorization of Jesus' deeds which had not happened at the time he was speaking. The authorization in question is that found in his 'hour', the moment of the Cross. That was the moment when, specifically as man, as a human being, the Word won by a human action of unsurpassable generosity, the authority he had always possessed as God.

One of the Holy Trinity has suffered for us. That is the ultimate authorization of the Gospel and so of the mission of the Church. That is why we can put forward an authoritative claim to have the most important message the world will ever hear. It is this Trinitarian person who was crucified for us and by us whose return we await in Advent. The Parousia will be the supreme verification of our faith. 'They shall look on him whom they have pierced.'

The Third Tuesday of Advent

Today's reading from the prophet Zephaniah is, like all classical Hebrew prophecy, a message of both woe and weal to Israel. It warns, but it also encourages.

The warning is dire. The city of Zion: Jerusalem, Israel's sacred centre and, as so often, the city which best represents her life, is told off in no uncertain terms—indeed in dreadful terms. Zion has learned her divine lessons so ill that—so the oracle of the Lord which now reaches her has it—in effect she has never really been the pupil of God at all. She that was meant to be the elect city has 'never trusted in the Lord, never drawn near to her God'. This is a devastating message in the ears of a faithful Jew.

And so, as if by way of anticipation of the turning of the early Church to the Gentiles, the prophet warns her that she will be displaced in the affections of God. Of all places, Ethiopia will take her seat, the rivers of Ethiopia 'will bring me offerings'. And it is in fact the case that the Church of Ethiopia was not only the first place in Africa beyond the Mediterranean littoral to receive the Gospel. More than this: Ethiopian Christianity, in strange fulfillment of this prophecy, has felt an especial call to make its own the Old Testament heritage, such that (for example) every Orthodox church-building (and many Catholic ones too of the Eastern rite) has at the centre of its sanctuary a craft-object that represents the Ark once housed in the Jerusalem Temple.

But the prophet also has a message of weal, of good tidings. A day will come when the Hill of Zion will be celebrated not for the pride of its people, but for their humility. As Christians we know when that Day first came. It was when Israel's Messiah, taking on his shoulders the sin of the world, mounted the Cross of shame, with at its foot the Daughter of Zion, the true Miriam, our blessed Lady, offering his Sacrifice in the name of the Church that was to be.

The One who is coming this Advent will certainly turn the human scene upside down, turn history around.

The Third Wednesday of Advent

Today's lection from the prophet Isaiah will be familiar to those who celebrate or attend the older Roman rite. It is the culminating Isaiah reading of the Third Week of Advent in the more ancient Lectionary, read in the age of the Latin Fathers as the last word from the Old Testament in the Vigil Service for Advent's final Sunday. This text is certainly worthy of the prominence it has been given.

It speaks in lyrical metaphors of the coming of the Saviour. His coming is like dew falling on the dry ground, and, again, as the barren earth transformed when salvation springs up. These lovely conceits have made their way into the *Rorate caeli*, the 'Advent Prose' which Anglicans like so much they have taken it into the *New English Hymnal*.

But notice the context of these beautiful metaphors. The context is impressive, perhaps, but it is also rather dreadful. It is the ascription to God of both light and dark, both welfare and calamity. What is this all about? It is all about Isaiah's claim that the God of Israel is the only God, the God of all, and therefore the God who has all history, in both its positive and its negative aspects, in his hand. All serves his Providence—not least, in the mind of Isaiah, the pagan ruler Cyrus whose uncharacteristically benevolent decision to allow Israel to return to its own Land is one of the conditions for the coming of Messiah. Just so, long after Isaiah's time, on the eve of the Incarnation, the rule in Palestine—and the rest of the Mediterranean world—of the emperor Augustus would play into the hands of the divine Planner. It was while all the world was at peace, and Roman roads could carry the news of the Gospel wherever the *Pax romana* held good, that God entered history as man.

Cyrus and Augustus. These are power-mongers, not saints. Not just liberators and the benevolent contribute to God's plan, so also do slave masters and tyrants. Unwittingly, all of them prepare the way for the Lord's Christ to come. Holy prophets and blood-stained human beasts; angels and devils; earth, heaven and the underworld: all are utilized because, as we recall in Advent, history is coming to its climax: at the first Coming, in Bethlehem and at the second Coming, in glory.

The Third Thursday of Advent

How do we know what God is like? One obvious way would seem to be by inference from the world. Through the things that are made, says St Paul in the Letter to the Romans, we know something of him who made them. But which creature is a better guide to God, a humming-bird or a sting-ray? There is a problem here. Again, we might think we can get at what God is like from looking at how his Providence guides history. But which is the better clue, the creation of the welfare State or the rise of militant Islam? So these approaches to God via the world are ambiguous unless there is a way of determining the ambiguity from outside the world. And this is what we call revelation.

Revelation is God's self-interpretation, pointing us to some areas of experience and not others as keys to unlock his mystery. That is what is happening in today's first reading, from the Book of Isaiah. Just about as many horrible things had happened to the Jews as had beautiful things. Did that mean, then, that God's wrath was at least as constitutive of his relation with his people as his mercy? This is the issue the prophet addresses, and on the basis of prophetic knowledge he furnishes an answer.

> *For a brief moment* I forsook you, but with great compassion I will gather you.
> In overflowing wrath *for a moment* I hid my face from you
> but with *everlasting* love I will have compassion on you,
> says the Lord, your redeemer.

In other words, the message of the oracle is the disproportionate predominance in God of mercy over against wrath.

But, you may say, it is actions that speak louder than words. Many modern Jews have been unable to sustain the faith of Israel under the impact of the Holocaust. Yes, actions *do* speak louder than words: this is why the definitive self-revelation of God is the Incarnation, Passion, Death and Descent into Hell of his eternal Word Jesus Christ. God proved his everlasting love by entering totally into the dark places of creation and history which make us doubt his character. And in the Resurrection he showed how he can write straight with crooked lines, and make all creation and all history serve his loving purpose.

The Third Friday of Advent

At the beginning of Advent, as at the origins of the Church, we find John the Baptist and today, as Advent moves towards its close, he is referred to again, but this time with hindsight, from across his grave. When we last heard of him, he was accused of excessive Puritanism — in effect, of hating the world, and our Lord was accused at the same time of having too much fun — in effect, of enjoying the world too much. The same duality of criticism has continued to be levelled at the tradition that followed. The Catholic Church is either too misanthropic, especially misogynist, spoiling the joy of this world by treating it as a vale of tears which we should get out of as fast as we can, her heroes life-denying monks and martyrs; alternatively, the Catholic Church is a vainglorious triumphalistic money-making institution which built the palaces of the Renaissance popes to satisfy its lust for power and display, and glorified human culture instead of glorifying God.

The recurrence of the same inconsistent criticism should give us confidence that the Church has remained faithful to her origins. In those origins there was a negative moment: the 'repent' of John the Baptist, repeated with incomparable force on Calvary. There was also a positive moment: the Kingdom is near, the good creation is to be restored, exemplified in the junketings of Jesus and the paschal meals of the post-Resurrection Forty Days.

So: negatively, we have to interpret our lives in the light of the Fall and also of the Crucifixion. We are a fallen race who merit reprobation and who brought the only Son of God to the death of the Cross. But also: positively, we have to interpret our lives in the light of the creation, the Incarnation and the Resurrection. Our fall is the fall of animals so created that they were only slightly defective angels, albeit embodied, and were loved enough by God to warrant the sending of his Son, which he did in such a way that our final glory will far exceed our first.

It is because St John expressed so forcefully the first, the need of a Saviour, that in today's Gospel he can be called 'a burning and shining lamp'. But the Saviour when he came so exceeded the measure of any strict need for him that John's light was over-whelmed, as a candle flame almost disappears when arc lights go on. So it was with the light of Christ.

The Third Saturday of Advent

The Third Saturday of Advent always falls on or after the 17th of December: see the texts for the days from 17th to 24th December given below.

THE FOURTH WEEK OF ADVENT

The Fourth Sunday of Advent (Year A)

When Catholics hear the words 'The Annunciation', they naturally think of the event of that name involving our Lady—the feast we keep in springtime, the first of the Joyful Mysteries of the Rosary, Mary's conception of Jesus, the beginning of the Incarnation of the divine person of the Word in her womb. That mystery has had a huge impact on art and literature, Marian piety and doctrine and also, not least, on the way we respect human life when it is still unborn, indeed from the first moment of its conception. So it's easy to forget that, actually, there is another Annunciation nestling somewhat more modestly in the pages of the New Testament. And this is the Annunciation found in today's Gospel, the Annunciation to Joseph.

This time it's not an annunciation made to utter innocence, as with Mary. Instead, it's an annunciation made to worldly experience and realism, made to a someone, moreover, in whom we might expect resentment, jealousy and anger to be battling with loyalty, anxiety and pity. If Joseph were unaware of the real origins of Mary's pregnancy he would surely have been awash with such conflicting emotions, indicated discreetly by the evangelist, perhaps, when he presents Joseph as 'considering these things'. This second annunciation, the Josephine one, may speak more powerfully to us moderns than its Marian counterpart since, typically, we are in a flux of conflicting emotions ourselves. As the moral certainties of traditional society, rooted ultimately in religion, are removed, people no longer quite know what to feel about major aspects of human life, like conception or mortality or marriage or sexuality. They no longer know what human weight to give these dimensions of existence: a distinctively modern quandary of a thought-provoking kind.

So this Gospel shouldn't be a difficult one to speak about and it wouldn't be if it weren't for the fact that St Matthew's understated description of emotional crisis and dream resolution is absolutely inseparable from angels. How can modern people find room for that?

It's one of the privileges of being a Catholic Christian—a bearer of divine revelation—that we don't have to take on board all the intellectual cargo which the fashion of the age would have us load up. It may be difficult to get outside the cocoon that modern education and the communications media weave for us, but if we don't we shall inevitably become convinced that reality is secular—that it carries no marks of the transcendent. We shall be overborne by a sense of the modernity—the essential secularity—of reality, failing to notice that modernity is itself something human beings have constructed. Modernity—understanding everything as basically secular—is an ideology. Unless we recognize the way it puts up a screen between us and reality, we shall not appreciate real reality, the reality of creation, a God-made and God-dependent world continually open to influxes from that on which it depends.

Revelation enters the world originally, with Israel, that unique people; climactically, with Jesus Christ, the God-man; and ongoingly, with the apostolic message as a word of life from the God of all creation and history to ourselves. And one of the things revelation shows us is that communication in this world is affected by principalities and powers. The high points and low points of human interaction cannot be fully grasped until we realize how intelligences that are other than human may be at work.

What we have in the annunciation to Joseph is an account of how one such intelligence brought a unique truth within the grasp of a human mind in turmoil. The circumstances that were giving Joseph such anxiety were the long prepared means by which the salvation hoped for by Israel was at last to come about on earth. A respectable tradition of exegesis has it that Joseph's deepest and most chronic anxiety was that, if Mary was indeed the Virgin who should bear a child of the Messianic promise, he was not worthy to be the husband of the woman who was carrying Israel's hope and the hope of all the world.

On Christmas night we shall think about what that salvation means. Today the Church asks us to reflect on how it comes to be known by us. It's no use denying its revealed origin and turning our faith into a rationalism or a moralism. No use—not just because historians wouldn't credit it: it would be making Christianity a different religion. But no use too because, detached from divine revelatory action, what was left of Christianity would cease to be of much use to our contemporaries who want their efforts to understand and evaluate the world to be steadied and confirmed in an authoritative way. Life—and a lot of people quite far from the Church appreciate this—cannot be lived as a seminar that never comes to a conclusive end.

So on the last Sunday of Advent we thank God for the gift of revelation that steadies and confirms reason and morals as well as expanding and enhancing them in a world that is ultimately a sacred world. And we give thanks too for the angelic communication, to be heard again as rapturous music over the fields of Bethlehem when on Christmas night the Word enters his creation as a babe by token of the same love that makes the world go round.

The Fourth Sunday of Advent (Year B)

Not many shopping days left till Christmas, days spent festooning our homes with tinsel and crepe paper, deciding what to give Aunt Edna, or recovering from that office party. In the midst of this bonanza of the consumer society, we listen to the words that started it all off—the story of what happened to an unknown girl in Roman Palestine two thousand years ago. However, today I don't want to concentrate on our Lady so much as on the more neglected actor in the Nazareth scene: the angel.

Angels get a raw deal: prettified and rendered almost indistinguishable from their pantomime equivalent, the fairy. Do we have to believe in them, people ask. But for Scripture, for the biblical experience, angels are anything but pretty and their existence is not in doubt. What, then, for Scripture is an angel?

Angels are moving intellects so immense when compared with ourselves that God can use them for his self-manifestation. The biblical writers regard them as the court of God, the assembly of his spiritual instruments in relations with Israel. I think it is fair to say that meeting God by way of his angels is typical of a relation with God that is not yet fully inter-personal, not at the level of God's desire to draw us in friendship into his own inner life.

In that perspective, the Incarnation, we can say, marks the swan-song of the angels. The period of saving history characterized by the dominance of angelic mediators is superseded when the Word becomes flesh. Instead, there is Emmanuel, God with us, God made human, God permanently present in our humanity as our kin, as our Brother.

The last words of the Gospel of the Annunciation to Mary sound like an anti-climax, 'And the angel left her'. But in fact it was a climax. The angel, the imperfect presence of God, left her, but it left behind the perfect presence of God: the Hope of the Nations began forming as an embryo in her womb. Strictly speaking, heaven and earth no longer need occasional mediators for humanity and divinity are totally united in the person of the God-man. Jesus himself alludes to this in the Gospels. 'From now on, you will see heaven opened, and the angels of God ascending and descending upon the Son of Man'. In other words, the angelic world is now restructured, so that its focus is a human being in whom the fullness of the Godhead dwells bodily. It is Jesus in Mary who is from the moment of the Annunciation on the ladder stretching from earth to heaven. From now on, to see what God is like we need only look at Jesus Christ, in the various states and mysteries of his life.

Let us remember at Christmas that we will not be listening to a moving human drama. We will be privy to the events by which the Creator of all things entered his own creation and the power behind the cosmos showed itself through the features of one like ourselves.

The Fourth Sunday of Advent (Year C)

Today, on the Fourth Sunday of Advent, with Christmas looming, the Gospel invites us to concentrate our attention on Mary, the Mother of Jesus. Similarly, on the Octave Day of Christmas, New Year's Day, the Church will invite us to celebrate the 'Solemnity of Mary as Mother of God', for that title, 'Mother of God', spells out in completeness what was involved in her being the Mother of Jesus. Jesus is the individual human being assumed from the first moment of conception by the Logos, the eternal Word, so as to be from the very beginning of his existence one single person with him, one person with One who is God.

So at Christmastide, which we might be forgiven for thinking of as above all a Christ-centred time, our celebration is framed in a Mary-centred way. This reminds us once again that in our Catholic tradition, the place of Mary is given and vital. Looking to Mary, having devotion to her, is not an optional extra. It is a regular feature of the Christian life.

Today's Gospel is one of those narratives about Mary which we read at this time of year. They are written in a heightened style meant to be a 'pastiche', a sort of copy, of the style of the ancient Scriptures. St Luke tells us in the preamble to his Gospel how careful he was to get eye-witness documentation for everything he wrote down. But this did not prevent him also 'writing up' his material, in a way that made people think back to their Bibles, to what Christians call the Old Testament.

Luke doesn't want us to think this is just a straightforward, rather charming, account of how one pregnant mother did a kindness to another. To bring out the deeper significance of what was happening, he uses the same sort of language about our Lady that the Hebrew Bible used about the Ark of the Covenant. He uses about Mary, in other words, the sort of language that the Old Testament used to describe how, on the wilderness wanderings and eventually in the Jerusalem Temple, the glory of God dwelt with his people. The cloud of the glory is not over her, as it went over the Ark in the desert. It is within her, in the person of her divine-human Son, now forming in her womb. She is the new Ark of the Covenant, as we salute her in the Litany of the Blessed Virgin. But how much more wonderful is the presence she houses than the Ark of old: it is our most human God, the babe who will be born at Bethlehem, our Brother.

The 17th of December

Why do people pay large sums to other people to look up their family trees? It might be snobbery, but since it's obvious that at all times aristocracies have been limited groups, so that my chances of being descended from Little Lord Fauntleroy are rather slim, it seems more reasonable (as well as more charitable) to suppose it comes from a search for identity, a desire for roots, of whatever kind.

Jewish interest in genealogical tables began after the Exile, when so many familiar landmarks had been thrown down, local traditions destroyed, and archival material looted or lost.

The genealogy of our Lord, as given by St Matthew, divides up neatly into three sets of names, each set being twice the biblical number of perfection which is seven. But the formal perfection claimed for this family tree doesn't match its content which included some of the most deplorable characters in Old Testament history, as well as some of the finest.

The perfection belongs not to the human stock as such, then, but to the divine plan which used that human stock, and used it so wisely, with such a sense of the ends for which the means were chosen. God writes straight with crooked lines, and he redeemed the tangled history of Israel by taking it up and uniting it body and soul with his own Word, his own self-expression, Jesus Christ.

The 18th of December

So a week to the day before Christmas, we are reminded of what is going to make it all possible—all the feasting and frolic, the carolling and carousing. It's not going to be anything we have achieved, anything any human being has achieved. It is going to be, as the insurance companies say, an act of God—in other words, something happening from beyond any human calculation and control, something no manager could ever have factored in, be he or she ever so competent or prudent.

And the act of God here is that the Father himself, who from all eternity has delighted in his Son, will now let this Son be in time as well. The Father will let the Son be the personalizing principle of a human conceptus, a human embryo. And all for this purpose: that our sorry world can also know true delight in him.

This is the gift that dwarfs all other gifts: that no matter how ungodly we seem and are, we can be co-enjoyers with the Father of all that the Son is. This gift that dwarfs all other gifts also, we can say, licenses all other gifts. Preachers complain too much about the materialism of Christmas. Christmas was about matter. Giving people things is a true echo of the divine action. We shall recognize this Christmas that we are not mainly achievers: we are first and foremost receivers.

The 19ᵗʰ of December

Today's Gospel describes a traumatic event: Zechariah's encounter with God's angel—God's angelic presence, his presence through the angel. It makes Zechariah speechless. Not just that it leaves him momentarily speechless, but it triggers a medical condition for which, I believe, the technical term is 'aphasia'. The encounter deprives Zechariah chronically of the power of speech.

At the surface level of the text, this misfortune is presented as a penalty for Zechariah's incredulity. But I wonder if something more subtle is not going on as well.

We remember Zechariah chiefly for his song of praise which the Latin church recites every morning in the Office of Lauds, and which the Mass of Christmas Eve will reproduce for us. There is a paradox here. We remember the silenced one for his speech, for exultant fulsome speech. But really it's not so surprising. To respond to the change represented by the Incarnation and the events that surrounded it, we have in a sense to abstain from language, to fall silent, so as to learn in a new way how to use language again, so as to speak of divinity humbling itself to become flesh and working marvels in the midst of the commonplace with a view to changing the commonplace for ever. The words come from our human resources, including the Old Testament, but how they are fitted together has accordingly to change. In this sense, the God of the Gospel is a new language for the world.

The 20ᵗʰ of December

During the Second World War there was a very strange case in Hanover, in northern Germany. A woman caught on the streets during an Allied bombing raid in 1944 was thrown to the ground by a bomb blast. She recovered from minor injuries but nine months later gave birth to a daughter with fingerprints, blood type, and other indicators, that were absolutely identical to those of the mother. The mother claimed adamantly she was a virgin, and medical tests supported this claim. Doctors came up with the hypothesis that the shock of the bomb may have affected a dormant cell in the womb which triggered parthenogenesis: a virginal conception and birth.

I know about this case because it forms the basis for a short opera, *Parthenogenesis*, by the Scottish composer James MacMillan. The reason why it attracted him—apart from being an extraordinary story—was that it's what someone has called a 'negative print' of the Nativity: the feast which we're just now preparing to celebrate.

Under the Hitler regime, Germany was a country obsessed by the possibilities of genetic experimentation, including what we now call 'cloning'. It was also a country whose political ruthlessness had led its enemies to set aside the civilized principle of warfare whereby non-military targets are never aimed at directly. The Hanover conception took place during a human descent into the abyss. In a sense the child born in Hanover did have a father. Its father was human evil.

Compare the Nazareth conception. It took place among a people who knew the only Source of human life to be divine and therefore that life is not to be manipulated. A nation who accepted through ancient prophecy the possibility of parthenogenesis—not, though, as a repetition of what is already in people but just the opposite: as opening up an unimaginably different future, the Kingdom of God. At Christmas the Bethlehem birth will tell us not of evil as father but of the Father of mercies, the Father of superabundant peace.

The 21st of December

Today's Gospel—the Visitation—has always formed part of the readings for Advent, and that for fairly obvious reasons. It tells of our Lady's pre-natal experience, or more exactly the one recorded out-of-the-ordinary event that happened to her while she was carrying, while she had the Coming One (Advent himself, you might say) in her womb.

Between pregnant women there is, I imagine, not only a strong sense of solidarity but also a heightened sensitivity to everything touching their condition—a device of Mother Nature, perhaps, to ensure that the human mother and her offspring are bonded together from the word 'go'.

And certainly this is a very womanly Gospel, an intimately female encounter quieting for a moment in the Lectionary cycle the male voices—the oracles of the prophets, the calculations of St Joseph, and the preaching of that very masculine figure St John the Baptist.

But of course the evangelist expects us to find more in the Visitation episode than just two pregnant ladies as it were patting each other. The Gospel points to something the historian would overlook—and that is the primacy of the Messianic Child. To the historian, John the Baptist and his movement account for Jesus and his movement. Jesus was a disciple of the Baptist who, after the Baptist's execution, began to give a creative twist to the Baptist's teaching and in that way emerged as his successor. In reality, however, Jesus was the cause of John. He was what the Scholastics call John's 'final cause': what finally make sense of John's life and death. 'He who came after me', says John in the Fourth Gospel, 'ranks before me since he existed before me'. The Messianic Child in Mary's womb is the Word of God in person, his humanity endowed with the fullness of the gifts of the Spirit. John moves, repositioning himself in the womb, as when he is born and grown up he will move and reposition himself in the world. Because the Word made flesh, the Son to whom the Spirit is given without measure, draws near.

Something like that is true of us too. In terms of our conscious history we are the prime movers. We decided to take the claims of Jesus seriously, or, if we are cradle Catholics, to carry on with the practice of the faith. But in reality he is the final cause, drawing us to himself. As he told his disciples, 'You have not chosen me, I have chosen you'.

The 22nd of December

So Hannah sings at the birth of Samuel, and Mary bursts forth into her Magnificat. Two pregnancies, two imminent births. It's not surprising that these women are given songs, lyrics, call them what you will. Traditional cultures have a repertoire of music for the high points and low points of life, for happiness and sorrow. And no doubt, with the aid of these chants (happiness) or dirges (sorrow), the individuals who inhabit those cultures have fewer life problems than we do as a result.

But more is involved here than simply providing emotion with an appropriate and satisfying expression. In the Bible such outbursts are essentially—not accidentally but essentially—doxology, the praise of God. They belong within a whole objective order, wider and deeper than ourselves, a creation directed from the very start to God's glory in which even non-sentient things are to share in their way.

> Let the wilderness and the dry-lands exult,
> let the wasteland rejoice and bloom,
> let it bring forth flowers like the jonquil,
> let it rejoice and sing for joy.

In this Gospel, Scripture has left an echo of the life of our Lady as a song of praise, music that magnifies God for the crowning of his creative work in the redemption of the world. In the Latin church we recall that every evening in the Office of Vespers. We recite her Magnificat not just to remind ourselves of the origins of our salvation but in the hope that it will start singing in us, that some of it will rub off on us, so that we enter more into this union of the creation with God which this music implies.

Today is also the anniversary of the approval of the Order of Preachers by Pope Honorius III in 1215. One of the mottoes of the Order is *laudare, benedicere, praedicare*—praise, bless, and preach. This Order is, then, inherently a liturgical Order since it understands preaching, even (or especially) the preaching of doctrine, the awakening and development of a Christian intelligence, to be inseparable from the movement of worship that bears us towards God.

The 23rd of December

Every so often this priory, like all priories, has a canonical visitation. At each such visitation, the Dominicans ask, Is anything likely to change? This points up a difference between a canonical visitation and a divine visitation. On a divine visitation the one thing you can be certain of is that something will change, and the only question is what. The prophet Malachi's account of such a visitation is the classic one in the Hebrew Bible, though you've really got to hear it set to music by Handel in *Messiah* to appreciate its full force: you may remember the bravura effect the baritone voice has to produce for the words 'He will shake'.

In today's Gospel, Zechariah and his family are also shaken. Aphasia, suddenly finding you can't speak, is a reaction to trauma, and the business of the name shows that the trauma is connected with an intervention that has caused something to change. In traditional societies, the choice of names is often governed by very strict rules. There are some relics of this in the modern West: Danish kings can only be called either Christian or Frederick. Here, in the case of the infant John, the name taken from outside and against all custom, rule and convention, signifies divine interruption.

In Scripture, visitations affect one person, or, some, or many, and they have the effect of hoisting salvation history up onto a new level. The parallel between the unusual births of John and Jesus, each with their own annunciation, may make us think that the Nativity of Christ is in the same class as the visitations of the past. That is a temptation of low Christologies: interpretations of what happened in Jesus Christ that don't do its novelty proper justice.

This visitation and this visitation alone has changed things not just for one, or for a few, or for many, but for all, because the Incarnation of the Word will change the fundamental relation between God and the world. What that means we shall have to wait for the Masses of Christmas to discover.

The 24th of December

In the Roman rite we say or sing the Canticle of Zechariah, the Benedictus, each morning in the Office of Lauds. Presumably the main reason why it has been chosen as the Canticle of Lauds is because of the way it compares salvation to the dawn, to first light: something which makes this Canticle obviously suitable for Morning Prayer.

But it is especially suitable so to do on Christmas Eve. The atmosphere of the Benedictus is one of expectation trembling on the brink of realization. And that is exactly the atmosphere of Christmas Eve even for those of us who are grown old in sin and cynicism. Christmas Eve conveys very well a sense of the anticipation of something wonderful.

But what is it, for St Luke, that we are expecting? It is a Child who was God and therefore—we can go on—a childlike God. That the divine nature could express itself as a child speaks to us about the eternal freshness, the everlasting creative novelty of God.

And here in the divine Child is an outcome that, unlike all other births, does not in some way disappoint. Our existence may be unsatisfactory, so may humanity's, history's, the world's. But it is all held within the embrace of something of wider range that defeats cynicism, the jaded sigh of Ecclesiastes: 'What has been is what will be, and what has been done is what will be done, and there is nothing new under the sun'. Our God is an eternal Child who can restore to us our innocence, our happiness. As the older Roman Liturgy of the Mass opens: *Introibo ad altare Dei, ad Deum qui laetificat juventutem meam*: 'I will go to the altar of God, to the God who gives joy to my youth'.

CHRISTMASTIDE

CHRISTMAS AND ITS OCTAVE

Christmas: The Mass at Midnight (1)

For most British people, Christmastide is nearly over now. The shopping spree is at an end, and there are only another twenty-four hours or so to go before the partying and either the cooing or the fretting over the children are ended likewise, and people can start looking forward to New Year instead. In the Church, however, Christmastide is only just beginning. If we are attuned to the Liturgy, not a single Christmas carol will have been heard until tonight, and the Christmas season itself will extend for another three weeks until the feast of the Baptism of the Lord, or, on a different reckoning, for another six weeks until the Presentation at Candlemas. Two such different rhythms of time alert us—almost as much as anything anyone could say about their beliefs and values—to the difference between two world-views. That at least is a strict clerical view of the matter.

Is it too harsh and schematic? Some sociologists would claim that what is happening in England today is not that the Christian faith is dwindling or disappearing but that it is becoming vicarious. People don't want to practice religiously themselves, or even to believe in any obvious sense. But they do want other people to believe in their place, to carry out religious observances in their place, to receive sacraments in their place: strange as that may sound. If this be so, perhaps such vicarious faith is amazingly profound—or, on the other hand, perhaps it is nothing of the sort. Such residual interest in the theological Christmastide as there is on the part of the general population seems to be rather trivial in character, largely centering on chocolate-box images of the Nativity.

In what way have they got that wrong? When in the Middle Ages the Western iconography of the Nativity became fully established it showed the manger of Bethlehem as at once an altar and a tomb. Quite unsentimentally speaking, the Child who is born tonight was born to die in a far stronger sense than with any other human being. The Baroque age, which liked to spell out dramatically what the mediaevals said in a coded way, produced an image of the Nativity which shows a plump bouncy baby under whose right arm is a skull with a half decomposed lower jaw, while the floorboards the baby is resting on are shaped like a cross. Both image-types are saying the same thing. This Child cannot come to his destiny without a Sacrifice which will disclose how estranged we are from the God of life and also how far the God of life wants to go to meet our need and indeed to surpass our needs, thanks to his philanthropy, his love for humankind.

In the Paschal mystery, the Cross and its outcome, the first Christians experienced the Creator God engaged in redeeming his creation so as to bring it through to the goal he has for it. It was for this reason that they searched out memories of Jesus' origins, realizing that, centred on the Cross and what came of it, there was divine purpose in everything connected with his story, right from the start.

And if we ask what that purpose was, the answer of the New Testament runs, it was to restore all things in Christ. This is what the angel voices are saying in the fields over Bethlehem. Everything is to be reconciled: God and man, God and the world, the world and man. And it is all to be done in a way which will at once unite everything and yet leave it as integrally what it is. 'Not by the conversion of the Godhead into flesh', says the Athanasian Creed of the mystery of the Incarnation, 'but by the assumption of manhood into God: wholly one not by fusion of substance but by unity of person'.

And this is it: the philosopher's stone, the key to all mythologies, the foundation for a theory of everything. The union of divinity with humanity, and the union therefore of the Source of creation with that creation in a new way that has the power to resolve all conflict and all frustration of the good: this is where we take our stand. It is from here that we can see how right we are to feel at home in the world and yet drawn beyond it. How humanism is both right and wrong; how Islam (which is against not only fusion but union) and Buddhism (which is against substance) have each got half of the jigsaw puzzle and so can never put the bits together; how Hinduism has a weird and wonderful guess at a truth it could never know. Emmanuel. God with us: really with us, on our side of the Creator/creature distinction, and yet at the same time really

God, without diminishment of his perfect being. This is the Gospel that made England Christian and it is the mind-blowing, heart-pacifying truth we offer the world at Christmas.

Christmas: The Mass at Midnight (2)

The founder of the movement called Christian Science was the late nineteenth century American matriarch Mrs Baker Eddy. Mrs Baker Eddy was not opposed to Christmas as such. But she was very opposed to giving Christmas presents. Or rather, she was opposed to giving material Christmas presents, sending people what she called 'gross and sensual' gifts. Far more helpful, she thought, was to sit in a chair and think beautiful thoughts about one's friends, in that way sending them spiritual Christmas presents.

It fell to our own G. K. Chesterton to disabuse her. Her proposal, he commented, did not lack a 'certain economic charm'. But it had a fundamental theological flaw. At the first Christmas, the divine Father did not in point of fact think beautiful thoughts about us. Instead he gave us the aboriginal Christmas present which consists of the divine Word, eternally one in substance with him, and as of this night embodied as a human baby, in our flesh. Mrs Baker Eddy was emptying out the whole meaning of Christmas which is precisely to embody good will in something material.

At the time Chesterton wrote the phrase 'the consumer society' did not yet exist. But even in the Edwardian period a Cockney barrow-boy could press his nose against the window of a great London store and see a world of wondrous material things, any of which might be a gift if the right buyer came along. Great shops represent an alliance of commerce with art. They accept that many people will cross the threshold mainly for the experience of being in the shop rather than for anything they are going to take out of it. People go into it as into a dream-world, to see something they may fall in love with.

The seventeenth century Dominican priest-tertiary St Louis-Marie de Montfort writes that almighty God has an emporium or opulent shop where he has put on show everything that is most precious, beautiful, and splendid. It is Mary as giving us Jesus.

This is the emporium into which we are invited by the shop-window of the Liturgy of the Church this Christmas. To find the true goods of the Church we have to come on in, past the window. The goods we are to find entrancing are a Child held in its mother's arms. Not any child, however, though every child is an image of this Child in vulnerability and personal innocence. Instead, a Child in whom the Creator of the universe has taken on our nature to show us his glorious selfhood in ways we can appreciate.

Often there is nothing useful our religion can do for us. But always it is this enchanted world where the beauty of God shines out in the gift which cannot be bought by anyone precisely because it is for everyone: cannot be bought but can be commonly enjoyed. So back in conclusion to Chesterton: 'The Christ-child stood at Mary's knee,/ His hair was like a crown,/ And all the flowers looked up at Him,/ And all the stars looked down.'

Christmas: The Mass at Midnight (3)

Wherever we are in the world, at Midnight Mass on Christmas Eve we are in spirit at Bethlehem where the Saviour was born. There, earlier tonight, crowds will have gathered inside and outside the basilica of the Nativity, waiting for the Latin patriarch to arrive from Jerusalem to begin the Christmas celebration.

Some of the families present claim to date back to the time of Christ, and it was through such families, presumably, that the memory was passed down of where exactly Jesus had been born — a cave among trees at the end of a ridge, or so it was said. It was by reference to such reports that some fifteenth hundred years ago the Jerusalem bishop persuaded the emperor Constantine to build a church.

If we went there ourselves, what should we find? Leaving aside the pilgrims, we should find a community that is dwindling, if not dying. That is, Christian Bethlehem is dying. In the new Israel, it is hard for Christian Arabs to find good work, nor could they expect better under the Crescent of Islam. Slowly but surely, they are drifting away.

This is very sad, but it is not wholly incongruous. When the Son of God took our nature, the situation he entered was marked by homelessness, rejection, fear for the future. There was no room for him at the inn and soon, owing to Herod's hostility to Messianic ideas, he was on the run for his life, carried to Egypt by Mary and Joseph. He came, after all, to find us in our lostness, and, as the stranger at the inn, sharing that lostness in his own mode, he sought to bring us to a different home.

In the Gospel according to St Luke, from which the Gospel of the Mass of Christmas Night is taken, the inn at Bethlehem is not the only inn that is mentioned. There is also the inn of the Cenacle, the Upper Room, where the Lord Jesus instituted the sacrament we are celebrating now. With his enemies closing in on him he offered his own the most exquisite hospitality: the feast of his presence, his very Body and Blood. At that moment God in Christ made himself their home, their inn, the place where their desire would be nourished, their thirst quenched.

All homes now are only pointers, and inns do not just have signs: rather, they *are* signs—of the ultimate warmth and shelter that is the life of God.

Christmas: The Dawn Mass

On hearing the news of Charles Dickens' death in June 1870, a Cockney barrow-girl is said to have exclaimed: 'What! Dickens dead? Then will Father Christmas die too?' The Christmas of Dickens, the Victorian Christmas, the family Christmas, the English Christmas as found in the modern period, has now become inextricably confused with the traditional Christmas of Christianity. It is hard to imagine the extinction of the family Christmas without supposing the dying-out of Christmas altogether.

The Dickensian Christmas has not been without its critics. One obituarist remarked sardonically that Dickens' contribution to Christianity lay in the discovery of the immense spiritual power of the Christmas turkey. The joviality of Christmas at Dingley Dell, does it have much to do with the original Christmas at Bethlehem, with the Christ-child lying in a place fit only for animals? Dickens himself thought there was a connexion. At his public readings of 'A Christmas Carol' he would give special emphasis to a passage where he had written: 'After a while they played at forfeits; for it is good to be children sometimes, and never better than at Christmas, when its mighty Founder was a child himself'.

The common connexion, then, lies in the theme of the childhood of God: the childlikeness of God and the actual childhood lived out by God in the God-man Jesus Christ. What does this mean for our attitudes to maturity, to seriousness, to what is important in life? It seems that it was unnecessary for the Word of God, when he took to himself a human nature, to grow old or even to become middle-aged. Yet it was necessary that he knew childhood, for there is something about the Word which cannot be spoken *except in the form of a child*. As the young man he was when he ministered and died, his name for his Father remained a child's word: *Abba*, 'dear Father'. He was a child in love with the Father, who prayed on the Cross the Jewish child's nighttime prayer, 'Into thy hands I commend my spirit'. His utter trust of the Father replicated in time and space his eternal responsiveness to the Father as the eternal Word. It was the power of that everlasting Childhood that broke through the tyranny of death in the Resurrection.

From divine revelation we know that this world is essentially a child's world, a world made for feasting, not a tragic world whose sorrows are beyond repair. Dingley Dell is not a faithful image of the world as it is empirically, but it is a true image of the world as it was meant to be before the Fall, and as it will be eschatologically, in the End. Scrooge's nephew says he regards Christmas 'apart from the veneration due to its sacred name and origin, if anything belonging to it can be apart from that, as a good time; a kind, forgiving, charitable, pleasant time; the only time... of the year when men and women seem by their common consent to open their shut-up hearts freely, and to think of people below them as if they really were fellow-passengers to the grave, and not another race of creatures bound on other journeys'.

We ask God this Christmas to give us the grace of spiritual childhood, to open our hearts to those in need, and above all to place our trust in the ultimate Goodness of things whose name is the Father of Jesus Christ our Lord.

Christmas: The Day Mass (1)

The Gospel of the Day Mass of Christmas is, then, the Prologue to
the Gospel according to St John, this great text which Christopher
Columbus declaimed into the wind and waves each day from the
poop of the Sancta Maria on his voyage of discovery of the other
side of the world.

Among its many virtues, the Prologue draws to our attention
what should be our reasons for Christian believing.

The study of reasons for believing, or what we call 'apologetics',
is a much-needed discipline sorely missed in much Catholic
religious education in recent decades. This is a good time to start
practicing it again. Leader-writers and commentators in the press
give the impression the Church is on the intellectual ropes, battered
to a pulp in fact by the forces of secularism especially in its robust
scientific variety, and that if any religious body will be alive and
kicking in a century's time it will be Islam.

So let me give you, drawn from today's Gospel, reasons why
we should neither be secularists nor Muslims. In each case, the
reasons have to do with the claim that in the beginning was the
Word and the Word was with God and the Word was God.

To begin with: a reason for Christian believing over against
secularism (which I shall take to be more or less synonymous with
atheism). One perfectly legitimate way to paraphrase the statement, 'In the beginning was the Word' is: 'In the beginning was
rationality'. The ultimate reality of the world is order that is filled
with thought. If you are an atheist it is impossible to make this
claim.

Secularists may prize reasoned argument, and the orderly
exploration of the world by the physical sciences, but on their own
principles these are chance by-products of evolution. It is purely
accidental that human animals can do these things. Rationality is
not the foundation of the world. It is a sport. It arose by a
one-in-a-million chance. There is no creative thought, no rationality
in act, behind the world. For scientific secularism, rationality is, in
this sense, alien to the basic character of the universe.

Yet to say this is virtually to contradict oneself. To speak of
rationality at all is to claim that in a universal kind of way all things

are penetrable by reason, subject to reason. The only justification for this claim is bound up with the Christian conviction that in the beginning was the Word—creative thought—and the Word was with God, and the Word was God.

This same text also give us a useful reason for Christian believing over against Islam too. Another perfectly legitimate way to paraphrase the statement that 'In the beginning was the Word' is 'In the beginning was communication'. God is not a bare unity for whom communication is something that goes on, if at all, only by his choice in deciding to set up relations with a world outside him—which is what Islam holds. Rather, from the beginning God is *in his own life essentially communicative*. From all eternity, he has his Word, and his Word exists as sheer communication with him because it is, precisely, the *Word* of God: it is essentially communication and what communication does is to communicate.

Relationship is not something God sets up beyond himself if he so chooses. It in inherent in his being, it is essential to who he is. If this were not so, how could we be justified in saying—as most modern Western people want to do—that relationship is the most important thing that exists, that it is what concentrates the highest values there are, that the sharing of knowledge and love with another takes us to the heart of what is really worthwhile in life? In saying things like this, we should only be making a claim about the preferences of one particular animal species, our own—or, to be more precise, the preferences of the higher-minded animals among us. We cannot say that being in communication, being in relationship, is foundational to reality unless we can say with today's Gospel, 'In the beginning was the Word and the Word was with God and the Word was God'.

On Christmas morning we remember this affirmation and we also remember, and more especially, the affirmation that follows it. To set beside the philosophical claims that need divine revelation for their full securing, we have the following totally unexpected theological assertion (made today while kneeling down, at the appropriate point in the Creed), 'And the Word was made flesh and dwelt among us'. In the Incarnation the communicative rationality behind the world, the communicative rationality that rules out of court as serious contenders for our attention both secularism and Islam, united itself to our human nature in the babe born at Bethlehem, so that we might be re-made: regenerated as rational communicators ourselves, and, more than that, lifted up to begin to share that endless divine life which the Word enjoyed with the Father in the Holy Spirit from before the world was made.

Christmas: The Day Mass (2)

Not without reason, perhaps, high-minded Christians seem always to be complaining nowadays about the commercialism and materialism of the modern Christmas. A witty example ends with the injunction, 'Get thou behind me, Santa!'. Sometimes this complaint takes the form of saying, Christmas should really be about the home, the family. Hence the recent custom of sending people photographs of yourself, your spouse and your children rather than of anything more directly theological. A sometime prior of Blackfriars Cambridge adjured me in preparation for the Day Mass of Christmas, 'Now remember, it's a family service, not too much about the Trinity'.

Of course, a presentation of the Christmas message which did not take into account the sanctity and vulnerability of home and family of Jesus would not be true to what happened to Mary and Joseph at Bethlehem and Nazareth. Nor for that matter would a version of the Christmas message that sought to exclude gift-giving—and, in that sense, materialism and hence commerce if not (one hopes) commercialism. The manger was not reserved to shepherds who came in from the fields empty-handed. It also included the magi who brought costly gifts including the very symbol of commerce, gold itself. What we hear today is that the Eternal entered these institutions and practices, and validated them in such a way as to point to their ultimate meaning.

And here I am afraid I cannot manage not to use the 'T' word: 'T' for the Holy Trinity. The Word became flesh so as to demonstrate that these ordinary processes get their full sense only from something greater than they are—from the way they can be made to reflect the boundless Generosity that the Trinity is. Since the Incarnation, the only way to be properly human is to be Christian. To be attuned to the music of the cosmos is no longer possible without taking seriously the music of Christmas. So I give the last word to that amazing poet Christopher Smart:

> Where is this stupendous stranger,
> Swains of Solyma, advise,
> Lead me to my Master's manger,
> Show me where my Saviour lies?
> O most Mighty! O most Holy!
> Far beyond the seraph's thought,
> Art thou then so mean and lowly
> As unheeded prophets taught?
> O magnitude of meekness!
> Worth from worth immortal sprung;
> O the strength of infant weakness,
> If eternal is so young!
> Nature's decorations glisten
> Far about their usual rim;
> Birds on box and laurels listen,
> As so near the cherubs hymn.
> Boreas now no longer winters
> On the desolated coast,
> Oakes no more are riv'n in splinters
> By the whirlwind and his host.
> Spinks and ouzels sing sublimely,
> 'We too have a Saviour born',
> Whiter blossoms burst untimely
> On the blest Mosaic thorn.
> God all-bounteous, all creative,
> Whom no ills from good dissuade,
> Is incarnate, and a native
> Of the very world he made.

Sunday in the Octave of Christmas, The Holy Family (1)

The family today is under threat in the Western world as never before, and so thought has to be taken for how families should be trained: how they should have a discipline of life suited to the process of sanctification as that goes on specifically in the family setting. In a priory like this one, a novitiate is offered suitable to training people for the Religious life, for life in a Religious community, in what we can call the monastic church. So likewise there is also a novitiate suited to training people for life in a family community, life in the domestic church. But this family novitiate is not offered by clerics, it is offered by the Holy Family of Nazareth themselves

There is an obvious parallel between the mother of a family and the Mother of Jesus. The mother of a family has to nurture her child within her own body and then, once that child has come forth, to continue that nurture by all possible means. That includes a responsibility for spiritual nurture, by teaching her child through deed and word the human vocabulary of the love of God with which the New Testament Scriptures and the lives of the saints are filled.

Likewise, there is an obvious parallel between the father of a family and St Joseph, the adoptive father of Jesus. The father of any family has to honour God the Father by exercising his fatherhood in an upright fashion: by guarding and protecting the mother and children of the marriage, and exemplifying in his own life obedience to the law of God. And that means developing a sensitivity to everything opposed to that law which might undermine the children's good, undermine their human and spiritual wellbeing.

When a human child is enfolded in the protective love of the father and the nurturing love of the mother, it becomes an image of the Child of Nazareth who in time was enfolded in the love of Joseph and Mary just as, in eternity, as the Son he was enfolded in the love of the Father and the Holy Spirit.

In the face of an often false modern sophistication, such a Nazareth novitiate will entail re-learning key qualities of natural and supernatural life. We have to re-learn the beauty of generosity and self-giving, of fidelity and chastity, as well as the basic dignity of womanhood and motherhood, of manhood and fatherhood.

At the first Christmas, the requirements of the census obliged the Holy Family to go to Bethlehem to be counted. But the Church's families too need to go to Bethlehem in this sense: a Catholic family must not be afraid to stand up and be counted, to stand out, and be accounted different from others in its ethos. As the Second Vatican Council notes, it is a 'domestic sanctuary', it is the most basic cell of Holy Church. It just *has* to be different.

Sunday in the Octave of Christmas, The Holy Family (2)

The title 'The Holy Family' —meaning the inter-relation of Jesus, Mary and Joseph—comes from the end of the nineteenth century. Before that, for four hundred years, what we now call the Holy Family had gone under a different title: not everywhere but in a good deal of visual art, preaching and devotion. It was called *trinitas terrestris*, 'the earthly trinity', understanding the inter-relations of Jesus, Mary and Joseph as a sort of mirror on earth of the divine Trinity of Father, Son and Holy Spirit: Jesus embodying the Son, Mary symbolizing the Holy Spirit, and Joseph playing the role of the eternal Father.

Whatever one thinks of that title or that idea, it does have one distinct advantage. Not all of us live in nuclear families. Some of us live alone, or come from broken families, or belong to some wider group whether linked by blood or by other ties, as in a Religious community. But all of us, I hope, have homes. When the Holy Family was known as the earthly trinity it seems to have been the patron of a much wider variety of such homes than it became later—from the cottage of an unmarried peasant to the palaces of Catholic dynasties like the Wittelsbachs or the Habsburgs.

Today's feast tells us that somehow we have to sacralise our homes, to make them open out toward heaven—not only by living out the moral virtues in them but also by letting them signal that they have a reference to the heavenly home of which the opening prayer of today's Mass speaks: the Father's house that is the new temple, with at its centre the throne of God and of the Lamb.

Household prayers, grace at meals, having holy pictures in the house or even an icon corner like the Orthodox and Byzantine Catholics do is part and parcel of this—these are features of Catholic practice that point us to what we can call 'ultimate home'. Making the earthly trinity of Jesus, Mary and Joseph patrons of our home belongs there as well.

For the days between 26th December and 29th December inclusive, see Volume 1 of this Homiliary, The Sanctoral Cycle.

The 30ᵗʰ of December

So the Child whom on Christmas Day we worshipped as Emmanuel, God-with-us, starts to grow not only in strength but also in wisdom. The teaching of the New Testament about Jesus Christ is baffling unless we have got hold (preferably explicitly but if not then implicitly) of the key which the first Seven Ecumenical Councils of the Church give us, since all those Councils, in one way or another, were concerned with the question, Who is Jesus Christ?

Only if Jesus Christ is one divine person in two natures possessed in their full integrity, only if he is fully God and fully man, can we make sense of the various Gospels of Christmastide. The Child Jesus grows in wisdom in his humanity by coming to share ever more comprehensively in the wisdom that his divinity is. So, as or Lord's life and ministry develop, the humanity assumed by the Word comes to reproduce, insofar as humanity can, the essential qualities of the Word himself.

And what that means in the last analysis we shall see only at Easter when loving response to the Father takes the Son to the Cross and to Hell.

The 31ˢᵗ of December

It seems at first sight a bit rum that the last day of the year has for a Gospel reading the beginning of the Gospel according to John, 'In the beginning was the Word', the Gospel we heard on Christmas morning at the Day Mass. What has an ending—the final day of the expiring year—got to do with a beginning?

Actually, there must be some correspondence between ends and beginnings if time (and thus creatures who live in time) is to be fulfilled in a way that is coherent, consistent, congruent. For St Thomas, all creation as it comes out from God as its beginning is moving towards God as its end. The Source and the Goal are closely inter-related. And that is true in a special sense of rational creatures like ourselves whose souls were created by God with a natural desire to see him, which, thanks to God's grace, will be slaked—unless disaster intervenes—in the vision of God at the end.

But of course we shall not, at the end, return to him just as we were at the beginning, as though time and history were just an exercise that added nothing of abiding importance to the spiritual soul. On the contrary, we shall go back to God with all our experiences of each other, of nature, of the world, and not least of his grace as concretely shown to us in Jesus Christ and the sacramental living of the Church.

When our Lord came forth from God into the world at the Incarnation he was to return to him at the Ascension but not just as he had been before. He takes his human experience with him to the Father and not least he takes with him the family of his disciples who ever since the Ascension have been following him to his right hand.

So today, the last day of the old year, we think of our beginning and how it guides us to our end, but also of the difference that everything in between will make. It is a mysterious day, more significant than New Year's Day, perhaps, and with a curious patron, St Sylvester, the Christian who was pope when the Church became an official religion of the Empire in 314 but about whom, strangely, almost nothing is known. Sylvester appears again in legends and prophecies of the Apocalypse, the end not of the year but of time itself, as if to say that how things were at the beginning of the Church's role in human civilisation—a painful struggle through the darkness of hostility, indeed, persecution—so will they be at the end when finally she steps forth into the light of everlasting day.

1st January, The Octave Day of Christmas, Solemnity of Mary, Mother of God

The most popular Christmas card, among people who are in any way religious, must surely be the Mother and Child, Mary with Jesus. Today is the culmination of the Octave of Christmas, the eight day celebration of the feast that started on Christmas Eve. We keep this Octave Day as the Solemnity of Mary, Mother of God. In other words, we don't let Christmas end without looking explicitly at the role of Mary, the indispensable part she played in the Incarnation and thus in our whole religion.

Would it be true, then, to say that today we turn away from Jesus to his Mother? Not at all, because if we look at the great artistic images of the Madonna and Child we find that the Mother points us back to her Son. Mary is contemplating Jesus, perhaps, or indicating him with her hand—as in the kind of Greek icon which is called *hodegitria*: literally 'pointing the way'. In St John's Gospel, our Lord calls himself 'The Way', so there is an interesting ambiguity here. Mary points the way by pointing to the way that is Jesus himself, who is our way to the Father and also our way of life. And even when Mary is not gazing directly at Jesus or pointing to him, images of the Mother and Child still show their unity which artists can underline in subtle ways, by the arrangements of limbs or clothing, in line and colour.

The natural bonding which holds together a mother and her baby gives an obvious basis to this unity of Mary and Jesus. But here the unity is more profound. Here the Child is also Mary's Creator and her Saviour. His humanity has been assumed from the first moment of its conception by God the Word who is himself the self-expression of the Father, the Source of all. So he is his Mother's Creator. And it is by his gracious anticipation of his own redeeming work as man that Mary, at his birth as before it, is full of grace. So he is her Saviour too.

She has been prepared for this role since the beginning of God's involvement in the history of the human race. She represents what is best in the Jewish people, just as the Jewish people represented what was best in the religious experience of mankind. The affinity between this Mother and her Child—Emmanuel, God with us— will be, therefore, as deep as it is close, and it will lead to an extraordinary commerce between them. Between Mary and Jesus an exchange is taking place so deep that its significance is endless.

From one point of view, Christian spirituality consists in being taken up into that interchange, that relationship. We look with Mary at Jesus and with Jesus at Mary, so as to understand the union of God with humanity and, by grace, to begin to share in what it means, to begin to become saints.

This is the real meaning of the Western Church's most wide-spread Marian devotion, the Rosary. In the Rosary, we look with Mary as the events of the life of her Son: events joyful, luminous, sorrowful, and glorious. We salute her, but we place our greetings, our Hail Marys, between two other prayers. Before the Hail Marys comes the only prayer Jesus gave his disciples, the Our Father, and after the Hail Marys comes the doxology or 'Glory be' which is the Church's outburst of praise of the divine Trinity. In the interrelations of the Mother and the Child, the Trinity reveal themselves as the true God: the Father sending her the Son and enabling her to conceive in every sense of that word by the Holy Spirit.

That is why, as the anonymous mediaeval poet has it,

> There is no rose of such virtue
> As the rose that bare Jesu.
> For in that rose contained was
> Heaven and earth in little space.

It's all found in an image which is not just for Christmas but should be permanently in our homes and work-places: Mary, Mother of God, with Jesus her Child.

CHRISTMASTIDE

2nd January, The Holy Name of Jesus

It was in the year of St Thomas's death that the Order of Preachers was entrusted with the task of promoting veneration of the Name of Jesus. Our Lord had taught his disciples to pray to the Father the words, 'Hallowed be thy Name'. But soon enough the Name of Jesus itself began to be hallowed, treated as holy, as the New Testament letters indicate. And that reflected the concern of the Christmas Gospels for the significance of this Name. 'You shall call his Name Jesus for he will save his people from their sins.' So here the young Order had got hold of something very evangelical that went right back to the beginning.

Not that nothing had happened in between St Paul in the first century and the Dominicans of the late thirteenth century. There are a number of texts, very much to the point, that have come down to us from the Fathers of the Church, not least in the Christian East. In time, the monks of Eastern Christianity came to give the prayerful repetition of the Name of Jesus a major place in contemplation. Indeed they regarded it so highly that in the Russian monasteries on Athos just before the First World War it was commonly taught that the Saviour was really present whenever his Name was uttered in a spirit of confession and glorification — about which claim controversy grew so heated that a number of monks had to be taken off the Holy Mountain by frigates of the Russian imperial navy. In mediaeval monasteries too devotion to the Holy Name often aroused great fervour: the hymn by St Bernard in honour of the Holy Name became known as the *magna jubilatio*, the 'Great Outburst of Joy'.

This is what Dominican (and also Franciscan) preaching took out among the masses — often holding up as they did so a disc containing the trigram, the first three letters of the name 'Jesus' in Greek.

But what does it all mean? We know that primitive peoples were deeply concerned about getting right the names of their gods. It's less often pointed out that modern philosophers treat it as equally important to work out how God should be named, how language about him is justified when we call him, for instance, 'The One' or 'The Good' or 'The Beautiful'. God's 'Name' is his reality insofar as that can be known by us. The Old Testament is jealously protective of the Name of God, precisely in order to secure God's right of initiative in making himself known. The New Testament casts caution to the winds, because in the Son the Father has laid bare his own inner nature for our salvation. The Holy Name of Jesus gives us the key.

The 3rd of January

In today's Gospel we look forward to the feast we shall shortly be celebrating, the Baptism of Christ. In this passage, John the Baptist witnesses to its supernatural aspect, the visionary or, if you prefer, miraculous aspect: when Jesus went down into the waters John saw the Spirit descending upon him 'like a dove'.

Doves feature quite a lot in the Old Testament: notably in the Song of Songs where they are a symbol of love. Birds feature even more widely, if sometimes also allusively — as in the opening verses of the Bible where, in the act of creation, the Spirit 'hovers' over the waters, suggesting a broody bird about to hatch her young. The modern commentators are not quite sure how to take the description of the Spirit as a dove at the Baptism of the Lord, but perhaps these two references will do for a first interpretation.

At the Baptism, the Messiah, who is in the process now of being 'revealed to Israel', descends into the waters of the Jordan, and as he does so, the Spirit also makes himself known. The Messiah goes down into those 'waters' which so often in the Hebrew Bible stand for the chaotic aspects of the world, and he does so in the power of the Holy Spirit who at the beginning hovered over the chaos waters to make of them a cosmos. The Spirit acted in the beginning to bring the natural cosmos, a physically ordered world, out of primeval chaos. Now the Messiah is to bring a spiritual cosmos, a spiritually ordered world out of the moral chaos of fallen humanity.

It will mean for the Messiah a hard road ahead. The earliest Christian hymn-book, *The Odes of Solomon*, links to Christ's descent at his Baptism the other descent still to come, his descent on Holy

Saturday into Hell. 'The dove fluttered over the Messiah', says Ode 24, 'and sang over him, and her voice was heard… The abysses opened, which had been hidden'. Yes, in the Paschal Mystery, the full extent of our alienation from God will be laid bare, but this will also be the moment when the divine Love is revealed in its fullness in our pardon, reconciliation, and ultimately deification. The dove of the Baptism was not only a sign of the remaking of the world. The dove was also a symbol of the Love of Father and Son, the Love who personally is their Holy Spirit.

The 4ᵗʰ of January

This is the second time in the opening chapter of St John's Gospel that the evangelist recalls for us the exclamation of the Baptist on seeing Jesus, 'Behold, the Lamb of God!'. The Lamb of God: a very important title for Christ. In the time around the Epiphany, the newer Roman Lectionary reserves the first of John's acclamations of Jesus for a Sunday, but that only happens in two years out of every three. So it is good that, every Christmastide, those who come to weekday Mass can always be sure of hearing today's text and having a chance to ponder what this title tells us about the person and work of our Lord.

It is a sacrificial title. It looks back to Isaiah's prophecy of how the Servant of the Lord would be led like a lamb to the slaughter: he, the One in whom God's plans for his people—and not just for that people but for all the nations—was to come to fruition. The slaughter of lambs was no mere agricultural necessity for those of Isaiah's contemporaries who lived by the meat of sheep as well as by their wool. It was part and parcel of Israel's sacrificial cultus: these animals, so precious to the peasantry of Judah, stood proxy for their owners, the worshippers who vowed their lives to God in these sacrificial gifts.

It belongs to the Epiphany season to remember that the divine Son came to save us not so much by his birth as by his sacrificial Death, and by the Resurrection which was the unmistakable sign of the Father's acceptance of that gift. We do not leave the celebration of Christmastide without recalling the Baptism of Jesus: his descent into the waters and rising up again onto dry land as

the Spirit hovers over him like a dove—all of which is an anticipation of his Baptism of Blood on the Cross, the outcome of which is
his Resurrection and the Outpouring of the Holy Spirit.

So the title 'Lamb of God' is not just a statement of our need for
One who can make atonement for us. That would be, no doubt, a
relief to hear of, but a sombre message all the same. No, the title
'The Lamb of God' is a prophecy of joy ahead. 'The marriage of
the Lamb has come!' This is how in the Book of the Apocalypse St
John tells his hearers that the whole work of salvation has been
accomplished in Jesus Christ. The Baptism of the Lord, which we
shall be celebrating in a few days time is, as the ancient Liturgies
like to call it, the 'bridal bath' of the King.

The 5th of January

In the Christmas Octave we soon saw how the Liturgy of Christmastide does not stay fixated on the Babe in the manger—the
peaceful pastoral idyll with shepherds and domestic animals—but
looks directly ahead to the saving death of Christ, through the
Christmas feasts of the martyrs. Similarly, in the days before
Epiphany the readings invite us to contemplate the universal
mission of the Child who tomorrow will receive the homage of the
Magi.

Yesterday we had the call of Andrew and Peter whom tradition
regards as the chief sources of Eastern and Western Christianity
respectively. Today in the call of Philip and Nathanael the horizon
extends even further. Here the key statement is that the angels will
'ascend and descend upon the Son of Man'. It's a statement about
the limits or boundaries within which Christ will work—or, rather,
the overcoming of such limits and boundaries.

The call of Andrew and Peter, seen in the light of tradition,
which associates Andrew with Byzantium, Peter with Rome,
already implies that the sphere of the Messiah is not going to be
confined to Israel. But now with Philip and Nathanael there is
something more. It is the boundary not this time between Jews and
Gentiles but between earth and heaven that is collapsing. In Jesus
there is a direct opening to the transcendent, to what human
philosophy can only treat as a limit for thought, and human culture

only hint at in its myths and symbols. The invisible world of God
and his glory is breaking into this one, so as to give us direct access
to God himself.

That is what we shall see, we hope, in the glorified humanity
of Jesus in heaven, and it is what the gold, frankincense and myrrh
of tomorrow's Solemnity will signify. So the message of today's
Gospel is: the sky's the limit!

6th January, The Epiphany of the Lord

It has been fashionable in some circles to dismiss the stories of the
infancy of Christ as pious legend. But the pendulum of scholarship
has started to swing again. What, after all, is more probable than
that writers who believed Jesus to be Israel's Messiah and the
Saviour of all peoples (as Luke and Matthew did) would have been
curious about his origins, his ancestors, his birthplace, his family-
circle, and any memories that pointed to his later fate? In this sense,
it is the absence of such material in the other two evangelists, Mark
and John, which requires some explanation.

On Matthew's account of the infancy of Christ, the roughly two
year stay of the Holy Family at Bethlehem included an astronom-
ically-inspired encounter with wandering astrologers from the
pagan cultures to Palestine's east. To us, astrology means reading
your horoscope for a lucky week in the *Daily Express*. But as it
existed in the high cultures that practiced it, astrology was more
than that. It combined primitive science with speculation about
great religious and historical themes or trends.

There are now available plausible reconstructions of how
astrologers to the east of Palestine could have got hold of the idea
that a universal ruler was emerging among the Jews. Herod the
Great's reported reaction to such rumours was in keeping with
contemporary attitudes. Astrology made rulers jittery. At one point
in the later New Testament period, the emperor Domitian had
those born with the horoscopes of potential emperors identified
and executed. So the setting of the Epiphany is historically quite
credible.

In any case, if we believe that the Church has inherited a special
insight into the revelation entrusted to her (and there is no other

serious reason for belonging to the Church than this), we need to say that her methods can take us further than those of neutral scholarship. And she certainly celebrates the Epiphany liturgically as a genuine event.

Let us, say, then, that something significant happened. The text of the Gospel, and the texts with which it is surrounded in the Liturgy, tutor us in what that 'something' was. It has to do with the glory of God revealed in the child in Mary's arms and the universal importance—for all peoples, all individuals—of what his birth means.

The Wise Men stand for the wisdom that lies outside Israel, beyond the confines of the Land of the Promise. They represent a knowledge and an understanding of the world which was alien to the religious and cultural tradition in which, most immediately, the Word became incarnate. And yet despite this, they manage to come to Christ, to the incarnate Wisdom of the God they barely knew.

What those questions are become apparent from the gifts they carry. Gold is the metal from which royal insignia are made, and in which world trade is or was carried out. It stands, then, for politics and economics—questions about the nature of power and how it might be used for the human good.

Frankincense is the material of worship, used in the cult—the service—of God or the gods. As Wise Men, the Magi necessarily have searching questions about the divine, searching theological questions.

Lastly they bring myrrh: the stuff used for mummifying the dead, and death, we can say, is the great question-mark set against all human activity. In that sense we could call death the philosophical question par excellence, because philosophy is the discipline which asks in the most general way possible after what, how, and why the world is.

So the Wise Men have questions about the political and social order of the world, they have theological concerns, and they have philosophical anxieties. And these they bring with their own kind of faith and hope to this unique Child whom the Church of the Gentiles will eventually proclaim as universal King—the ultimate answer to the questions of politics and economics; as God from

God—the ultimate object of theological concern; as Victor over death—the ultimate resolution of philosophical anxieties.

By the presence of these pagan intellectuals at the opening of the Gospel, St Matthew anticipates the ending of his gospel-book. That is when the risen Christ will tell the disciples to go out and preach the Good News to every creature. The Epiphany is the proclamation to those who are not Jews, and whose faith may be far from simple, that they too shall be brought into the presence of God made man, the truth they seek in his own person, and rejoice there, as the evangelist records, with exceeding great joy.

The Second Sunday after Christmas

Today's Gospel is probably the most important paragraph of the Bible where orthodox Christianity is concerned, and this explains, no doubt, why the Roman Lectionary gives it us not only on Christmas morning and on New Year's Eve, but also now when we are well and truly into the Christmastide celebration. For orthodoxy turns above all on how we understand the Incarnation.

Why was it that Fathers of the Church, writing commentaries on the Gospel according to St John found it so hard to get beyond this Prologue? It has to do with the difficulty of leaving behind this phrase: 'The Word became flesh'. Just four words, but each could elicit a chapter in a book.

First, 'The Word'. The Word is God's self-expression. Besides the Father for ever and ever there is in the divine personality One in whom the Father has put the whole of himself.

Next, this Word 'became'. At the Father's behest, the Word compromised his divine changelessness without, however, abandoning anything proper to the nature of God. In his own person, he entered the realm of time, of history, with all its messiness and ambiguity. He became affected by the world which was made through him. One who was divine became one of God's own creatures. One who was of the same nature with the Creator became one of those things he had made, became part of his own creation, in order to show solidarity with it.

And lastly, *what* the Word became was 'flesh'. 'Flesh' for the Bible is man as subject to decay and death, subject to transience, to passing away into nothingness, at least for our body which is integral to ourselves. So far as secular historians are concerned, the Word ends his career at the Cross. And since the Cross was the supreme expression of his solidarity it was also the supreme expression of his glory, his glorious divine goodness. We saw the glory of the Word incarnate, says John on behalf of the apostolic witnesses: and he was full of grace and truth.

Sermons are supposed to end up with a moral, with a practical application, with something 'relevant'. But there is nothing we can do adequate to the meaning of today's Gospel except contemplate it in amazement as we walk back home. The Maker of everything we see around us, for our sake became a part of this world and a most vulnerable part at that. This tells us what the divine Generosity is like, and therefore into what kind of existence we have come. 'The Word became flesh.' They are the four most important words in the world.

The 7th of January

The Liturgy has given us so many wonderful themes for our contemplation at Christmas and the Epiphany that we may fall into a sort of religious reverie, assisted by the fact that at this time of year we have an excuse to do less or no work. But in his first Letter, St John makes sure that we don't lose contact with the messy world, a world of conflict, a world in which, as he says, we may *meet Antichrist*. The figure of the Antichrist is too deeply rooted in the New Testament for Catholics to leave it to Protestant Fundamentalists to deal with.

Some of the mediaevals thought a good deal about the Antichrist, using to interpret this figure the ancient metaphysical categories of the One and the Many. St John gave them the cue for this. He himself regards the Antichrist as both many and one. The baptized are to prepare themselves for the possible arrival of the Antichrist, yet many antichrists have already come. In other words: those many individuals who set themselves diametrically against the Gospel, and the Gospel community, share in the reality of what we might call 'Antichristhood', if there were such a word. And this is so even though there is only one person—*the* Antichrist—in whom that perfect antithesis to Christ will one day be summed up.

This is a potentially dangerous area for the religious imagination to play in. But just as in the ordinary moral life we have to develop a nose for how virtues may tip into their opposites and become vices, so here too we have to be on the look-out for Antichristhood rearing its head—which it will do, we can be sure from the New Testament record, precisely by telling us that it has come to save us. Antichristhood takes the disguise of Christhood.

Two modern examples are Soviet Communism and Western hedonistic humanism. The one persecuted the Church, the other made her irrelevant. Looking at the relative abilities of organized Communism and disorganized consumerism to damage her, we might think the latter had the edge. So on the basis of our modern experience, we might expect the final Antichrist to be subtle, not blatant.

That brings us back to St John: the faithful will need all their powers of spiritual discernment—'the anointing from the Holy One'—to find him out.

The 8ᵗʰ of January

In today's Gospel, our Lord sees that the people are like sheep without a shepherd and so he begins to teach them. This raises a question of importance for the contemporary Church, and it's the relation between pastoring or pastoral care on the one hand, and, on the other, doctrinal teaching: the communication of revealed truth.

Evidently, in this Gospel the two are so closely united that the evangelist sees no difference between them. We, however, may be tempted to set one over against the other. What people need is care, looking after, helping, being given moral or practical support, we hear—not being fed a diet of propositions, or metaphysical or similar truths which, after all, are essentially abstract ideas that have little to do with so-called 'real experience'.

But even in general terms, leaving aside for a moment the Gospel, this contrast cannot be sustained. Take the case of someone who has been bereaved: what counts as appropriate consolation will depend on the view one or both parties take of immortality. Or more widely, with any major setback that has befallen someone, beliefs about Providence, and, perhaps, the role of purification and detachment in human living, or, contrarywise, the absence of such beliefs, will dictate the whole spirit of a pastoral approach. Without doctrine (somebody's doctrine—even if it be the humanist's or indeed the atheist's) there is no context in which to determine what should count as an appropriate, helpful response.

The great nineteenth century French Dominican Père Lacordaire once said, 'The greatest work of charity is to teach doctrine to others'. He meant of course Christian doctrine: no other. Life cannot be nourished, the sheep cannot be fed, without a grasp of the wider realm in which life is set, without well-founded convictions about what is to count as legitimate expectations in life and which human practices really are virtuous. For the Church, that means in the end the entirety of the revelation set in our midst by the One who became incarnate at Christmas.

The 9th of January

Today's epistle has a rather ambivalent message for us about the extent of salvation. On the one hand, we hear that 'he who abides in love abides in God', and this sounds generous enough. All we have to do, it seems, is to be benevolent. On the other hand, we also hear that 'he who abides in God is he who confesses Jesus Christ as the Son of God'. Here what we have to do is to be doctrinally orthodox, to be credally correct.

The general tendency in our own age is undoubtedly to think in terms of ethical, nor credal, conditions for salvation. That God gives everlasting life to the good seems plausible. That he gives it to the correct seems altogether more dubious.

The trouble with such an approach is this: it treats the life everlasting as a prize for competitors who are engaged in a game that in itself has nothing directly to do with the prize at all. The prize is religious, life with God; but the game is only ethical, not cheating your neighbour.

This is why it is better to say with the apostle that there can be no abiding in God without a transformation of heart and mind by *both* love *and* faith, *both* faith *and* love. Faith in Jesus as the Word incarnate opens our minds to the mission of the Son who waits at the door of our soul and knocks. Love, understood not, of course, in the romantic sense nor, for that matter, as general benevolence, but as a facsimile in some way of the sacrificial self-giving of the Cross, opens our hearts to the mission of the Holy Spirit who makes faith in the Son fruitful in good works. And without these twin visitations by the Son and the Spirit we cannot abide in the Father.

Where does this leave the unbeliever or the adamant heretic, who are deficient in faith? And where for that matter does it leave the apparently unrepentant sinner or the morally misguided man, who are deficient in love? The Church commends all to God's mercy but she does not do so by obscuring the revealed way of salvation, which the Bible teaches and she herself is commissioned to preach.

The 10ᵗʰ of January

Among the Luminous Mysteries which Pope John Paul II added to the traditional Rosary, at any rate as an optional extra, the one that seems to stick out rather is the central one, the third, entitled 'The Proclamation of the Kingdom and the Call to Repentance'. Like the traditional Rosary mysteries, Joyful, Sorrowful and Glorious, the other Luminous mysteries are one-off events. They are episodes which are readily set as scenes. They can be visualized. It's not quite so easy to visualise an ongoing process such as our Lord's proclamation of the Kingdom in the overall course of his public ministry.

The episode described in today's Gospel is helpful here. If we are to attempt a visualization of this particular Luminous Mystery we might do worse than start at this point. For St Luke, this scene is the beginning of the proclamation of the Kingdom. The messianic Spirit, who will bring about the reign of God and realize the divine plan for the world, now rests in fullness on Jesus, and so the entire hope of Israel is concentrated on his person. He is the Kingdom in a nutshell. All its energy is concentrated in him in advance.

Proclaiming the Kingdom, he can't but draw attention to himself. 'This text is being fulfilled today even as you listen.'

If we want to visualize this moment, we could if we wished make use of the classic Byzantine image of Christ the all-ruler which shows him blessing with one hand and holding out a book with the other. The book no longer contains a text from prophecy: Isaiah or Jeremiah. Instead, it carries an inscription drawn from one of the great New Testament confessions of faith in Jesus himself—precisely because the prophecies are now realized, and all the prophets are summed up.

Like all mysteries, the mystery of the Proclamation of the Kingdom confronts us with a challenge: how are we going to react? In our spiritual sluggishness, not everything about us wants to react at all. The modern hymn says, 'Let all that is within me cry, Praise him'. But very often that is the last thing all within us wishes to do. When Jesus spoke, says Luke, he won the approval of all, seeming to imply there was a hundred per cent favourable reaction. But then he adds, they were *astonished* by the gracious words that came from his lips, and that 'astonishment', with its connotations of both surprise and disturbance, a rupture in normal expectations, points ahead to the conflicts which will punctuate the ministry and ultimately to the Cross.

It is the Cross that is the real Luminous Mystery. *Per crucem ad lucem*, as the old saying has it, 'Through the Cross to light'. That is when we see the redemption in full act, and are bathed in the radiance of crucified Love which is what the Kingdom turns out to be all about.

The 11ᵗʰ of January

In today's Epistle, St John says of our Lord that he came not with water only but with blood, and that water and blood, along with the Spirit, are testimonies to his coming, as, precisely, the Son of God—for this section of John's First Letter (and indeed the Letter as a whole) is at pains to emphasise the centrality to Christian faith of belief in the divinity of Christ.

So what *are* these three witnesses—water, blood, and Spirit? They are, respectively, two events and one person. The events are the Baptism of Christ (hence water) and his saving Death (hence blood); and the person is the person of the Holy Spirit who inspired the apostles to proclaim Christ's Lordship—Jesus' sharing the prerogatives of the Father as God of Israel. At Jesus' Baptism, the Father's voice was heard echoing on the air, 'This is my Son, the Beloved'. At Jesus' crucifixion, a Roman centurion, standing in here for the response of the peoples, declared 'Truly this was the Son of God'. What was meant by the Father's word of paternal ownership of Jesus? What did the centurion—presumably a pagan—mean by his confession of the Lord's sonship? Who can say? And the answer to *that* question is that the third witness can say—the Spirit can say—since he is the promised Spirit of truth who is to lead the apostles into all the truth.

Through the biblical Canon as a whole, through the Liturgies, the Fathers, the Creeds, and the sacred iconography of the Church, the Spirit adds his witness. The Baptism of the Lord was indeed a theophany, a manifestation of the entire Trinity of whose saving outreach the Son is the central figure. And, though we are less used to thinking of it in these terms, so was Calvary likewise, the climax of the Church year in Holy Week. Calvary too is an epiphany of the Holy Trinity, as the Son gives himself to the Father in the Holy Spirit with world-changing effect.

The 12ᵗʰ of January

As used in the Lectionary, the Gospel for the last feria of Christmastide sets the scene for tomorrow's festival, the Baptism of the Lord, which itself is in a way the climax of the Christmas cycle. Though we have seen great things—the Incarnation of the Word as a tiny baby on the 25ᵗʰ of December and his exhibition to the representatives of the world religions on the 6ᵗʰ of January, one thing we have not yet done is to be shown the Holy Trinity. This is what tomorrow will be about.

At the Baptism of Christ God shows himself for the first time as who he is and begins, therefore, to renovate the created world. I say 'therefore' because when God visits his people he doesn't just stop to say 'Hello'. He makes an impact that changes the way things are. At the Baptism, the heavens, we are told, are thrown open. There is a falling of the barrier separating this world and the transcendental world within which our world is set. And what is revealed, then, under this now open heaven?

What is most obviously revealed (for there will be more to say tomorrow) is the descent of the Son of God, his going down into the depths of our material world, so as to take it up with him: to redeem it, to make it able to be the vehicle of God's glory.

As used in the Liturgy, today's Gospel sets the scene for this by showing how, though there is a revolutionary breakthrough—this is *fresh revelation*—nevertheless it *doesn't cast aside the whole natural and religious development that went before it*. Its context is John the Baptist's activity as a preacher of penance and critical debate within Judaism about what is involved in purification. All the noble, if also confused, expectations of humanity about a new start, a purgation of guilt, being better in future, will come to their fulfillment tomorrow when our Lord steps into the Jordan. The entire prophetic tradition of Israel will be crowned when John acts as the impresario of the Baptism of Christ: and then John, the keeper of Israel's conscience, the steward of her religious patrimony, if you like, and thus the representative of all that is best, under the Providence of God, in man's religious history, will see his moment pass. He will decreases as Christ increases.

This is what we all have to experience in our lives. Our best moral efforts are asked of us, yet we are not, thank God, limited to them, or we should be in real trouble. They are overtaken by the amazing grace of God in Jesus Christ.

Sunday after the Epiphany, The Baptism of the Lord

For early Christians, the thought that their Lord had himself undergone baptism was disturbing, embarrassing and even scandalous. Could the Immaculate Lamb, the altogether holy Jesus, really have submitted to an act of ritual purification? Could he have admitted by implication that he too was part of unclean, guilty, sinful, humankind? It says a great deal for their honesty that they did not attempt a cover-up, but left this seemingly controversial episode as it stood in the Gospel tradition.

But soon enough, when this event could be better contextual-
ized in the wider whole of the Church's developed faith about
Jesus, Christians came to glory in the paradox of the Baptism of
Christ: the moment when the Sinless One came to a sinner to be
washed. They gloried in it because they saw it as an expression, in
the life of Jesus, of the stooping down of God in loving-kindness
to man, his condescension to the level of this world. The way they
gloried in the paradox was by stressing at one and the same time
the humiliation it involved for the Saviour and also his undimin-
ished Godhead.

Let me give you three brief testimonies from the Fathers as
found in the Roman Office of Readings. St Proclus of Constantino-
ple: 'Come then and see new and overwhelming miracles: the sun
of righteousness bathing in Jordan, the fire immersed in water, and
God being sanctified by human ministry'. St Hippolytus: 'He who
is present everywhere and is absent nowhere, incomprehensible
to the Angels and withdrawn from the gaze of man, has come to
baptism as was his good pleasure... Could anything be more
wonderful? The Source without limits that engenders life for all
mankind and is beyond all understanding is covered by the poor
waters of this world'. St Gregory Nazianzen: '"I have need to be
baptized by you", says the lamp to the Sun, the voice to the Word,
the friend to the Bridegroom; he that is above all those who are
born of women to him who is the First-born of every creature; he
that leaped in the womb to him who was adored in the womb; he
who was and is the forerunner to him who was and is to be
manifested'.

In wonderful language, these Fathers register the paradox of
how it is the Infinite in human form who comes to John and
undergoes at his hands a rite of cleansing. The obvious question
is, Why? What is the rationale for this paradoxical act? We look
back from the vantage point of the Paschal Mystery, of Eastertide,
and we can see why. The Cross and Resurrection show how the
generosity of God is total in his self-giving; it went to the lengths
of the Cross and the descent into Hell. That is how the apostolic
letters can re-define God in terms of love. But if analogy from our
side is worth anything at all, it is, surely, characteristic of love—
above all, of perfect love—that it does not hesitate before risk.

When it comes to the aid of the beloved, it does not wait to see whether it might be misunderstood or compromised. It cares not a fig for these things. It makes itself vulnerable and if necessary accepts the hurt.

At his Baptism, the Saviour chooses to be with us where we are, to enter into solidarity with us, sinners as we are. In so doing, he laid himself open to the malicious tongue, the wagging finger. What, in this perspective, makes the Baptism great as a festival of the Church is that in this way it is the preamble of the Crucifixion. The whole destiny of Jesus is contained within it. It is the culmination of Christmastide because it is the source of the impetus that will carry us on to Easter.

This is what the Byzantine icons tell us. Christ goes down into the Jordan as on Calvary he will sink into the chaos waters of death. The river is dark with the murk of evil, but the shimmering gold which surrounds the figure of Christ cleaves it like a sword. It is the overture of his Sacrifice when on the Cross he will enter the darkness again and this time transform it into the radiance of the Resurrection light, offered to us all as joy and peace in the Holy Spirit.

LENT AND PASSIONTIDE

ASH WEDNESDAY WEEK

Ash Wednesday

All men are mortal. No one is going to dispute that proposition at least. But generally we put it in the third person. 'People die' rather than 'I too shall die'. In a moment, however, we shall be carrying out the ancient ritual whereby, as we submit to it, we shall—for once—be saying, 'Yes, I too shall die'.

Our secular culture tends to place a taboo on death. It makes people reluctant to visit cemeteries or even to see the seriously ill in hospital. Over against this we give what Newman called not a notional but a real assent, one that carries with it our emotions and imagination, to the truth of this proposition, 'I too shall die'.

So why do we have this reminder of my/our mortality at, in particular, the start of Lent? There seem to be two main reasons. First, in confessing my mortality I recognize my creatureliness and so my dependence on the Creator for the gift of life. Pride, lust, greed, and the other deadly sins which, in the Lenten warfare, we propose to root out from ourselves, derive from a childish failure to take on board the fact that I am not a god.

I can only act on the assumption that the world exists for my pleasure and self-aggrandisement if I suppress the awareness of my own mortality and finitude. And so at the beginning of Lent, when we re-dedicate ourselves to holy warfare against the disordered passions, we begin by becoming aware in our bones that as animals, albeit ensouled animals, we are dust, raised up for a short span and falling back again to the earth, our common (natural) mother. The word 'humility' is connected to the word 'humus', meaning 'the earth'.

There is also a second reason for drawing attention to our mortality at, above all, the beginning of Lent. On Ash Wednesday, we use the ashes to point up a contrast between our present condition and the free gift of our divine destiny made over to us in the Paschal Mystery of Jesus Christ. The rites of the Church tell us not only of dependence on the Creator. They speak too of the purpose for which the Creator came as the Redeemer into this world. By grace—that is, by gratuitous affection for us, love not only unnecessary but even, we could say, groundless, without foundation, except in the divine will itself, God chose that our human nature should not peter out in spiritual ruin and material decay but should enjoy life and communion with himself as an everlasting possession.

It was to confer on me a share in his own deathless life, something to which as a mortal, sinful creature I could never aspire, that the Word assumed my nature in Mary's womb and bore that nature throughout a human life determined by the realities of sin and death. This he did so as to become in the Resurrection the source for me of a new kind of life—a life I could never possibly claim—and to give me in the Holy Eucharist the medicine of immortality.

The Thursday after Ash Wednesday

Today's readings are quite sharply contrasted. Deuteronomy holds out a very this-worldly picture of happiness: to enjoy length of days in the land that God has given, the land of Israel, a land flowing with milk and honey. The Book of Deuteronomy shows signs of what we might be tempted to call 'humanism'—a religious humanism, of course, stressing how much God loves his people and how therefore they should be drawn to obey his commands, and yet a humanism nevertheless.

When we look by contrast at the Gospels, we soon realise that our Lord can only be called a humanist in a very strange—some would say a very forced—sense. His teaching highlights themes like repentance, sacrifice, renunciation, and these go against the grain of humanism as generally understood. Nowhere does he suggest that developing the potential of creation, or of human nature as such, will bring us to salvation.

The doctrine of the Church concerning the Fall of man and the Atonement convey much better the atmosphere in which the original Gospel message was presented. Only the death in our nature of One who was personally God could suffice to make reparation for the sins of the human race and to give humanity a new divinely originated principle of action, one that can carry us forward to our destiny. Lent reminds us that where human nature is concerned, optimism is misplaced.

Fortunately for our peace of mind, Easter tells us that, similarly, we should not be pessimists either. The recreation of our nature in the glorified humanity of our Lord salvages the old creation, which God in the beginning declared to be 'very good'.

We are not humanists, then, not even religiously-minded ones, but nor are we anti-humanists either. If you want a word for it, we could do worse than take one from the Greek for the Last Things. We are *eschatological* humanists. Catholic Christians believe that our true happiness is a gift from the crucified and risen Lord of history who lets us anticipate this happiness by glimpses now. But it is fully ours only when we come to share his glory in the End.

The Friday after Ash Wednesday

Fasting enters into all the great religions of the world. It is a symbolic action undertaken almost instinctively by religious people. But what is it symbolic of?

Perhaps the single most common factor in the use of fasting in different religions is the idea of the need for the divine. I put all my other needs into perspective by deferring the satisfaction of my most imperative need, which is the need for food, and in this way I express, and in expressing deepen, my need for God or for the divine. 'For God or for the divine': one can't be more specific because it all depends on the context—which religion we are talking about. In connexion with today's Gospel we *can* be more specific, because today's Gospel is an admirable statement of the *Christian* doctrine of fasting.

And as we heard, in Christianity fasting is related to the presence or absence of Jesus Christ in whom, as the Only-begotten Son made man, God is united or 'married' to mankind.

When this Bridegroom is present, the disciples will not fast. Instead, they will feast and celebrate. But when he is absent, then they will fast. When he undergoes his Passion and Death the time for mourning will come with a vengeance, but the destruction of the humanity of the Son does not in fact bring down 'vengeance'. Instead, it brings the Father's gifts of forgiveness and divinization through the Resurrection of Christ and the sending of the Holy Spirit.

The Son made man becomes present to us again in the Spirit in a more intimate and final way than before, and yet this doesn't alter the fact that the world to which he is present is still a world that every day by sin refuses to receive him, a world that absents itself from him. The sin of the world by which the Church's members remain wounded means that the Bridegroom who, *from his side*, is ever present with his righteousness yet mercy and love, is *from our side*, still absent as he was in the tomb and the Descent into Hell. So fasting brings home to us our essential incompletion. Our redemption is unfinished.

The Saturday after Ash Wednesday

Isaiah has been called the Shakespeare of the Bible. But his book contains a large number of texts which seem to come from rather different periods, and if that is so—little in biblical scholarship can be regarded as definitely proven—scholars ask why they were joined together with the oracles of the Jerusalemite prophet after whom the whole collection was named. One possible answer is that all these texts tend to link salvation to the effort to create a righteous order in society: to make the actual social order (or disorder) correspond to the divinely right order of things.

In yesterday's reading, the fast God chooses was said to be 'to share your bread with your hungry, to bring the homeless poor into your house, and when you see the naked to cover him', while in today's reading the hearers are to 'pour themselves out for the hungry and satisfy the desire of the afflicted'. And because the Church, inheriting the Scriptures of the Old Testament, regarded herself as the legitimate continuation of the Synagogue, the ancient People of God, Christians have never been lacking to preach down the ages the obligation in justice on the rich to share their excess goods with the poor.

However, the more typical vocabulary of the Church is to speak not so much of justice as of mercy. Feeding the hungry, clothing the naked, and so on: in tradition these have been described not as the 'corporal works of justice', but the 'corporal works of mercy'.

Why this significant shift of vocabulary? Justice is usually defined as the virtue whereby we habitually give each his or her due. But what in concrete terms is actually due to anyone is indefinitely debatable. By contrast, mercy is a virtue which doesn't tempt us to calculate nicely what we should keep for ourselves and what give away. Instead, it inspires large gestures of not counting the cost, often beyond what moral reason would dictate.

Our Lord uses both words but mercy is more characteristic of his value system. In identifying with publicans and harlots, our Lord did not express solidarity mainly with what the Victorians would call the deserving poor—those who suffered injustice since they did not have their due. No doubt the publicans and harlots were in some ways harshly treated, but they were not the most obvious categories of persons to choose when looking for socially deprived groups. Realistically, if unflatteringly, he calls them 'those who are sick'. What he does is to have mercy on them.

It is said that if you are on the political Right when you're under thirty, there is something wrong with your heart, and if you are on the political Left when you're over thirty there is something wrong with your head. The tendency of ageing to fixate us on our bank balance is perhaps less likely to freeze our generosity if we develop the virtue of mercy rather than dispute the conflicting claims of justice.

THE FIRST WEEK OF LENT

The First Sunday of Lent (Years A, B, and C)

In the Our Father, we say 'Lead us not into temptation'. And yet in today's Gospel, on the Sunday of Temptations, the First Sunday of Lent, we find the Spirit of God leading out Jesus into the desert precisely in order to be tempted. Although the evangelists never ascribe the Temptations of Christ to God himself, they make it clear that the fact of the happening *was* God's will. And there is something paradoxical here.

We are morally imperfect and can grow in virtue through struggling with temptations. But according to the Our Father, we should ask to be spared temptation. By contrast: as God made man, our Lord is morally perfect and thus incapable of moral growth except in the sense of moving from one indescribably exalted condition of perfection to another. But in today's Gospel he is led by the Holy Spirit into the wilderness so as to face temptation. What on earth is going on?

To understand what is happening on the First Sunday of Lent we have to think in terms not so much of individuals as of humanity at large. In the episode of the Temptations, Jesus took up the task of purifying the corporate imagination of his people, the Old Testament People of God which was the bearer of the divine plan for humanity as a whole. He faced not his own demons, his own evil thoughts, for he had none. Rather he faced the evil thoughts that had haunted his people ever since their own desert wanderings as described in the opening books of Scripture and so often referred back to in the prophets.

The Gospels according to St Matthew and St Luke tell us what those temptations were. There was, first of all, the materialism which led people to sell out the spiritual vision given them. Then, secondly, there was the love of power which made Israel want to be a nation like other nations and dominate the rest. Thirdly, there was the doubt which, when cultivated, bred mistrust of the goodness of God. In his spiritual encounter with Satan, our Lord exorcises these internal images as each temptation is presented to him.

It is the evangelist Luke who makes one thing clear, however. Though Satan is frustrated in the events narrated today, he will return. Today, on the Sunday of the Temptations, Jesus as the New Israel—indeed the New Adam, all humanity's Representative—conquers the corrupt imagination of the human race. On Good Friday, he will do far more. On the Cross, once Satan has led Judas to betray him into the hands of wicked men, Jesus will struggle with the actual realities our own disordered thoughts image: the powers of sin and death. That is why Easter is the real magnet that draws us in Lent, draws us on toward a change of life.

Meanwhile, we ask not to be led into temptation, that is: that we may never know the accumulated weight of evil as the Word incarnate knew it. We pray that our tasks in this world will not be beyond us, and that the power of the Saviour will strengthen us in all our trials, above all in the hour of our death.

Monday of the First Week of Lent

Many—if not most—of our ideas about how to deal appropriately with other people come from the Bible even if they can be paralleled elsewhere. The moral code in the Book of Leviticus, for instance, from which we heard an extract in the first reading, has its parallels in the law-codes of the pagan societies surrounding Israel in the Ancient Near East. As Catholics, this is what our tradition of 'natural law' thinking would lead us to expect.

And yet the revealed moral law as we find it in Leviticus has at least one quite startling difference when compared with natural law, and that is the way the moral life is entirely centred on the holiness of the God of Israel. The most important reason given for performing right actions is that 'You shall be holy, for I the Lord your God am holy'.

We can see something analogous in the Gospel for today, the Parable of the Last Assize. This has been an important Gospel in the emergence of the theme of the corporal works of mercy which, in their heroic exercise, are an index of sanctity. I don't suppose there is any religion or any society so bereft of all natural feelings of human decency that it denies some value to such works of mercy—though we have to allow for corporate blind-spots such as the present-day secular West shows on the topic of abortion. And yet the whole atmosphere is changed when these works of mercy are seen as acts of service to the Christ who is invisibly present in the needy. The presence of Christ in those in need is an aspect of the solidarity of the Son of Man with those he came to redeem.

Though we can separate out elements of a social ethic suitable for statesmen or social workers whatever their religious faith or lack of it, our morality as Catholic Christians is essentially a mystical morality. It is bound up with the mystery of God's own holiness and the presence among us incognito of his incarnate Word.

Tuesday of the First Week of Lent

So in today's Gospel our Lord gives his disciples the Our Father, just as in Lent in the early centuries of the Church's history this same prayer, the Lord's Prayer, would have been solemnly 'handed over' to people preparing for Baptism. It was a high point of the catechumenate, the programme of initiation into the Church.

But what was all the fuss about? It is after all just a prayer, consisting of a few lines among the thousands of lines that make up the New Testament, and a prayer moreover which active Christians are likely to treat as commonplace—recited every day, several times a day if they come to Mass and the Liturgy of the Hours or say the Rosary. That is the trouble—we have domesticated the *Pater*. Familiarity has bred not contempt, surely, but at any rate taking something too much for granted. Somehow we have to get back to a position where, like the catechumens of the patristic age, we can be surprised by this prayer, really react to it as amazing, as a revelation.

A small beginning would be to reflect a little on the opening invocation. 'Our Father who are in the heavens': that, when you think about it, is an extraordinary combination of words. 'In the heavens': that means God as surrounded by the worship of the hosts of Angels. It declares God's transcendent holiness which is incandescent, burning. No man can enter his presence and stay alive, says the Hebrew Bible. And yet this One who is 'in the heavens' is, we hear, 'Our Father', our *Abba*, that intimate word which the New Testament writers thought so important they passed it on in the original language, rather than the language in which they were writing. He is 'our dear Father', if we bear in mind that behind the words 'Our Father' lies that 'Abba' mode of address. We call God 'our dear Father' only because our Lord licensed us to do so, and even—and this is really stupendous—commanded us to do so. He has told us to enter into the mystery of the Father as intimately as the Son himself who shares the Father's life from before the world was made.

It is a beginning that is aweful and endearing, dreadful and sweet, a combination that is literally marvellous.

Wednesday of the First Week of Lent

Jonah, evidently, was a figure that fascinated our Lord and the early Church. A prophet who had been swallowed by a sea-monster, who spent three days in its belly and survived, just as Jesus would go down into the depths and come up again in his work of redemption. A prophet who travelled a long way to preach a message of repentance as Jesus had come a long way, all the way from the heart of God. It's not surprising that for the ancient Church Jonah became a symbol of salvation and so he appears on the walls of the catacombs.

Within the Gospels that is, if anything, the emphasis of the evangelist Matthew when Jonah's name comes up. In the Gospel according to St Luke, from which we are reading today, the stress lies on Jonah the preacher of repentance. Here we might ask ourselves: do we need one? Would we be here in church, at a weekday Mass, praying, unless we had already repented? The foundress of the English Dominican sisters, Mother Margaret, used to say, 'I don't fear Hell because I know I'm not going there' (you can get away with saying things like that if you're a candidate for beatification). 'What I *do* fear', she went on, 'is the abuse of grace'.

How often do we go to Holy Communion, and how much do we profit by it? More than we think, we hope, but hardly as much as we should. Nor will we unless interiorly we are dying to ourselves, so as to get into the rhythm of Eucharistic life. By that rhythm our life through grace should have a basic undertow of perpetual thanksgiving, for that is what the word 'Eucharist' means. Whatever befalls us we can always give thanks perpetually inasmuch as, in St Paul's words, all things are ours because we are Christ's and Christ is God's.

Thursday of the First Week of Lent

Today's Gospel raises the problem of petitionary prayer. This usually comes in the form: We ask God for things, we don't get them, and so we say that God has not answered us, and perhaps even that he does not exist.

The logic of this is strange. If I am asked for something and feel I have to refuse, this does not normally elicit the complaint that I have not given an answer, much less that I don't exist. The difficulty is rather the opposite: the answer has been only too clear, and my existence only too effective. To this extent, the problem of petitionary prayer, thus posed, is a pseudo-problem.

The real problem is the one found in the ancient world and actually treated in today's Gospel. Given that people will inevitably ask God for things since man is a naturally praying animal, how does such asking affect the relation between God and human beings?

In cultures where it was not taken for granted that the divine principle was intrinsically benevolent, by praying one might be laying oneself open to sinister consequences. Or again, the divine 'No' might be a sign of caprice in God's dealings with humans, a sign of his arbitrariness. In this Gospel our Lord reassures his hearers that since God's goodness infinitely exceeds that of a good parent his 'No', if it comes, is neither malevolent nor capricious. God knows better than we do what is best for us in the longest possible run. His response to our petitionary prayer is based on that knowledge, shared, if at all, only with the saints.

Friday of the First Week of Lent

Two readings, one from the prophet Ezekiel, the other from the Gospel according to St Matthew, which are difficult ones for those of us who want to proclaim a Gospel of grace, a Gospel that is really good news.

Or are they? Certainly, these texts set their demands high, morally speaking. For the prophet, if the upright man reneges on his former integrity of life, God will take into account none of the good he did previously. His fate will simply be to die. For our Lord in the Gospel, the righteousness of the disciples—their adhesion to the moral law not just in its broad outlines but in all its fine-tuning—must exceed that of the scribes and Pharisees, who as moral theologians were famous for being sticklers.

So how can these Scriptures be used to forward a Gospel, precisely, a message of good tidings? Well, firstly, the Gospel couldn't be good unless it upheld right morality. There is no goodness without what is right in all its beauty. And secondly, the Gospel is not a Gospel of grace through being a Gospel of forgiveness on the cheap. Free forgiveness and cheap forgiveness are not at all the same thing. Cheap forgiveness says, 'There, there, nothing you did or failed to do matters really'. Free forgiveness says, 'It matters dreadfully—but the blood of Jesus Christ, the blood of One who was God, can reverse the sentence and wash the stain away'.

Saturday of the First Week of Lent

'Be perfect, as your heavenly Father is perfect', our Lord tells us in today's Gospel, echoing yesterday's message: 'If your righteousness does not exceed that of the scribes and Pharisees, you will not enter the Kingdom of heaven'. These words have to be reconciled with his other teaching, formulated most clearly by St Paul, to the effect that salvation is essentially the gift or grace of God, the result of his mercy, freely poured out.

Somehow we have to integrate two truths: first, that we are saved by grace, but secondly, that our salvation demands from us a strenuous effort if we are to make it our own. If we deny the first truth, we become Pelagians who think you have to save yourself;

if we deny the second truth, we become Antinomians who regard the keeping of the moral law as irrelevant to salvation.

The Church's doctrine of salvation seeks to unify these elements in a satisfying manner. In justification, when we begin our Christian lives—normatively as adult converts undergoing Baptism, it is God alone who initiates our salvation, infusing into us the gift of an orientation to himself that means for us living faith, faith that will be spontaneously fruitful in charity, in love like that of God.

In sanctification, the next stage, through which my own personal appropriation of salvation develops, God does not (in St Augustine's phrase) 'save us without us'. Our freedom is no longer just an absence of resistance to grace. Now it has to mesh with God's continuing gracious gifts so that by perfect charity, our righteousness may indeed go beyond even the ethical practice of the best of the Jews of our Lord's time. This is how the saints lived and live.

THE SECOND WEEK OF LENT

The Second Sunday of Lent (Years A, B, and C)

Today's Gospel is the story of the Transfiguration, a very untypical example of a Lenten Gospel even if it has occupied this place in the worship of the Roman rite for a long time. The typical Lenten Gospel, surely, is the one we heard *last* Sunday.

In his Wilderness Temptations Jesus was confronted by the Evil One who presented him with the classic wrong choices made — according to the Old Testament — by his people, the House of Israel. Taking up that cue, in Lent we remind ourselves liturgically how horrible the human race has been and is. We call to mind that we share in a general tendency to criminality.

This Lent, as every Lent, the newspapers will reinforce the work of the Liturgy for us. They will show us how in human beings everywhere the demons of anger, avarice, lust, jealousy and pride (and not forgetting gluttony and sloth), live, move and have their being.

But just as we're starting to come to terms with that in the Lenten project, the Church presents us with a very different Gospel, to put it mildly: the Gospel of the Transfiguration. The Jesus whom we have just seen — last Sunday, in fact — enveloped by evil, is now, this Sunday, bathed in the Glory of God: God's radiance, his bliss, his joy. At the Transfiguration the deepest reality of Jesus's being broke through and showed itself to his disciples.

Why? Or indeed, How? To understand what on that occasion was going on, we need to share the faith of the Church — as indeed we do in order to get the hang of the biblical revelation as a whole. So what *was* going on? In the womb of Mary, the human soul of Jesus had been assumed by God the Word. It was united personally to the Word who himself had shared the Father's overflowing goodness before all time: before the Big Bang, and whatever preceded it, if anything did — *before all worlds.* At the Transfiguration, for one brief moment the body of Jesus, his face, and even his clothes became the picture of his soul — his soul as united personally to divine being, to the Word, and, through the Word, to the Father.

Nothing could be more natural, then, that in this unique moment of the public ministry the disciples saw in him the splendour, the fullness, the authority, of God himself.

There's nothing accidental about the way the Church gives us this episode to hear about while Lent is in mid-course. It's an ancient tradition which, fortunately, has survived in the modern Lectionary — and ancient traditions must have a lot going for them if they survive the razor-cuts of modernity. So why have people — ancient and modern — been so keen on this seeming disparity, this apparent incongruity?

The message to us of the Transfiguration in its unlikely Lenten context is that the last word in the struggle of the Christian life does not, actually, lie with *struggle*. The last word does not belong to *coping with temptation*. On the contrary, the last word lies with *seeing the glory of God*.

What Peter, James and John saw on Mount Thabor — the traditional site of the Transfiguration event — we too shall see if we stay faithful. We shall see the glorified humanity of Jesus Christ. The glory with which he was surrounded on Thabor was not just an episode. What happened on the mountain was that, to strengthen those three key disciples for the ordeal of his coming Passion, there took place a real anticipation of what was going to be with his Resurrection and Ascension an abiding state of affairs. The Lord Jesus has in permanency now that glorified humanity, that transfigured condition where the glory of the Godhead shines out through his human nature for our sake. He has it: he lives in it and he lives *as* it. True, he continues to carry the marks of the Passion, which are his wondrous trophies. But he is now beyond all suffering, standing before the Father's Face in the Fire of the Holy Spirit.

One day — the day of our personal judgment — the Light of Thabor will penetrate our souls, initially to judge them but then, please God, to warm them forever. So too in the General Resurrection, when the material cosmos comes to its final goal, that same Light will be reflected in the glorification of our bodies also. And this is what makes all the struggle of life, the struggle of Lent, worthwhile.

Monday of the Second Week of Lent

There are many philosophies that offer an account of what justice is. Everyone with even a minimal morality has some sense of what is due to others, what is their *ius* (from which we get the word 'justice'), what is their right. But it is mercy that seems to be the more specifically biblical virtue, and, in the light of the Cross of Christ, a centrally Christian virtue.

In today's Gospel, our Lord explains its basis. 'Be merciful, as your Father is merciful.' It's not too much to say that all our doctrine is contained in that little word 'as' — which I take to cover both 'since' or 'because' and also 'in the way that'. Be merciful because your Father is merciful. Be merciful in the way that your Father is merciful.

Why do I say that all our doctrine is contained there? Spelling out the force of that 'as', you would have to touch on the major dogmas of our faith. As the Father is himself merciful; as he has sent his Son into the world to communicate that mercy to guilty creatures; as on the Cross he showed what mercy was and in the Resurrection with the gift of the Holy Spirit showed what mercy can do; as the Church his daughter is a merciful Mother, with sacraments of mercy for the forgiveness of sins—you see, all our doctrine is laid out there. And *as* all this is the case, our Lord continues, so you too are to be merciful; you are not to insist on the strict fulfillment of the obligations others have incurred towards you.

Shakespeare wrote: 'The quality of mercy is not strained. It droppeth as the gentle rain from heaven upon the place beneath… It is an attribute to God himself. And earthly power does then show likest God's when mercy seasons justice.' Whether Shakespeare was a Renaissance humanist or a dogmatic Christian, perhaps a closet Catholic, has been much discussed. When we hear Portia's speech in *The Merchant of Venice* we can at least say, He knew what Christianity was.

Tuesday of the Second Week of Lent

In a particular time or at a particular place, some portions of the Gospels may seem to us rather superfluous or tilting at windmills. Some elements in today's Gospel could be an example of that. Warning people about being over-ostentatious in their religious dress, or going over the top in their use of religious titles, or, more generally, treating piety as a means to social one-upmanship, seems unnecessary advice in contemporary Britain. This is a society where priests in clericals, never mind cassocks, and Sisters in Religious habits, have more or less disappeared from the public square, where bishops are selling off their big houses and want to be called just by their Christian name, and most Catholics would die—well, not literally—rather than be caught saying the rosary in a railway carriage.

Nothing could be less like the Jewish society of our Lord's day, a sacral society with hierarchies of different sorts but all visibly labelled, where religion was publicly acknowledged as the most important element in life. One can see how in such a society piety might well become a tool of self-aggrandisement, a means to secure status and influence.

In our very dissimilar situation, however, there are probably other parts of the Gospels which take precedence over this, and notably the sayings that presume a community of the disciples will be *apparent*: a light on a lampstand, a city set on a hilltop, and that they will be engaged in highly public witnessing.

We must take care that our religion does not vanish from the public arena—except when the media choose to lampoon it and so people do notice it, but not for the right reasons. As secularism becomes more aggressive, what seemed in the 1970s more humble, and therefore more in the spirit of the Gospel, may now be more timorous or downright cowardly, a sinking-back into welcome anonymity. This is a more comfortable choice, no doubt, but is it a more evangelical one?

Wednesday of the Second Week of Lent

The situation of today's Gospels seems pretty clear. James and John, together with their mother, have come to accept Jesus'

Messiahship, but, against the Old Testament background, they understand it in mainly this-worldly terms. God will put down the wicked and enthrone his Messiah as king of a world-wide theocracy. So James and John as favoured disciples—along with Peter they constituted the inner core of the apostolic group—wish to be his vice-regents, sitting one on his right hand, one on his left.

They haven't heard properly the message Jesus has been giving them, not least at the start of today's Gospel. Not only is his Messiahship on another level from that of worldly power. More than that, he will enter on its effective exercise only with his own literally excruciating death.

Our theology helps us to understand what this means. The uncreated Son of God, now existing in our human nature and at the moment captured in this Gospel-passage talking with his fellow human beings, cannot make that humanity share in the divine Glory until it replicates or mirrors what he is in his divine reality: the only Son of the Father. And that will happen on the Cross when his Sacrifice, offered for our sake, perfectly represents what Christ is from all eternity. As the divine Son, he is eternally turned to the Father in love, in a self-giving which is divinely fruitful, because from it there comes the Holy Spirit.

The Cross pictures what the Trinity is like, and, more than that, by conforming the created structure of our humanity to the inner movement of the Trinity, the Cross enables that humanity to share in God's Glory, first of all in Jesus, and then in dependence on him, in all whose Saviour he is. To revert to the language of Scripture, it is by the Cross that he is lifted up as the Messiah-king, a fact revealed in the Resurrection.

The rest of today's Gospel flows necessarily. If divine Glory is divine sacrificial love, then the meaning of power, dignity, honour, greatness, is changed. Hierarchy is turned upside down. The greatest of all is the servant of all.

Thursday of the Second Week of Lent

By the time of our Lord's ministry, Jews, or at any rate the kind of Jews whose company Jesus chiefly frequented, saw judgment as taking place in a realm beyond this one. That's reflected in today's

Gospel, in the story of Dives and Lazarus. The observable fact is that rich people can be horrible to poor people without any divine intervention to right the balance in history. If you wish—and some of his contemporaries *did* wish—you can keep hold of the idea that judgment takes place inside history but postpone its working out to the end of history, the last historical generation when the successors of the goodies and baddies get their just deserts, possibly through an almighty bust-up of the Armageddon variety. But that doesn't say much about the Lazaruses, or the Diveses, who have lived and died in the meanwhile. Part of our Lord's intention in this parable is to re-state for his Jewish interlocutors the reality of a divine judgment beyond history, after our deaths, and to re-state it by arguing that only this belief makes coherence sense of the Law of Moses and the teaching of those of the prophets who defended that Law and applied it. The overall thrust of Scripture, he is saying, is towards a real judgment for everyone at their personal ending, at their death. And since all Jews can get this message from Moses and the prophets, let them hearken to them.

This is also a salutary warning to us who are, as Pope Pius XI put it, 'spiritual Semites' on whom the Word made flesh, Jesus Christ, has laid the duty of almsgiving to the poor—which for the tradition of the Church is not just something generous minded people go in for because they like that kind of thing but, as we remind ourselves in Lent, a divine precept. One of the points on which we shall be judged in eternity is whether we have shared our goods with our brother in his need.

Friday of the Second Week of Lent

In today's readings we hear of what might be called three 'descents'. The first occurs in the Old Testament lection: it is, of course, the 'descent' of Joseph into Egypt, sold down the river by brothers jealous of his gifts and his father's favour. The remaining two are in the Gospel: the 'descent' of God's servants the prophets, who so often got negative reactions, including physical maltreatment, from their contemporaries, and finally, then, the 'descent' of our Lord who was humiliated unto death, even death on a Cross, and who, as we say in the Creed, 'descended into Hell'.

It is noticeable that the descents in question get progressively worse. The patriarch Joseph did extremely well in Egypt, a rich and fascinating civilization as the novelist Thomas Mann brings out so beautifully in his *Joseph and his Brothers*. The prophets by contrast, were in tighter situations—but let us not exaggerate: many of them had court connexions which gave them kudos and access to wealthy and influential people (though admittedly such privileges could backfire). Lastly, then, we come to Christ's Descent which, though imaged in these earlier experiences, is not just part of the series. In bringing the series to its climax, what our Lord experienced changed its whole character.

He does not just die. For our sake he tastes what Scripture calls the 'second death': he bears the burden of the world's sin in all its ferocious malice as well as its repetitive tediousness. Staggering beneath that burden—being 'made sin', as Paul says, though he knew no sin, the only Son of God goes down to Sheol and enters by co-feeling with others that condition of perceived estrangement from the living God which by his Resurrection he will sweep away for the just for evermore.

Saturday of the Second Week of Lent

Here we have another of those Gospel stories that are so familiar we have them almost by heart. But this one is a story where we can miss the telling details.

The details I have in mind concern especially the restoration of the prodigal son by the father. Our Lord has ransacked the Old Testament for references that will show how this reconciliation between father and son isn't just kind and generous: a nice thing for the father to do. We're meant to think, it's more than generous, it's overwhelming. The picture is built up by accumulating allusions to the Hebrew Bible which the first hearers knew better than we do.

Thus, for instance, the father fell on the son's neck and kissed him: the classic expression for blissful reunion in the Book of Genesis. He showered on him rich clothes and ornaments: recalling how for the prophet Ezekiel God had metaphorically clothed the abandoned infant Israel with shoes, fine linen and silk when he chose her to be the elect people. The father in the parable sent for the fatted calf: the same gastronomic honour the patriarch Abraham had paid to his three angelic visitors at the Oak of Mamre. He put a ring on the son's finger: the symbol of authority Pharaoh gave Joseph. And it goes on...

And then we think: but the prodigal son is *us*. He was and is meant to be none other than ourselves. It was on those who, left to their own devices, were estranged from God that the Father — the true Father, the Father of Jesus — has heaped up blessings. The privilege of being the friends of God, of partaking in his mysteries, of being called with saints and angels to share his Glory, and to taste even now on earth the fruits of the world to come.

This is all for us: amazing! In our Lenten penance and meditation we are to let that response — 'amazing' — sink in all the way.

THE THIRD WEEK OF LENT

The Third Sunday of Lent (Year A)

The story of the Samaritan Woman is one of the great stories of the Gospels. The Samaritans were a community of mixed racial descent living just to the north of Judaea, the Jewish heartland. Really they were a Jewish sect but were not recognized as such by Orthodox Jews. Excommunicated for their doctrinal peculiarities, they set up their own counterblast to Jerusalem—an alternative Temple on Mount Gerizim where some of the main events of the Old Testament had taken place. In effect, the Samaritans reacted to their expulsion from official Judaism by claiming that the Jewish tradition was all theirs anyhow, and naturally this only made matters worse. Religious antagonism is frequently more bitter between sub-divisions of the same religion than between those of quite distinct faiths. And the Samaritans had undoubtedly created difficulties: putting obstacles in the way of the restoration of Jerusalem after the Babylonian exile and later helping the Hellenistic monarchs in Syria in their wars against the Jews. In the time of our Lord, Jews were particularly strict about not eating and drinking with Samaritans. Hence the woman's surprise when Jesus asks her to operate the well for him—'What? You are a Jew, and you ask me, a Samaritan, for a drink?'. Are you so desperate that you cannot be bothered to observe the proprieties?

His reply does not delay on the issue of communal relations. Instead it goes straight to the mystery of his identity and what it is he can offer. 'If only you knew what God's gift is and who it is that is asking you for a drink, you would have asked him instead, and he would have given you living water.'

At one level, Jesus is just another traveller: weary, hot, dusty, thirsty, in a hostile countryside. But at another level, he is the Source of the Holy Spirit, the Life-giver, and so he can provide 'living water'. By 'living water' she, however, thinks he must mean running water as distinct from well water which could be flat or stagnant. But the water table is far down and the streams are dry. So how, she asks, are you going to get it? And with unconscious irony she enquires whether he is greater than the patriarch Jacob who used to water his cattle there.

He now speaks more explicitly. What he can give her is a taste of the life of God. It will be like a perpetual spring inside her, refreshing her now and for ever. In the light of the Christian experience of grace, we can reach some understanding of what this means: this is the water which the first century martyr-bishop Ignatius of Antioch called in his letter to the church at Rome, 'water that lives and speaks in me, and calls out to me from within, "Come to the Father"'. The Samaritan Woman too begins to get the hang of it. It has something to do, she divines, with ultimate happiness. Oh yes, she says, give me that water—I could do with a bit of that.

But she still shows no sign of interest in who Jesus himself might be. So he takes the initiative and, using his supernaturally informed insight, refers, delicately enough to begin with, to her private life which was not exactly a paragon of marital fidelity. Defensively, she lies to him, 'I have no husband'. Or perhaps it is meant to be ambiguous, 'I have no "husband"'. Jesus uses this answer to uncover her past. The evangelist John has already warned his readers that those whose deeds are evil do not go near the light since they are afraid their actions will be uncovered. So here we come to a dramatic turning point. Will the *Samaritana* turn towards the light, or will she turn her back on it?

With psychologically convincing realism she does a little of each. She brings up the subject of worship, suggesting that a deepening process is under way though this could also be a diversionary tactic aimed at getting herself off the hook. She says, 'Our fathers worshipped on this mountain... But you say that Jerusalem is place where we ought to worship'. Jesus deftly turns this change of subject to his own ends. The day is coming when the criterion for being God's daughter or son will not be worshipping in a holy city but worshipping in the Holy Spirit, worshipping 'in spirit and in truth'. When that day comes, all that can cut a person off from God is not an accident of birth but one's own evil: unfaithfulness, lovelessness, hardness of heart—the very things implicit in the six husbands and the botched attempt at a cover-up.

And so the story comes to its climax. With a rush of half-understood intuition she stammers, 'I know the Messiah is coming'. And he replies, in a phrase that may also entail a claim to Godhead, 'I am he'.

A credible enough story, then, within the presuppositions of the Gospel tradition; a story that captures the atmosphere of Jesus' world, a story which illustrates certain of his qualities: his irony, his supernatural insight into the human soul, his freedom in communicating with women and with the unorthodox. But the Church gives us this story in the Lenten Liturgy not for any of these reasons but *so that we can take it to heart*. In the Samaritan woman we are to find ourselves: compromised, muddled, shifty, our theology often not all that it might be, but capable nevertheless of admitting Jesus Christ into our lives. Divine relationship is not just for exceptional spiritual heroes. It is also for the mediocre majority and even for downright nasty pieces of work if they are willing to kick over the traces and begin again.

In Holy Week we shall meet Jesus again in the midday heat and hear him say again, 'I thirst'. A mediaeval Franciscan poem, the *Dies irae*, illuminates today's Gospel by bringing it together with the Passion narrative: *Quaerens me sedisti lassus, redemisti crucem passus*, or in the English translation, 'Thou with weary steps hast sought me, Crucified hast dearly bought me'. The loving-kindness of God, by choosing to include us in its own communion, brought the eternal Son to the death of the Cross. But though that Sacrifice required nothing from us, it was not meant to leave us unchanged. *Redemisti crucem passus, tantus labor non sit cassus*: 'Crucified, hast dearly bought me, Have thy pains no profit brought me?'. This is what we ask ourselves in Lent and Passiontide. Have I let the Spirit of Christ enter heart and mind so that love for God and neighbour rules my life? I must turn again to the Cross, where he opened his heart for me and receive that living water of the Spirit that flows unceasingly from his riven side.

The Third Sunday of Lent (Year B)

The Liturgy of the Word today presents us with two partial but ultimately unsatisfactory ways of experiencing God, and by implication it contrasts these with the way we as Christians experience, or ought to experience, what he is like.

The first way is the way of the Ten Commandments, the ten supreme 'Words' of the Jewish Law, which express the Old Testament experience of God as moral Lawgiver on Mount Sinai. We all have consciences. We are aware of the difference between the concept of right and the concept of wrong. We are aware not only of how things have been and are but of how they ought to be. We have a sense of ethical imperatives that bind because they are objectively true, because they accord with practical reason. The moral law is not something we make up as we go along, it is something we *recognize* or *receive*. It may be discovered by a process of reflection about the good; or, alternatively, it may be disclosed to us. For Israel, the moral law was above all something *disclosed*, and in giving the Law God had revealed to Israel in his love for her what the good life is like—and made it known more comprehensively, as well as more readily, than was the case among the Gentiles. Hence that lyrical outburst of the responsorial psalm in praise of the Law: how perfect and trustworthy it is, more desirable than purest gold and sweeter than honey.

Nevertheless focussing one's sense of God and relation with God on the Law has its drawbacks. Inevitably there is something impersonal about it. The moral law is universal or it would not be moral *law*. And a divine command, even if it reflects the divine goodness, is not God himself. Jesus will tell his disciples that he will not call them any longer servants, he will call them friends. Stating obligations, however necessary and desirable, is not in itself friendship.

The second less than fully satisfactory way of approaching God comes in today's Gospel, the Cleansing of the Temple. The Jews weren't just moralists. The Psalter shows they were contemplatives too. One main way in which they contemplated God was through his Temple presence. If you were feeling miserable and you wanted a shot of God's presence, you could always go on pilgrimage to Jerusalem, up the Hill of Zion. 'I remember, and my soul melts within me;/ I am on my way to the wonderful Tent,/ to the house of God.' Not that God was confined to the Temple sanctuary, but that was where he had chosen to put his Glory.

And once again there are drawbacks. The mystique of Jerusalem may be a very moving thing in Judaism—I think of the cemeteries

of the Hasidim on the westward slopes of the Mountain of Olives
so located that at the resurrection of the righteous they can face
the Holy City. But that mystique is also a very restrictive thing.
Anywhere that is not Jerusalem is religiously disadvantaged. And
even Jerusalem is of little use unless one is a Jew. What our Lord
objected to at the Cleansing was not so much—so it has been
argued—the commerce for its own sake (money changed hands
when people bought animals for sacrifice) as the way Israel had
nationalized her worship (money-changers were needed to prevent
Gentile coins that defiled the bearers from coming into the sanctuary in people's pockets). The Temple was not in practice the house
of prayer for all nations that the more far-seeing of the prophets
had described.

So finally, then, Jesus offers his own way into the experience of
God. 'Pull down this temple, and I will rebuild it in three days'.
And the evangelist adds, 'He was speaking of the temple of his
body'. His own body is a temple, a sanctuary, because in his
humanity, his embodied humanity, he is himself personally the
Word of God and the Glory of the Trinity expressed for us. Since
he shares our humanity, we can respond to God in him in the way
that is least partial and unsatisfactory for human beings: we can,
as he himself taught, respond to him as Friend, in a shared
inter-personal communion of knowledge and love.

In this body of his he will undergo violent death. He foretells it
now, but we shall witness it liturgically on Good Friday. Yet his
murder will be an opportunity for fresh building. In his risen body
he will be even more accessible to us, set free in the Holy Spirit to
communicate as the God-man with people everywhere. He will
reach out to touch them wherever—through, not least, the Church
which is now, as we say, his Mystical Body and his sacraments
which are her mysteries.

The Third Sunday of Lent (Year C)

In today's Gospel our Lord both confirms our common sense view
of things and also gives us a shock. First, he confirms what we
would think anyway. Natural disasters don't imply that all who
suffer from are specially wicked. But then he goes on to say

something that pulls us up with a start. Nevertheless, he says, all deserve punishment since all are infected with evil.

This is a dogmatic claim. It states one of those all-encompassing truths that don't so much need explaining as explain everything else. The Fall of humanity has brought us all to spiritual ruin.

Though this is a truth of revelation, not of reason, there is a side to it we can check out. One of the great themes of all literature is the sickness of the heart. When we read of it in newspapers we only think of malice in concentrated form: spectacular crimes that hit the headlines. But malice doesn't only exist in concentrated form. It comes in diffuse form as well: less clear-cut, less focussed, but just as real.

Again, we generally think of how by malice people do things that are wrong. But the novelists show us how malice can enter into the mixed motives behind even deeds that are right. So without repentance we shall all be cut down.

This is a hard saying, but like all the hard sayings of our Lord it must be seen in the light of his Death and Resurrection. God is holy, and by his nature must judge evil relentlessly. But through the Paschal Mystery, the Father turns that judgment to a word of forgiveness and reconciliation. We shall see as much at Easter.

Monday of the Third Week of Lent

A prophet has no honour in his own country. As Jesus makes clear, this isn't just a reference to himself. It's a reference to the stories of Elijah and Elisha and by implication to the entire tradition of prophecy in Israel. And in this way it raises the question of what we can call the mystery of Israel.

The word 'mystery' can mean one of two things—either a riddle, a puzzle, or a reality so deep we shall never get to the bottom of it. In this case, it's a bit of both.

Israel manifests extreme reactions. She is either passionately attached to the word of God or else she violently rejects it. From the Jews come God-intoxicated souls: people like Isaiah or St Paul. But equally, from the Jews come those determined to exclude God totally, to remove him from human consciousness, human society: people like Freud and Marx. The mystery of Israel is that God chooses a people as his very own and also allows many—even most !—individuals within that people to harden their hearts against his coming.

That is the problem, the puzzle, which the mystery of Israel contains—at least as Christians see it. The totally positive and the absolutely negative are bound up together. But then, as Christians see it—indeed, as the New Testament presents it—there is a divine answer.

The answer to the problem is revealed in the Resurrection of Christ. There it was shown that the absolutely negative part could serve or help forward the totally positive part. The Cross, the work of the enemies of Christ (admittedly these included Romans as well as Jews), in one obvious sense destroyed his mission, put an end to it. And yet—with the cooperation of the Daughter of Zion, the Mother of the Lord, who stood by on Calvary—Israel's Messiah, the Son of David, made of the destruction of his mission the perfect oblation he offered to the Father for the salvation of all the world.

At Easter, the Resurrection will show how the Cross—the victorious Cross we shall hail it even on Good Friday—was the real triumph of his mission, how that Sacrifice was efficacious. It became the source of endless thanksgiving, both for the Church of the Gentiles and for the Church of the Circumcision, the Church of the Jewish Christians which includes, we can hardly fail to note, all the apostles on whom the whole Church is abidingly built.

Tuesday of the Third Week of Lent

The Liturgy gives us to read today the Prayer of Azariah, from the Book of Daniel. Its combination of qualities makes it a magnificent prayer. We are likely to be struck by its personal aspects: the dispositions it stresses as just what is needed when coming into the presence of the Lord. 'With a contrite heart and a humble spirit may we be accepted.' And certainly the prayer's emphasis on absolute sincerity, on repentance, on trust, on the whole-hearted seeking of the face of God, can and should be mirrored by us when, as individual persons, we come to pray.

Yet I venture to say that the distinctive character of the prayer does not lie in these qualities as needed by individual suppliants for their personal life. It lies, rather, in the appeal to the Lord to remember for the sake of the common life of the people the significant past. That past includes not only the Covenant promises he made to the ancestors but also the merits, thanks to their election, of those same ancestors. It is on that basis that God is asked to be merciful now lest an incongruity arise with the 'marvellous works' he did of old. The prayer is made by someone conscious of how reduced, drained, marginalized, and rudderless, Israel has become, and it begs God to remember the fathers and show mercy.

This prayer inspired, I feel sure, the English Catholic prayer sometimes recited at Benediction which takes up an exactly similar attitude. Only in the second case it is the saints of this island who contributed to its original conversion that enjoy the place Azariah gives to Abraham and the other patriarchs. In the Catholic prayer we ask that God will hearken to the intercession of the missionary saints who made England Christian, that he will not allow their work to fall into oblivion, since to do so would be to introduce a contradiction into his own economy of grace. How often do we who long for the reconversion of England to the Catholic faith pray in this manner—this biblical manner which the Liturgy sets before us today?

Wednesday of the Third Week of Lent

In what sense does the Law revealed to Israel still abide, still retain validity? In the circle of St Matthew's first hearers, Moses' phrase in Deuteronomy 'the whole Law' or 'all this Law' would, I imagine, have conjured up in people's minds not just the moral law but also the ceremonial law, the cultus Israel was ordered to perform. Such Jewish Christians as St Matthew combined with the earliest Liturgy of the Church attendance at synagogue worship, and in many ways it is a pity that there is no continuing Jewish-Christian community with a ritual life peculiar to itself, to witness to the continuity between Israel and the Church. After all, the Church consists of the Church of the Circumcision, those of the original Jewish stock, as well as of the Church of the Gentiles.

Be that as it may, the Law included, then, not only moral precepts but ceremonial precepts too. However, the sense of the Church has always been that what our Lord is speaking of in today's Gospel is, crucially, the moral law — above all the ten pillars of that law, the Ten Words, or Ten Commandments. The gift of the Commandments to Moses on Sinai, as reported in the Book of Exodus, has been called the 'creation of the moral universe' to parallel the account of the creation of the physical universe in the Book of Genesis.

We believe that Jesus Christ has bestowed on his Bride the Church a certain freedom, a certain authority, to actualize or apply the teaching by which he presented the Law. And just as she has chosen to interpret literally his prohibition of divorce and to interpret spiritually his prohibition of oath-taking (which, then, becomes a general exhortation always to be truthful), so she has held fast to his solemn warning about relaxing any of the moral commandments but has let go the ceremonial precepts that defined the way of worship in which for pious Jews the practice of the moral commands was embedded.

This may sound like an impoverishment. Here Blessed John Paul II's letter on fundamental morals, *Veritatis splendor*, may be helpful. On the one hand, it underlines the teaching of our Lord about how no moral command of the Law can pass away, stressing how actions that are morally evil can never, even in special circumstances, be countenanced. But on the other hand it also draws an important spiritual lesson from that fact. Each commandment suggests a direction for moral living where in some respect we can always grow in living more generously. To live the commandments in their fullness, says the pope, is to live by grace, in the power of the gift of the Holy Spirit who at Pentecost came from the risen Lord. We are not to be minimalists, paring down the commands to the bare minimum we could get away with. We are to be maximalists who put no limit on what moral growth, fed by the Spirit, can attain.

Thursday of the Third Week of Lent

In today's Gospel, we find our Lord defending his activities as an exorcist by pointing out a flaw in the arguments of his opponents. If his own exorcisms are diabolically inspired, then evil is divided against itself and will collapse. But nothing that is known about evil suggests it would seek to abolish itself. So the case against him is false.

We today are likely not so much to be impressed by the logic as rather embarrassed that he considered evil to be a personal force at all. Isn't 'evil' just another word for 'very, very wrong'? I think this conclusion would be premature.

The evil angels, though no longer much preached about in the historic churches of Europe and North America have not necessarily ceased to harass human beings. What they may have done, as ever in human history, is to change their masks—the manner of their self-presentation. In different periods and cultures, the evil angels have shown themselves in different ways. They can be pagan gods leading human beings into immorality; or demons experienced as inhabiting people. They can manifest themselves in totalitarian visions of politics or pan-sexual pictures of happiness. They can come over as neuroses that sap our capacity for charity towards God, neighbour and ourselves.

Those are some of their masks. They have something in common. Wherever they appear they disfigure the image of man, his nobility and dignity, which the Fathers speak of, on the basis of Scripture, as the image of God. In one way or another they brutalise us, they make us howl.

Why? What's in it for them? Theologians suggest that, through the Fall of these angels, their wills can no longer attain the Supreme Good for which they were made. So they use their abundant energy to disrupt the existence of lesser spiritual beings, ourselves: beings that in his goodness God is drawing to himself.

That is why the decisive victory over the evil powers was not Jesus's exorcisms but his Death and Resurrection which took our humanity in a definitive way into the divine life.

Friday of the Third Week of Lent

The Law was the centre of the Jewish faith, and the theologians of Judaism were lawyers, or, as English translations of the Gospels usually put it, 'scribes'. In the time of our Lord, it was not unknown for scribal theologians to seek a formula that would sum up the essence of the Law, or the Covenant. There were two reasons for this: one was a practical reason, to have a short explanation of Judaism for non-Jews interested in becoming converts; the other was more theoretical or conceptual, trying to pinpoint the central or essential thing about the Jewish faith so that all its other teaching and practices could be suitably arranged around that.

This is what is going on in today's Gospel. The scribe comes up to Jesus and asks him his opinion: 'Which is the first of all the Commandments?' Our Lord's answer puts together two precepts occurring in different parts of the Hebrew Bible: one is love of God, the other is love of neighbour. Some rabbis had come close to this but in his case there was a difference. Taken in the context of the whole impact his coming made, he began a process of bursting the bounds of the Law until Judaism turned into Christianity.

The moral truths disclosed by the Law remain valid for Christians. And yet no law, no matter how wise and holy, can fully specify love. No law can say exhaustively what love will lead one to do. Illuminated by the mission of the Son in the Incarnation and Atonement, and the mission of the Spirit at Pentecost, the earliest Church found that love has no boundaries, only a horizon: the horizon of God himself, who as St John the Theologian says, 'is love'.

Through the intimate relation with the Father his divine Sonship gave him, Jesus understood that love is the source and goal of our lives, it is what we are made for, and no matter what other attainments we may have we are nothing without it. I am talking, of course about charity-love, not any other kind. To see an image of it, go to Gethsemane, go to Calvary, look at the materials of the Mass: broken bread and outpoured wine. To say that God is love is not only to reassure, it is also to disturb.

Saturday of the Third Week of Lent

This is one of the most famous of the parables, but, as with any piece of Scripture, if taken out of context it could mislead.

The contrast between the Pharisee and the publican is so familiar it has entered popular speech. If we say of someone that he or she is 'a bit of a Pharisee', we could be referring to a number of the sayings of Jesus but most likely it is this parable we have in mind.

The parable may give the impression we are meant to choose between two human types, both rather unattractive. The more obviously unattractive figure is the Pharisee, a model of moral probity of a highly self-conscious kind. He readily writes off people less ethically exacting than himself and probably puts their backs up by the aggressiveness of his zeal for their improvement.

Is the publican much better? He is given fewer words to say, but none of them speak of moral reform. He may be the sort of character who rather rejoices in feeling part of the human mess and doesn't particularly want to get out of it. He could well be the kind of person who thinks the virtuous rather dull. Evidently, he hasn't made much attempt to emulate them. He may think that God will enjoy showing him pity by a really spectacular act of his merciful nature. The French have a name for this: they call it 'the Pharisaism of the publican'.

Something, clearly, is missing from this sort of analysis, and it is the fact that our Lord is not comparing personality types at all. He is assessing their readiness for sanctification by grace. He is pointing to the necessity for everyone of the grace of conversion — and that includes the grace of continuing conversion, of ongoing conversion. And this grace can never be received without a humble contrite heart. Both the dutiful, like, say the well-known girl who became St Thérèse of Lisieux, and the penitent, like, say the less well-known girl who became St Pelagia the Harlot, need that grace in their lives.

THE FOURTH WEEK OF LENT

The Fourth Sunday of Lent (Year A)

St Thomas tells us that the senses most clearly connected to understanding are sight and hearing. The case of hearing is, I suppose, obvious. If you can't hear what people say to you, then there is a great deal you don't know. But what about sight? A world denuded of colour would be aesthetically impoverished, sure enough. But do we actually need sight so as to understand the world?

Well, without sight we wouldn't be able to situate ourselves in reality so intelligently. Sight is meant to be our most objective method of contact with the world we inhabit. It should open up the world to us in its widest possible prospect. It ought to bring distant objects close and make nearer objects stand out more clearly. We have sight so as to distinguish between objects and relate them to each other, putting them in their proper place, their proper perspective.

Let's hold on especially to that last word, 'perspective'. There's a continuum in experience, or so it seems, between the way physical sight gives perspective, and having perspective more generally: having what we call a sense of priorities, of what is (or should be) more commanding in our lives and what is (or should be) more towards the margins of the picture. Seeing, it turns out, is a sort of lived metaphor for really understanding.

In the miracle of the Man born Blind, the God-man restores sight to the visually impaired. Is there some sense in which he does this for us too? Of course! 'Illumination' or 'enlightenment' was a common name in the Church of the Fathers for Holy Baptism. The person who is baptized is enlightened—something given ritual expression in the lighted candle the newly baptized are handed with the advice to keep it burning. In Baptism and Confirmation, the act of faith is amplified by the graces needed for the development of faith, and this makes possible a new kind of seeing: we could say, a new sense of perspective, a new way of positioning ourselves in the field of objects in this world. The Lord now enlightens us by making us understand the life he has won for us by his Incarnation, Death and Resurrection, and the way this puts into a new context all the other realities we have to do with.

We sometimes see references to 'The Enlightenment'—an eighteenth century movement of philosophy stressing universal reason. At least in the Latin-Catholic parts of Europe, this movement was consciously anti-Christian in character. We should remember that the Church had the word 'enlightenment' first, and that for her it means a perspective even more comprehensive than philosophy, a perspective that positions us on a spectrum reaching from Genesis to the Apocalypse. It's a perspective that shows the world painted in the colours of the divine plan, the divine purpose for creation—colours even more amazing than those found in nature.

Colours both brighter and darker, since, unlike the rationalist Enlightenment, we know not only of this world but also of Heaven and Hell: the gracious God, Heaven, and the loss of the gracious God, Hell. 'Once you were darkness', says St Paul, 'but now you are light in the Lord.' This carries implications for us. We have to become what we are. So he adds, 'Walk therefore as children of the light.' And again: 'Expose the unfruitful works of darkness, for whenever anything is exposed by the light it becomes visible.' And yet again, 'Be blameless and innocent, children of God without blemish in the midst of this crooked and perverse generation, among whom you shine as lights in the world'. Those who are enlightened by faith in Baptism have to be the visibility of charity, for the newly enlightened are given not only a lighted candle but a white garment, which is the robe of Christian love. If we are to be lights for the world, we have to keep this robe unspotted.

Do you *see*?

The Fourth Sunday of Lent (Year B)

As today's Gospel opens, Jesus is describing his destiny by a rather strange comparison. He is comparing himself to the symbolic bronze snake which, during the wanderings of the Israelites through the desert of Sinai, Moses lifted up on a pole for them to look at. To grasp what is going on we have to think about what could be symbolized by snakes.

On the whole most people do not care for snakes, despite the frequent beauty of their skins. Nasty, creepy-crawly things, they tend to say, even if in this island we have only one poisonous variety and that is not lethal except perhaps to small animals and children with certain allergies. However, these unpleasant associations were not the main things that came to mind when people in the ancient world thought about snakes. There snakes were symbols of healing. Why was that? The general habits of snakes were no different now from then. But what impressed people was the way snakes could shed their old skins and appear all glistening, decked out in new ones—an instant skin graft that combined wound repair with cosmetic surgery in a single action. The snake thus became a symbol of healing and so, as can happen after some operations we undergo ourselves, a new life, a new start.

In this context, the meaning of Moses's gesture is plain. It was a sign of hope to the sick, the footsore, and the weary in the wilderness, and especially to those who, on top of everything else, had just got snake-bite as well. It was a striking episode as well as a strange one because for the snake-bitten the occasion of suffering was also the symbol of its overcoming.

And that is what made it in the Gospel a perfect image of the Passion, which is the life-giving death of the Lord. Jesus is saying that the Cross on which he is going to be lifted up, the instrument of his suffering and death, will be the means of our liberation from spiritual suffering and unending death—just as the venomous snake, by its ability to get rid of an old skin and appear all arrayed in a new, is a symbol of healing and new life.

This reminds us that the trial and execution of our Lord will not be a regrettable accident cutting short an otherwise promising career. It was for his Passion—his 'hour'—that the Word incarnate entered our world. That is why in the Church of the Byzantine rite bishops don't have the tops of their episcopal staffs shaped into crooks like Latin bishops do. They have them made into the likeness of a snake instead.

It is from the death of Christ and nowhere else that the fullness of revelation and grace come to us.

The Fourth Sunday of Lent (Year C)

The parable of the Prodigal Son is so beautiful that one can hear it over and over without getting bored by it, or so I find. Some background also helps.

By the Jewish standards of the time, the father in this little drama has already overdone the milk of human kindness in the first act. The Hebrew Bible warns fathers not to part with their goods before they die: in doing so they may put themselves in jeopardy. And it was against the Law to divide an estate in this way: the whole inheritance should have passed to the first-born. So the father is already reckless to the point of illegality.

The prodigal son, having squandered his substance, is keeping alive by herding pigs—just about the most abhorrent profession there could be for an orthodox Jew. The pig is ritually taboo, probably because it figured in the idolatrous religions of Israel's neighbours. No sense of remorse seems to drive the prodigal back home. It seems to be just self-interest: 'How many of my father's hired servants have more food than they want and here am I dying of hunger'.

But then in act two, while he is still far off, a tiny but just recognizable figure on the road, the father sees him, runs out to meet him, falls on his neck and kisses him. And then begins a restitution of the son which condenses a whole range of Old Testament allusions. He's given a ring like the stranger Joseph was by Pharaoh; the fatted calf is slain, as it was by Abraham for his angelic visitors. Far from remonstrating with the prodigal over what he has done, he lavishes honour on him in his relief and rejoicing.

This is a contrast between expectation and reality which it is the role of the elder son to make clear. He has always been a good lad: hardworking, trustworthy, uncomplaining. Typically he's still out in the fields, at work, and only hears about the party because he hears music coming from the house. His reaction is waves of anger: perhaps the first time in his life he won't accept his father's decision, rejecting what he has done as unjust and outrageous. From any ordinary point of view he is right, and the father can only repeat that love has made him do this. He defends his behaviour by echoing the words of the patriarch Jacob clasping Joseph to his bosom: 'It was fitting to make merry and be glad, for this your brother was dead and is alive, he was lost and is found.'

In a famous painting by one of the Van Eyck brothers, a tiny mirror at the centre of the picture-space exactly reflects the room where a betrothal is taking place. In the parable of the Prodigal Son we are meant to see a whole world refracted, a greater space, and it is the world of God's gracious relations with ourselves. This parable is a miniature of the Gospel of grace. Here we have as a story what St Paul will articulate as a doctrine: the doctrine that though God is in his own nature burning righteousness, nonetheless, so as to save us, he becomes for us a gracious God, a God of excessive mercy, a God of love.

In the dispensation of salvation he awaits us at each moment, like the father in the parable scanning the horizon from his farmyard gate, looking down the road for the prodigal to return. Where sin abounds, there grace abounds the more. Now we see the God of grace as he is: the merciful Father who beckons us as our goal at the end of the world.

Monday of the Fourth Week of Lent

Today's Gospel *could* just be another healing by Jesus, albeit on St John's reckoning the first, significantly, in the series of such miracles. But as always with this evangelist, there is more to it than meets the eye.

The 'more to it' centres on the phrase, 'The man believed the word that Jesus spoke to him'. Discussing religion with the man in the street one soon finds there's great confusion over the word 'faith'. Does it mean believing something reassuring against most (if not all) of the evidence? Does it mean convincing yourself of something you know can't be true but which it would be psychologically helpful to believe? Is it a general attitude of hoping for the best in an uncertain life? And the answer is of course that it is none of these things. Faith—in the sense Catholic doctrine uses the word—means entrusting your mind to the word, the testimony, of God. Faith is when grace moves the will to give its assent to the truth of God and to stick to it, whether what that truth teaches is something we should like to believe or not. Liking doesn't come into it.

Faith so understood has to come first and foremost in the attitude we should have in our relations to God. St Thomas calls it our primary bonding to God, *prima conjunctio ad Deum*. This is why Jesus makes faith in himself, as the living Testimony of God, the condition of his miraculous actions, requiring it even from those he loved most, like the family at Bethany, and deliberately limiting the effect of his power when faith is absent, as at Nazareth, even though it was 'his own country'.

The testimony of God that we have accepted by faith so as to be members of the Church is that Jesus Christ is God's own Son, sent for our salvation and given for our sanctification. That is the conclusion St John intends us to take from his Gospel-book as a whole.

What is especially relevant to us in Lent is that such faith is the root of all holiness. The more *this* faith takes charge of our life, the more ardently we put it into practice, the more conjoined we are to God. Like the official's son, we shall live—but in a more pregnant sense of 'live'. We shall live to God.

Tuesday of the Fourth Week of Lent

Our faith is based on things that really happened. God gave us a message through events that took place. So it's important for us to feel confidence in the records—above all, the holy Gospels—as well as, of course, to get the message God is giving us. Today's Gospel, from the Gospel according to St John, is a case in point. It's a real event and an important message all rolled up in one.

Time was when the scholars thought St John's Gospel was nothing but symbolism, a sort of poem in prose. The author was a mystic having profound thoughts, but those thoughts didn't have much to do with anything that actually happened in the life of our Lord. The portico with five pillars by the pool of Siloam was thought to be a literary fiction: an allegory for the five books of Moses. The message of the mystical evangelist was that Christianity has fulfilled Judaism. He expressed this in a piece of symbolism made up for the purpose: at a place where nothing could be done for a cripple, Jesus gave healing.

Imagine the surprise of the critics when archaeologists claimed to have uncovered the remains of the five-pillared portico and found it just as John described it. That was part of a re-think that renewed confidence in the historical value of St John's Gospel and so of the portrait of Jesus in the Gospels as a whole.

It is *through* Jesus's historical reality, his really doing things that actually happened, that the message comes to us and can be known as trustworthy in what it says. And yes, the message today *is* how the Gospel goes beyond the Old Law. That at least the critics didn't get wrong.

It is a Gospel passage with a message about the power of the Saviour that is relevant to us as well as to Jews. In Lent we recognize that we are in the same position as the man at the Pool of Siloam. We are spiritually lame, one-legged men, and in some areas of our lives and relationships paralysed, hardly able to move. Jesus is not only the man who really lived in Palestine. He is also the living Lord of the Church who can still make people spiritually able-bodied, enable them to walk in peace with their neighbour free of crippling resentments and petty dislikes, enjoying instead the liberty of the children of God under God's blue sky.

Wednesday of the Fourth Week of Lent

In today's Gospel our Lord tells his hearers that the hour is coming when those who are in their tombs will hear the voice of the Son of God and all who hear it will live. It's an opportunity to remind ourselves of what we believe will happen to us after our deaths.

So far we've known a two-stage existence on earth. We were called into existence at our conception. At stage one, we were enclosed for nine months or thereabouts in the darkness of our mother's wombs. This was something of a 'part life'. We enjoyed the sub-conscious bliss of an intimate relation with our mother. But we weren't as fully 'there', and certainly not as fully active, as we would be at stage two when we were born.

There is a parallel here with the after life scenario. 'Those who are dead will hear the voice of the Son of God and live.' There will be a new existence in Christ for the souls of the dead. If they have not made themselves hellish, they will know a life in company with him, but, like our pre-natal life in the womb, it will be, to begin with, life in only a partial sense. True, it will have the merit of an intimate relation with God. But in Purgatory, or in Heaven before the General Resurrection, I shall not be completely me. The life beyond is, at stage one, only a life of the soul, and as St Thomas says, *anima non est ego*, 'the soul is not me': not the entire me. In Purgatory and Heaven there will be rather restricted activity, like in the womb only in a different way. My soul will be engaged in mental activity—loving mental activity, certainly—but mental activity all the same.

But then comes birth to the fulness of the life everlasting. We declare in the Great Creed we recite at Mass, 'I believe in… the resurrection of the body', while the Apostles' Creed used at Baptism says, even more forcefully, 'in the resurrection of the flesh'. The flesh is where we are at home, and it's where we carry out all sorts of activities that delight the spirit. That is what makes stage two so important for our future hope: it's the life not just of the mind but of the *world* to come when we shall be as variously active as we are now but all through God, with God, and in God, unlike now.

Thanks to the first Easter, our flesh will flower again, in that unity of soul and body which together make up the complete me.

Thursday of the Fourth Week of Lent

In today's Gospel, our Lord speaks of four sorts of witness to him. What are they?

First, there are the Scriptures, above all the Torah, the Law given through Moses. Christ is the key which unlocks the door of the ancient Bible of the Jews and unifies and makes sense of its various aspects and claims.

Secondly, there is John the Baptist, the last of the prophets, whose burning zeal for God's revelation to Israel had led him to identify his cousin Jesus as the long-expected Messiah.

Thirdly, there are Christ's own works, his wonderful actions in healing and transforming creation done in favour of, especially, the handicapped, the sick and the mentally disturbed.

Lastly, there is the voice of the Father—a reference, presumably, to the 'theophanies', moments of direct divine manifestation which the Gospels describe on two main occasions, the Baptism of Christ in the river Jordan and his Transfiguration on a mountain.

On the basis of all these taken cumulatively, then, Jesus regards his own claim as, in one sense, sufficiently attested. And yet in another sense—as he says—he makes no claim at all. In his own words, 'he does not receive glory from men'. His whole discussion of claims is in the context, solely, of what the disciples need for their own faith—'signs of credibility' (so later apologetics would call them) which we need to consult in order to validate the rational element in our belief in Christ. 'I say this that you may be saved.'

Why does he make no claims for himself for his own sake? Why does he not, in his own words, 'seek glory from' human beings? The explanation lies in his deepest identity as the Word of the Father. As One who is divine precisely in the mode of receptivity, of openness, of dependence on the Father (he is, to repeat, the Father's *Word*), he shows his Godhead by being sheer relationship to the Father rather than some sort of terminus in himself, some sort of end in himself.

He is not a terminus, not a goal. Instead he is the Way to the goal. Yet as the unique Way, in his own person as the only-begotten Son irreplaceable by any other mediator, he is not only the way but also for the world the truth and the life.

Friday of the Fourth Week of Lent

In this Gospel, the Jews doubt that Jesus can really be God's ambassador on the grounds that we know where he comes from.

This might seem an odd problem to have until we re-phrase the objection in more modern terms. Can someone so drenched in particularity as Jesus—a Palestinian Jew, a Galilaean, a Nazarene, a carpenter's son—can such a person really be a universal mediator? The implicit reply of the evangelist is that the Jews *don't* know where Jesus comes from: though born in time, he comes from the bosom of the Father whose eternal Word he is.

In a sense, however, this answer simply re-states the original question, for how can the universal Word be embodied in a particular individual without frustrating the Word's own universality in action? A clue to the solution can be found by looking ahead to the fruits of our Lord's saving work in the Church to which the evangelist belonged.

The Christian experience of grace is not the obliteration of distinctiveness but the transfiguration of particularities. For the painter Stanley Spencer to show us the Parousia is to show it us in a particular Berkshire village, while for the poet Francis Thompson, the vagabond alcoholic from Preston, Jacob's ladder, the connexion between earth and heaven, stands by the railway terminal at Charing Cross.

Saturday of the Fourth Week of Lent

In today's Gospel our Lord is reminded by the Pharisees that none of the religious authorities believe in him, only the crowds do—and they are accursed.

It would be easy to take this statement, turn it round, and make it into a demagogic glorification of 'the people' (whoever they are) over against 'authority' (whatever that is). But such a homily would be ideology, not theology.

The Pharisees are pointing out that those people who have studied the Jewish religion long and hard enough to have an opinion worth hearing don't give any credence to Jesus' claims— unlike the illiterate element in the population which didn't know the Law, the Torah, whether because denied the opportunity or by not bothering to make the effort and in either case becoming 'accursed', which is here a technical term for not sharing in the holiness of Torah.

How was it that people who knew so little nevertheless welcomed the Saviour? We should have to answer in terms of two principles—the intrinsic power and radiance of revealed truth once offered to people and also its fittingness to human nature. As St John's Gospel says of Jesus, he knew what was in man.

But in that case how can we explain the abandonment by large elements of a previously Christianised population of adherence to Christ? For instance, in Western Europe since the Second World War, perhaps the most thorough de-evangelisation process in Church history, unless the aftermath of the French Revolution can trump it.

Blessed John Henry Newman points out that acceptance of revelation is only reasonable or plausible or imaginatively possible if we have certain relevant prior attitudes or expectations in considering its claims. The Jewish crowd had those attitudes and expectations which came from a grasp of the rudiments of Judaism: there is a God, concerned with man, who shows his hand in history. But when those prior dispositions are wiped out—for instance by secularism, scientism, materialism—the capacity of the human mind to entertain revelation begins to break down.

Fortunately, not altogether. We do not know which of the faithful will persevere but we know that some will. As St John, once again, tells us, the body of the faithful is 'anointed by the Holy One', and this instinct for divine truth, planted sacramentally by the Holy Spirit in Christian initiation, can never be lost by that body as a whole, though many individual persons may be lost to the body. It is this supernatural truth and not any sociological optimism, much less a cult of the people, which grounds the hope and confidence of the Church.

The Fifth Sunday of Lent (Year A)

In ten days time or so, we shall be thinking of two hillsides. On Good Friday there will be Calvary of course, but we must not forget on Holy Thursday the Mount of Olives, where Jesus underwent the Agony in the Garden. And that second hillside is already on the horizon today. It is the huge dry outcrop of rock which separates Jerusalem from Bethany where, as we heard in today's Gospel, Jesus' friend Lazarus lived together with Martha and Mary his sisters. Near the top there is now a modern chapel in the shape of a tear because it is here that, according to the shortest verse of the Bible, John 11: 35, 'Jesus wept', wept for his friend Lazarus who was dead.

A chapel in the shape of a tear sounds rather a gimmick, but if it is a gimmick it succeeds very well. You look out at the world through a tear-drop, just as so often people do look at the world because of what the old Roman poet called 'the tears of things'. There are many things in this world which make it a vale of tears. If we could quantify the human tears that have flowed since the start of history we might find, however, that the greatest source of all human lamenting is grief—the death of loved ones, final separation from people we love, their going from us, where we cannot say.

It is this experience, grieving over a lost friend, which caused the only tears recorded of Jesus. He wept for Lazarus his friend, causing Christians centuries later to call this place, *Dominus flevit*, 'The Lord wept', and to build an altar on the spot where God himself had watered the earth by crying.

For according to our faith, Jesus Christ is God made flesh, God made man, so that what Christ is said to do, God is truly said to do also. Christ wept, therefore God wept—as man, certainly, for that is the only way God could weep, yet it was really and truly God who wept for Lazarus his friend.

Many of the doctors and divines of the Church have asked the question, Why did God become man? (the title of a famous treatise by St Anselm), but they have found few better answers than that of St Bernard: it was to know what it is to be man, from the inside. God became man in order to experience our condition, our life, from the inside: to know our joys and sorrows as we know them. Of course, God knows all things and unless he knew them they would not exist at all. But without the Incarnation he does not his creation *from within*, he does not know it as a creature, he does not know it as man. And in that place, on the Mount of Olives, when Lazarus lay beginning to stink in the tomb, One who was God knew what it is to weep for a friend, to grieve, to sorrow for one who was alive and is dead.

The tears of Christ at the grave of Lazarus do not give us a theoretical answer to the problem of physical evil. They do not prove to us it is reasonable for a young mother to die tragically of cancer, or for children to be knocked down by a runaway car, or for anyone we have ever loved to die—since in love, age is of little importance. What those tears do, however, is to help in practice. To realize that God has wept, that our own Maker has grieved for a human being, his brother, this is to know that God himself has been through the suffering we go through. It enables us to accept more readily the counsel that tells us, Grief is the price we pay for love.

It also reminds us, as we enter the season of Passiontide, that the God revealed in Christ is, as our mediaeval forebears called him, *humanissimus Redemptor*, 'our very human Redeemer'. Equally importantly, the events at Bethany remind us that, correlatively, our very human Redeemer is almighty God. The Incarnate Word did not leave this world unchanged by his coming. He did not leave it unchanged for Lazarus whose decomposing corpse he restored to human integrity. As the Byzantine Liturgy acclaims, 'Thou hast wept over Lazarus as a man, and Thou hast raised him as God'. And this miracle was a foretaste of his own Resurrection when he rendered our human nature glorious and immortal—in himself, first of all, but also, as the feast of our Lady's Assumption, the Easter of summertime, will recall for us, not just in himself since it was all done for our sake, so that the human family may follow where Jesus and Mary have gone before.

In the day of that consummation, so the Apocalypse of St John records, 'he will wipe away every tear from our eyes', he who had no one to wipe away tears from his eyes on the Mount of Olives, at the *Dominus flevit*.

The Fifth Sunday of Lent (Year B)

So in today's Gospel, Jesus hears of a request from some 'Greeks' — whether these were pagan Greeks or simply Greek-speaking Jews from the diaspora, Jews from beyond Palestine, we are not told. They approach the disciples of their own volition and with what is, plainly, a heartfelt and even urgent request, not a merely casual or voyeuristic desire. 'Sir, we should like to see Jesus.'

Hearing of this request, there wells up in the human mind and heart of the Word incarnate a terrific wave of praise and thanksgiving to the Father. And the reason is that Jesus finds, prophetically, in this spontaneous desire of Greeks to see him, an anticipation of the universal fruitfulness of his mission and, especially, his saving Death. He foresees, if you like, the catholicity of the Church.

A grain of wheat falling to the earth and dying looks as though it has come to the end of its life-cycle. But in fact if it dies, if it turns into seed in the earth, it may yield a rich harvest. So it will be with Jesus, with no 'may' about it. From his Death will flow the salvation of the world.

As he speaks these prophetic words, there comes an answering recognition from the Father. As the evangelist John describes it, the bystanders heard a curious sound which could be interpreted as either the weather or a voice. But our Lord, hearing it on his inward ear as well as his outward ear, tells the Twelve it is a promise from the Father. The Father will glorify himself by glorifying the Son. Exegetes have noted that this episode in St John's Gospel corresponds to the event of the Transfiguration of Christ in the other three.

Jesus' prophecy, 'When I am lifted up from the earth I shall draw all men to myself' proved correct. From the first Easter onwards, that 'drawing' began to affect men and women in ever-expanding segments of the earth's surface. We have only to think of the consequences in our own island. From the conversion of the Anglo-Saxons in the sixth century and following there issued our civilization which, historically, is a Judaeo-Christian one though with Greco-Roman and Germanic aspects. The culture— above all, the moral culture—of this island is unthinkable without the Conversion. Historically, our moral perceptions are inextrica- bly bound up with a sense of the fatherhood of God, the brother- hood of man, and the gift of grace to us through Jesus Christ our Lord. We could sum all that up in one simple formula: 'the sacredness of all human life, as loved by God in his Son Jesus Christ from the cradle to the grave'.

Where then, we ask ourselves, are we today?

The Fifth Sunday of Lent (C)

The story of the Woman taken in Adultery has to be among everyone's favourite stories concerning the Saviour—and we hope for the right reasons, which do not include condoning her offence. Catholic exegetes have understood the words of Jesus to the adulteress, 'Neither do I condemn thee', as an act of absolution, albeit expressed in negative form. In saying these words he forgives her, having thwarted the attempt to execute her (which is what the Law required), and doing so by the brilliant strategy of making her accusers feel their own hypocrisy whereupon they withdraw from the scene in silence. He does not challenge the Law, but he makes its adherents understand the difficulty of applying it with rigorous honesty.

And meanwhile he pours the salve of his forgiveness into the woman's moral and spiritual wound. We notice that her way of addressing him is already open to his saving power: that title *Kyrie* which may mean simply 'Sir' but which in other contexts is more charged and has the sense of 'Lord', as we are well aware from the words of the *Kyrie eleison* in the Liturgy. Did she have an inkling of their real relation, the relation indicated by St Paul in today's epistle: 'not having a righteousness of my own, based on law, but that which is through faith in Christ, the righteousness from God that depends on faith'—faith, in this case, in the right of the priestly Messiah of Israel to absolve, to dismiss with blessing?

His role in her going free is a transcending of the Law even if it is not, in strict legal argument, a rejection of its norms. His absolution of her is an example of how our Lord went beyond the Law of Israel in the name of a righteousness that, so far from mitigating, exceeded the Law's demands, because the righteousness of the New Covenant is the righteousness of charity, which has no limit. Ad so it is one way in which Jesus' career exemplifies what the prophet Isaiah was speaking about in today's reading from the Old Testament. 'Thus says the Lord... Behold I am doing a new thing; now it springs forth, do you not perceive it?' It is the novelty of redeeming grace we see in today's Gospel. That is the best of all reasons for making it a favourite.

Monday of the Fifth Week of Lent

The Old Testament lection given for today is the longest biblical reading of the year. In celebrating the chastity of Susanna it presents an interesting contrast to the Gospel of the Woman taken in Adultery with which it has long been yoked. Before 1970, when the Lectionary to be used with the Missal of Pope Paul VI was devised, these two texts were already linked together, but on the Fourth Saturday of Lent, rather than the Fifth Monday. They had been there for one and a half thousand years in the Latin West, and still are when it is the Missal of Blessed John XXIII that is employed at the Liturgy.

These readings—which, broadly speaking, concern sex and violence—what are they doing in the Lenten Liturgy?

Historians of the Liturgy tell us that each of the days of Lent was associated in Rome itself with a different so-called 'stational' church, a church where the pope stopped off on a circumambulation of his city so as to make a *statio*: that is, to celebrate the Liturgy of that day. These readings belonged to the *statio* at Santa Susanna, a church called after a third century women martyr who shared with the biblical Susanna not only a name but also the virtue of chastity.

The Gospel of the Woman taken in Adultery comes into the picture because to reach this church, the pope, along with the clergy and devout laity who accompanied him, had to make their way down a very notorious street, a haunt of prostitutes, pimps and lechers. Rather as might be the case in parts of Soho or central Amsterdam today, that Gospel of forgiveness yet rebuke—'Go, and sin no more!'—was relevant to those leading a sexually depraved life-style. The Susanna story is a story of justice, but the story of the Woman taken in Adultery is more typically New Testament: it is a story of mercy.

There is, however, a way in which we can think of Susanna in a real relation to the New Testament and that is when we consider her story as part of the Church's build-up to the events of Holy Week. As the Latin Fathers loved to point out, Susanna is a type of Christ, the Innocent One, who, like her, was accused by false witnesses and betrayed in a garden. He too will be sorely tried and keep silence when he is indicted. St Jerome tells us how when he read of the clamour raised for Susanna's execution he could not stop himself thinking ahead to Good Friday, and the cry, 'Crucify him'.

The tale of human misery, which includes Susanna's ordeal and the humiliation of the Adulterous Woman seems to go on for ever. But no! The execution of Jesus is not a further example of it. It is the mercy of God coming to end the tale for ever.

Tuesday of the Fifth Week of Lent

If you ever bump into an Eastern Orthodox bishop or even a Byzantine-rite Catholic bishop in full fig, you will find that they are carrying, just as it says in today's Old Testament reading, a serpent on a stick. Whereas a Latin bishop carries a shepherd's crook, a Byzantine bishop wields a staff with a stylized snake on it. What a horrid thing you might say, but you would be wrong.

On the feast of the Exaltation of the Cross we read this same story from the Book of Numbers, but we hear as the Gospel of the day how our Lord applied the story to himself.

He is the true Serpent lifted up on the Cross in the wilderness of this world. Like the bronze serpent Moses put on a stand for the Israelites to contemplate in the desert and hopefully be cured of snake-bite, the Cross is at once something ghastly and something re-assuring. It is an instrument of torture and death which by the power of God becomes a vehicle for healing and salvation.

This is typical of the saving divine power, that it turns the horrible into the wonderful. Of course, since it is power to revolutionise reality for the sake of the good.

In this Gospel, Jesus alludes to the same theme when he says, 'When you have lifted up the Son of Man, then you will know that I am He': meaning, that I am one with the power and being of God himself.

And he continues, 'He who sent me is with me, and has not left me to myself'. In a sense, so this passage of St John's Gospel is hinting, our Lord *is* his mission from the Father. He originates in a procession from the Father before all time, and when he enters the world as man that procession becomes his mission. It is a mission to heal the world's ills and we recognize that he *is* that mission when we say of him, that he personally is our salvation — when we call him 'our Saviour'.

In Holy Week we shall rehearse once again everything that involved.

Wednesday of the Fifth Week of Lent

It seems a bit strange that in today's Gospel our Lord's Jewish opponents say they've never been in bondage to anyone. After all, we've just heard in the Old Testament lection a story of some pretty beastly behaviour of the Babylonians to the Jews whom they'd just conquered. And at the time of Jesus' conversation Judaea was occupied by the Romans.

It's possible, no doubt, for a proud people to be officially annexed without ever really knuckling under, so that they maintain the spirit of liberty in circumstances adverse to it. Also, there was no totalitarianism in the ancient world. That was a discovery of modernity, with its technologically far superior methods of oppression. Under foreign rule, Judaea kept, in fact, a lot of its institutional life so such liberty wasn't just a matter of how people felt inside.

And in any case, the greatest motive force behind the Jewish experience of liberty was not civic but spiritual. It was the corporate conviction of being uniquely chosen, the outstanding recipient of divine blessings which give joy, assurance, confidence, and so a certain indifference to the attitudes of others.

And in a way this was the trouble. As St John of the Cross notes, divine blessings—including mystical graces of a very high order—can turn into snares and temptations if we start to regard them as effectively the same as God himself. That's why that Carmelite mystic thought a dose of the dark night was good for us: to prevent our mistaking God's gifts for God. Did Israel's sense of the gifts of God to her, of her uniquely privileged spiritual status, work against the plan of God for her? That status was intended to be a preparation for the Incarnation, but it easily turned into a rival to the Incarnate One.

And the result was a failure to distinguish between two levels of freedom—on the one hand, the freedom given by God through the revealed truth and spiritual life of the Covenant with Israel, and, on the other hand, the freedom which the Word of God Jesus Christ in his eternal origination from the Father personally is. The Jewish opponents of Jesus had had the gift. Now they were offered the Giver himself. In fact they preferred the gift. And so—for here Jesus does not mince his words—they made of the gift something perverse: if not diabolical then at least adversarial, inimical to, even contrary to, the saving plan the gift was meant to serve.

Thursday of the Fifth Week of Lent

So in today's Gospel our Lord tells the Jewish theologians that if anyone accepts his word they will never see death. It's spiritual death he is talking about, not physical death, though to be sure there is a connexion of a kind. In the Age to Come spiritual death will prevent one from enjoying the resurrection of the just. But his interlocutors misunderstand him—whether by an innocent mistake or maliciously is not made clear.

An angry exchange follows, or at least there is considerable anger from the side of the questioners. They want to know whether there is a sense in which Jesus makes a claim that goes beyond even the claim orthodox Judaism makes for Abraham, the father of Israel. And—despite the mistake over spiritual death—there is indeed such a sense, to which the Saviour gives discreet or oblique expression by saying Abraham saw—in hope and desire, we should understand—the day of the Incarnation.

When did Abraham see that day and how? The compilers of the Lectionary have given us a clue by providing a companion reading from the Abraham cycle in Genesis. For many of the Fathers of the Church it was the Logos—later incarnate as Jesus— who spoke to Abraham in the utterances and encounters which lay out the future plan for his posterity. Was the crucial occasion that recorded in Genesis 18, the meeting at the Oak of Mamre with the three mysterious figures whom the icons of the Church will call the 'Old Testament Trinity', the visitors who came to tell Abraham that Sarah would after all conceive? Or was it maybe the vision in Genesis 15 when a 'great dread and darkness' fell upon Abraham, an experience connected in some way, it is implied, with the divine plan for him? We do not have the answer to that question.

But the answer we *do* have is the confession of the Lord's pre-existence which the debaters force out of him. 'Before Abraham was, I am.' 'I Am' is of course a version of the divine Name. For a Unitarian monotheism, this is blasphemy; for the Church, with her Trinitarian monotheism, it is a wonderful and inexhaustible truth.

Friday of the Fifth Week of Lent

Here we have one of those passages of the Gospel according to St John that have furnished the Church with the building-blocks of her doctrine.

To have seen the Son is to have seen the Father because the Son is in the Father and the Father in him. The Son has his existence and his identity only through relation to the Father. At an abso- lutely basic level we might say of ourselves—or of any creature for that matter—we only exist at all in relation to our Source. In God, says the apostle, truly enough, we live and move and have our being. But in this passage we are told something further, the implications of which are electric.

The something further is that *the converse is also true*: the Father has his identity, his personhood, only by way of his relation to the Son. The God who is the origin of all worlds, from the macroscopic to the microscopic, is who he is only because of his relation to the One who Jesus is as man. Thus, and in no other way, is he the Father. The Father is in the Son in exactly the same sense as that in which the Son is in the Father. The Father lives, moves and has his being in the Son.

And what that tells us is: the person of the Son on earth lifts the curtain that veils the person of the Father in heaven. The visible Face of the Son is the unveiling of the Face of the heavenly Father, the Face of God to which Israel had looked in holy fear, in hope and in joy. This is why the great majority of Christian artists have preferred not to depict the Father as well as the Son, not to paint the Face of the Father distinctly from the Face of the Son.

It is also why we cannot let the study of the New Testament go in any direction its practitioners choose. We could ask—we *should* ask—of any overall interpretation of the New Testament, Does it allow us to worship the image of our Saviour as the very Face of God? Only that dynamic identification—the Father is so much in the Son that the Face of the Son on earth shows us the Face of the Father in heaven—can preserve the authentic character of Christian revelation.

When we venerate an image of our Lord, we do not simply pay it respect; we worship it as the Face of God. That is what we shall be doing on Good Friday as we 'creep to the Cross', and kneel to kiss the figure of the Crucified.

Saturday of the Fifth Week of Lent

The opening prayer of today's Mass is about those preparing at this time to be baptized. Indeed, many of the prayers of the Missal during Lent and Eastertide are about such catechumens: after Easter, the correct word would be 'neophytes': those new born from the waters of the font.

Originally, I believe, the Lenten fast affected only this group of people who in that way prepared for their initiation into the Church at Easter: their death to sin, both corporate and personal, and their rising to the new life of grace. Fasting on the part of the rest of us was originally an act of solidarity with the catechumens on the part of the whole Church.

The New Testament presupposes such solidarity and universal identification in its understanding of the redemptive significance of Christ's death. We have an example of that in today's Gospel. 'Jesus was to die not for the nation only but to gather into one the children of God who are scattered abroad.' Christian solidarity is not founded on our sharing a common humanity, as is the solidarity of modern secular humanitarianism, but on the elective and redemptive will of God who forms those he will into a regenerated humanity, a new body called by St Paul, the 'Body of Christ', and by the Fathers, 'the holy Catholic Church'.

This is not to say of course that common participation in basic humanity is worthless. Certainly not: the whole of the natural law tradition of the Church is there to tell us otherwise. But it is nonetheless a reminder that we must not reduce catholicity simply to 'concern for others'. Our primary communion is now with those who are of the household of faith. This is not because we like what the French call 'groupuscules' but because, with the coming of the Incarnate Word in our flesh, the emphasis in God's plan has shifted decisively to the making of a new people, on the basis of faith in Christ and life in the Holy Spirit.

HOLY WEEK

Palm Sunday

The vestments of the celebrants today are blood-red, because at the beginning of Holy Week we anticipate the week's end. The One who enters Jerusalem today is already, in the words of Keats, a 'murdered man'. And so it's blood we're thinking of already. You may say, so what? There's so much blood shed in the world: in road accidents, murders, natural disasters, political atrocities. Yes, but this blood is different.

This is redemptive blood, the blood Marlowe's Faust saw streaming through the firmament, and St Catherine of Siena perceived as soaking the Church in its flow. It is royal blood, the blood of the Messiah, to be shed in a self-giving whose effects are so wonderful that this Sacrifice is a triumph, and not a defeat. The red we wear today is also the red of regal triumph.

Today the Lord sought to enter his own city, Zion, the holy city, whose vocation it was to be the dwelling-place on earth of the truth, goodness, and beauty of Israel's God. It was a city that belonged to him by right, for in his divine-human person he is the measure of all of these—truth, goodness, beauty—taken together.

But the omens were not good. Scripture knew of cities that kept their gates firmly closed, to their loss. Jericho closed its doors against Joshua. Jerusalem, despite this morning's hosannas, later this week will close its doors on Jesus, it will have him crucified outside the gate.

So often we know this in our own lives. We close the door of our personality, snap it shut, when to have opened it would mean healing for ourselves and others. On Good Friday the Saviour will do the opposite to what Jericho and Jerusalem did. He will open his arms as wide as they can go, so that all the world may march in through the fissure in his side, into the spacious welcome of his Sacred Heart.

Monday in Holy Week

Today's Gospel invites us to think about the burial of Christ. One of the surprising things about the way St Thomas Aquinas presents the events of the Passion and Resurrection is the amount of space he gives to Christ's Burial. Something that appears to have worried his contemporaries was the opulence of it all. They pointed out how the rich and influential—Joseph of Arimathea, Nicodemus— played the main part. And they were also concerned at the sheer extravagance of it—the extravagance represented by the sheer quantity of the spices and perfumes (the embalming agents) that were used: one hundred pounds of myrrh and aloes, according to St John, poured onto the corpse. And part of this objection is that, in any case, a woman had already anointed him for burial, a reference to today's Gospel.

St Thomas agrees with the objectors that built into the meaning of the Passion is the ignominy of what Christ suffered, the humiliation of it, and therefore, as he puts it, the patience and constancy with which Christ endured these things: things that are the demonstration of the Father's love for us. Nevertheless, Thomas disagrees strongly with those who said it would have been more appropriate for Christ to have had the kind of burial that was the lot of the poor—chucked, like Mozart, into a pauper's grave.

On the contrary, judges Thomas, the honour given Christ in his burial was completely fitting. Such honour—the spices, perfumes and so forth—were a testimony to his divine power. In other words, the One we are remembering in Holy Week was not just a victim—not even a perfect representative of all the victims of history. No, he was God almighty, God himself taking up that role in order to change the situation of the world.

Moreover, adds Aquinas, the character of Christ's burial 'pre-figures the devotion of the faith who one day will serve the dead Christ': the Christ of Good Friday. That is a cue to us about the care and diligence with which we should arrange or attend the offices of the Sacred Triduum, and about what should predominate in our personal praying, reading and general consciousness in Holy Week.

Tuesday in Holy Week

Today and tomorrow, the last piece of Scripture we read as the Gospel at Mass is the story of Judas' betrayal. This makes obvious chronological sense in the narrative of the Passion. But taking two days over it, one of them the eve of the Paschal Triduum, suggests we are meant to find here a key that will open up the significance of what is going to be happening over the next few days.

The betrayal of Jesus by Judas exemplifies human evil. Throughout history people have betrayed their friends, their spouses, their parents or children, their fellow-citizens—in a word, their fellow human beings. Betrayal as a phenomenon points to the low price we have often placed on solidarity and communion. Now in Judas this wave of malice rises up and topples Jesus himself. And there is a peculiar enormity in this. As the Logos, the divine Word, Jesus is the ground of all the solidarity and communion there is—all positive relationship there is wherever it may be found. On Holy Thursday, the fate of the Logos will be settled by a corruption of relationship, by a traitor's kiss.

This handing over of Jesus to his enemies would be impossible without a prior handing over which takes place in God himself. From all eternity the Father has been handing over himself in the person of his Son. And the Son has reciprocated, in a total gift of self that produces the love-being of the Holy Spirit. Now that process of deliberately defenceless giving finds its expression in time, at the Supper and in the Garden. And the result? Judas's betrayal, though filled with the malice of the sin of the world, became the means whereby the Spirit of love was set free in the world at Easter and Pentecost.

During the Triduum, our Lord's humanity will become absolutely aligned with the self-expression of God. It will become the finite re-enactment of what God is. That is how from that first 'Three Days' there can come new life in the Holy Spirit, reconciliation between God and humankind, a share in the divine life for us: grace and glory.

Wednesday in Holy Week

Today, the Gospel continues to explore Judas's act of betrayal. The act of betrayal was seemingly very simple. Judas handed over a very simple secret for a very straightforward reason. What he betrayed was, quite simply, the whereabouts of Jesus in the hours of darkness. Why he betrayed was financial gain.

Some have found this too unsubtle. Surely what and why Judas betrayed must have been more profound than that? Isn't it rather a let-down if the climax of the Incarnation, the redemptive death of the God-man, was triggered by something as simple and sordid as a bag of shekels?

Actually, there is a deep fittingness in the betrayal for money of the Saviour of the world. Economists agree with philosophers that money is a mysterious thing. You might think nothing could be less mysterious than the pound in your pocket. But in fact it takes a lot of understanding. Money has been described as a kind of knot that ties together all the processes of society—whether this be for good or for evil.

If so, what more appropriate than that the life of the infinitely precious God-man, spent for the revaluing of humanity in the eyes of the Father, should be exchanged for hard cash.

Money is the symbol of all we value, all that matters to us. The exchange of money makes the world go round. And this is what through a 'marvellous exchange' the blood of Christ will start to do, from Good Friday onwards. It will become the medium in which to value—indeed, to re-value—all human life.

Holy Thursday

This afternoon's Liturgy is essentially a celebration of the Holy Eucharist. At every other Mass, we give thanks by means of the Eucharist. But in today's Mass, almost uniquely, we give thanks for the Eucharist itself, for its institution. As St Thomas Aquinas remarks, this holy sacrament is our *viaticum*, our food for the journey—not simply the journey through death, which is how the word was understood in more recent times, but our journey through life as well.

I say that today's celebration is *almost* unique because in fact the Church has just one other festival of thanksgiving for the Eucharist: namely, Corpus Christi which was introduced precisely in order to prolong the meditation we should be making today as we recall how at the Last Supper with his chosen disciples the Lord 'gave himself with his own hand', as St Thomas' great hymn for Corpus Christi puts it. For today, the theme of the institution of the Eucharist—this sacrament which is at the heart of the Church's life—is in some danger of being crowded out by other motifs, so thick and fast do the acts which make the Church and the Gospel what they are come clustering about us.

In this Mass we shall also be celebrating the *mandatum*, the 'maundy', the new commandment to 'love one another' which our Lord gave as his last will and testament. We recall how this commandment of charity is the basis of the Church's ethos. It is the revolutionary wind set blowing wherever Jesus' mission and message are heeded. We remember today how in practical demonstration of what charity involves, the Master made himself a menial and, to the horror of the disciples, washed their feet. After this homily we shall be re-enacting that scene to re-commit ourselves to its significance.

Also today throughout the world in every cathedral the bishop, as chief pastor of his local church, blesses the oils to be used in the coming year. They are for the initiation of new Christians through Baptism and Confirmation, for the strengthening of the sick, and for the making of ministerial priests to build up the Church's common life. Thus through the bishop, the Church on this day takes steps to secure her own future as the communion of charity.

And overshadowing it all, as the Liturgy of the Hours tells us, is the impending death of the Lord, for this is his long-awaited 'hour': the hour when the betrayer is at hand, who, having left the table, simultaneously leaves the communion of charity and enters the darkness that all who knowingly reject love inhabit. Judas goes out, and as St John comments so meaningfully, 'it was night'. By the light of the torches the traitor will guide the enemies of Jesus to their victim and in a grotesque parody of the love-command, betray him with a kiss.

Tonight, when Mass is over, the Church will continue to watch and pray with Christ in the sacramental presence of the Eucharistic Gifts. She will do so remembering that Christ our Head still suffers in his members, for whom he makes intercession everlastingly before the Father. He still bears in his body the marks of the wounds, and we may understand this to mean that his risen glory does not remove his will-to-share in the world's suffering, but enables him to exercise that will until time as we know it ends.

And so we come back finally to the mystery of the Eucharist, which is the real Presence among us of the sacrificial Victim, now gloriously accepted in his Resurrection. By a wonderful conversion the whole substance of bread and wine are changed into the personal being of our Lord, so that by encountering him intimately in Holy Communion we may be joined more closely to the Father and thereby to each other. We encounter him in the Holy Gifts as the Victim of Love who each day in the Sacrifice of the Mass invites us to enter the movement of his priestly self-offering. He is on the altar and in the Tabernacle for a purpose: that we should learn the hidden fruitfulness of self-giving. When we carry the Eucharistic Elements in procession we are acting out their deepest sense as our Food for a journey, the Food that makes us hunger for the Banquet of the City of God, the City that lives by charity alone, all pride and egoism burned away. 'You have given them Bread from Heaven, containing in itself every sweetness.'

Good Friday

Good Friday is the only day in the year when the rubrics direct the person giving the homily to be brief. The explanation might just be practical. After the lengthy Passion reading there will shortly be the equally protracted intercessions, and then your own approach to the sanctuary in two files, first for the veneration of the Cross and then for Communion with the pre-sanctified Species.

But there's reason to think more is involved in this demand for brevity in preaching than being economical with time.

Today the divine Word, the self-expression of God who for our sakes emptied himself to become a human being so that we might hear the words of God himself, this incarnate Word, Jesus Christ, is dead, and his voice is extinguished. The New Testament attests that without the Son no one can see the Father, nor can anyone come to the Father. There may be a sporadic knowledge of God in the world religions, but without the Son the Father is personally revealed to nobody. And this is the day when the humanized Son dies and the Father, accordingly, becomes inaccessible to us.

At the end of the Passion, when the Word of God is humanly dead, the Church herself has few words left to say. She is not to proclaim her faith or criticize society or organize works of charity or do any of the hundred things her members have taken to be manifestations of the Gospel. She has only to intercede, and, above all, to be united to Christ.

First, to intercede. Faced with this cosmic cataclysm, the human death of One who was personally God, what believer would be unwilling to pray for all sorts and conditions of men who are affected by this event whether they know it or not. And secondly, to be united, not so much in words as in gestures, with the Lord who today sinks down into death and Hell. And so we come to the Cross, to plant our kiss on the figure of the Crucified — the kiss which was for him the instrument of his betrayal, the kiss which is so ambivalent an act: the sign of love and friendship, but also the symbol of lewdness and moral disorder, and the token of formal and possibly insincere relations in polite society. We should look today to the purification of our motives, as the precondition of daring to approach the image of our so costly redemption.

And finally, we are invited to come to Communion under the deliberately deficient symbolism of the single Species. As orthodox Catholics we know that our Lord is wholly present in his full Godhead and his full manhood under either Eucharistic sign. Yet we also respect the different ways in which he allows himself to be given us in the prayer of his Church. Today we receive him, quite deliberately, by the symbolism of incompletion. This is not for those practical reasons which led the Latin church of the Middle Ages normally to reserve the chalice to the ordained. Instead, it is out of doctrinal conviction. Today we have only a truncated Eucharist, a mutilated Eucharist, for today Christ our Lord suffered the disintegration of his very being. The human body which was to be forever the fleshly medium of the eternal Word of God in his outreach to us lies lifeless in the grave by action of our kind.

Every Holy Communion should include an element of repentance, and it does: 'Lord, I am not worthy that you should enter under my roof'. But in today's Communion this is especially marked when our common Redeemer is wrapped in his bloodied burial shroud, sinful humanity's parting gift to him, and the silence of the tomb closes in, seemingly for ever, around the Word of God.

EASTERTIDE

EASTER AND ITS OCTAVE

The Easter Vigil (Year A)

In the so-called Enlightenment, at the end of the eighteenth century, it was predicted that long grass would cover St Peter's Square in Rome. After the Revolutionary period which in Continental Europe swept away most of the institutional markers of Catholic Christendom, the German poet Heinrich Heine asked: 'Don't you hear the bell ringing? Get down onto your knees. They are carrying the sacrament to a dying God'. Fifty years later, the apostate priest and biblical scholar Ernest Renan, spoke of how it would soon be necessary to take the faith and 'carefully roll it up in the purple shroud where dead gods sleep...' 'We have put out the lights of heaven', said an atheist politician after the successful campaign to abolish the schools of the Religious Orders in early twentieth century France, 'and they will never be lit again'.

Sometimes, when we look at the condition of culture, of the media, of science, of entertainment, of opinion, we may be tempted to agree. If so, we are forgetting the words of Newman at the end of his *Essay on the Development of Christian Doctrine*. 'It is true there have been seasons when, from the operation of external or internal causes, the Church has been thrown into what was almost a state of *deliquium* [i. e. total eclipse]: but her wonderful revival, while the world was triumphing over her, is a further evidence of the absence of corruption in the system of doctrine and worship into which she has developed. After violent exertion men are exhausted and fall asleep; they awake the same as before, refreshed by the temporary cessation of their activity, and such has been the slumber and such the restoration of the Church. She pauses in her course, and almost suspends her functions; she rises again, and she is herself once more; all things are in their place and ready for action.'

The point Newman is making is that the Body of Christ, his Church-Body, can never get away from the Easter story. Like Head, like Body. When public opinion turned against our Lord, who was in turn rejected by the crowd, condemned by the authorities and submitted to an ignominious death, he was not only written off, treated indignantly as wrongheaded or cynically as an irrelevance or anxiously as a threat to the status quo. More than that, he was treated as obscene, as an abomination. That was how the Law regarded a crucified man: 'Cursed be everyone who hangs upon the tree'.

There was, however, a surprise in store. Jesus the Son may appear to be cursed but in reality he is more than ever the Beloved of the Father. His obedience to the mission the Father had given him—to demonstrate God's loving mercy in risking his all for sinners—this obedience reaches its climax, its ultimate perfection, when he is raised up on the Cross.

And so now, at Easter, in the Resurrection the Father glorifies the Son who as man has so wonderfully glorified him. The Father communicates to the Son made man, precisely as the Crucified, the Glory that is the Holy Spirit, whom we call in the Creed, the 'Lord, the giver of life'. He seemed dead and gone but he was far more alive than ever before. 'Christ being raised from the dead will never die again; death no longer has dominion over him.' And we mustn't forget how that passage continues: 'So you also must consider yourselves dead to sin and alive to God in Christ Jesus'.

We mustn't forget it because it is the key. We have come to the end of an era in the Catholic Church in our country when it was easy to be a Catholic either because the institution was so successful, as in the 1950s, or because reforming it was fun, as in the 60s and 70s, or because Cardinal Basil Hume made it so popular, in the 80s and 90s. We have left an era when it was dead easy and are entering on a new time, when our motto will have to be 'Dead to Sin and Alive to God'. Continuing conversion, death to sin, real spirituality like the saints had, life to God. That is the only way the Church-Body can follow to the Resurrection her glorious Head.

The Easter Vigil (Year B)

Physically, it was one of the better-class tombs of the period. Not surprising, because the wealthy Joseph of Arimathea had given it over for the purpose. The kind of tomb that agrees best with the Gospels was actually the latest word in fashion. The poor were dumped down shafts a dozen at a time, but this was a one-man-one-grave affair, cut deep into the rock, the burial chamber just under ground level. Large families had a network of chambers pushed back into the hillside, joined up by little passages. There they could lie connected in death as in life. But the tomb of Jesus was a single tomb, a new tomb in which no one had been laid.

It was obligatory to seal the entrance by a large stone. You didn't want people stumbling in by accident. Once a three-day period of mourning was over, contact with the dead incurred defilement. The dead were unclean. They had fallen through the hands of God into the shadow world of which the Hebrew Bible declared, 'The dead cannot praise you, the shades cannot thank you; those who go down into the pit cannot hope in your faithfulness'.

So the women arrive at the tomb of Jesus, a tomb which represented, one might say, the antithesis of all he had stood for. It was a tomb of the rich, but he had identified himself with the poor and the weak. It was an utterly private place, but his life had been a very public life, a life lived in communion with others and in their service. And above all, it was a profane place, yet if any man had been God-filled it was he. Indeed, he had been the very expression of the Word of God, his human nature assumed by the Word to be its very own instrument.

The women probably didn't notice how that day was the anniversary of the act of creation. The first day of the week, the day after the Sabbath, had that significance in the Jewish calendar. It memorialized the opening day of the six-day creation account in the Book of Genesis. Not only was it the first day. When they came soon after dawn it was for the first sign of day. That no doubt had a practical rationale: they wanted to be able to see what they were doing. But it was the moment that mirrored the creative declaration, 'Let there be light!'.

For the body of Jesus to remain in that place, on that day, beyond that moment: this would have constituted a blatant contradiction at the heart of God's creation as well as within his saving plan. God could not endure that the body taken by his Word should remain a moment longer in that place. He reaffirmed the consistency of his own divine being as the Creator God, and as the Saviour God. He raised the body of his servant and Son from the grave, and in that act made the empty tomb the space which is at the heart of the Christendom to come. The Resurrection is good news, the best possible news, because it tells us that evil will not have the last word, that human communion is not just a dance of the molecules, that death and the collapse of meaning are not the end.

Why, then, in St Mark's account of the empty tomb, did the women react with fear? Was it not by a surmise of the scale of what had been done, of its world-shaking divine dimensions? The true God, the God of Scripture is—among other things, to be sure—in the classic phrase, *mysterium tremendum et fascinans*, the 'fearful and fascinating Mystery', not the nebulous but very flexible and highly accommodating God of modern-day liberal Christianity (we could try putting that into Latin as well: *mysterium nebulosum sed multum flexibile et valde accommodans*).

Tomorrow, at the Mass of Easter Day, and in the language of more intimate, indeed tender, encounter, we shall hear how the risen Lord came to his own, so as to confirm the message at the tomb. But already tonight enough is known for the Church to cry out, *Lumen Christi!*, the Light of Christ!, and for us to reply, 'Thanks be to God', *Deo gratias*.

The Easter Vigil (Year C)

All four Gospels begin their account of the Resurrection with the visit of the Spice-bearing Women to the tomb of Jesus. At the beginning of his narrative, St Luke tells us that these women, having prepared the spices and ointments, had first rested on the Sabbath, Saturday, 'in obedience to the commandment'. In other words, these women were pious observant Jewish women who were also disciples of Jesus. That is important and we shall return to it.

They reach the tomb in early light and are perplexed to find the body absent. Our religion begins with a real absence. It is into this unexpected void that the Easter proclamation—the *Praeconium paschale* which some minutes ago we heard sung over the paschal candle—was heard for the first time. For all that the Roman Liturgy is supposed to be a short and sober affair, St Luke's version of this proclamation is a lot less florid than ours has been tonight. It consists of the simple words, 'He is not here, he has been raised'.

The Resurrection had no witnesses. It was an event inaccessible to any eye and beyond comprehension. Necessarily so, because it is a new beginning of the creation, changing all the rules: rules of perception and rules of intellectual entailment. No longer are the laws of causality what they were, nor have our usual criteria for establishing meaning and truth stayed the same. The Resurrection makes possible a different kind of vision and understanding, and it is, we would say, the only one that makes perfect sense of the world. But it cannot be caught in the web of the old world, the original creation. The icons of the Spice-bearing Women at the Easter sepulchre show not the Resurrection but only the scene of its proclamation: the burial cave, the empty tomb, the linen cloths, and figures in white garments inviting the women, 'See the place where he was laid'.

These are, as I said, pious observant Jewish women who were also disciples of Jesus. The *Praeconium paschale* is made to them because it is expected that *accordingly* they will understand. They bring to the situation three things: their knowledge of the hope of Israel for a new relation between the world and God; their knowledge of Jesus and of his message that in his own person and work this new relation was actually coming about; and the tender love which moved them to prepare these spices, unguents, to honour the body of Jesus and discourage, so far as human skill could, its collapse into putrefying, stinking flesh.

All the male disciples would have shared with the Spice-bearing Women the first two of these advantages. It seems to be the implication of this Gospel that only to the tender love of these women could all the pieces of the puzzle come together.

Jesus had told them about the Father that he is the God not of the dead but of the living. Now the figures in white remind them of some other words of Jesus which had bewildered the Twelve. The Son of Man—the mighty angelic defender of Israel at the right hand of the Most High, this heavenly figure from the Jewish Scriptures, was himself to die and to be raised.

And now there comes the breakthrough: the penny drops, the ice breaks, there is a disclosure situation. The Father, the God of the living, had been in the Son—not an angel but their dear Master himself—all along. The scene they are part of marks the triumph over death achieved by God as man. And it is now the hope for all the world. Hence the troparion of the Byzantine Liturgy for tonight's festival: 'The godly wise women followed after You in haste with sweet-smelling myrrh. But Him whom they sought with tears as dead they joyfully adored as the living God, and announced to Your disciples, O Christ, the glad tidings of the mystical Pascha'.

Easter Day (1)

Our themes today are: losing and finding; absence and presence; mistaken identity and recognition; separation and communion. The Mass of Easter Day is about all of that. In the Gospel, we hear of three contrasting reactions: instructively contracting reactions, from each of Mary Magdalen, Peter, and John.

First of all, let us look at how Mary Magdalen reacts. Notice how physical—in the sense of material—her relation to Jesus is. For her, the Lord's body *is* the Lord. If we are theologically sensitive, we don't usually speak of the corpse as the person himself. But she does, unhesitatingly. 'They have taken away my Lord and we do not know where they have laid him.' It's rather pathetic. Her sense of holding and having, presence and communion, revolves around tangible things. This is the confirmed later in the narrative when she clutches at Jesus as if to prevent his Ascension. Nowadays, her reaction to the loss of the loved one might be to hoard up photographs and other souvenirs, or lockets of hair like the Victorians. In a sense, perhaps, she does not need the Resurrection. She has her memories. Our own relation to God in Christ can turn on memories of places or times when we were religiously happy. When the memories fade we complain we have no contact with him, and then this attitude is seen to be problematic.

Next comes Peter. Bluff, no nonsense Peter who is either hot or cold, yes or no, all or nothing. I think of Peter as large and muscular but a bit out of training. In the race to the tomb, John overtakes him. But while John pauses for a moment at the entrance, Peter dashes in and sees—nothing very much. He notices the discarded grave clothes, but they don't speak to him. They don't evoke anything Jesus might have said: any insight into what the God who is the Life-giver might have done for his crucified Servant and Son. Peter is strong on enthusiasm, but insight is not his *forte*. He hasn't much subtlety in this business of losing and finding, absence and presence, mistaken identity and recognition, separation and communion. He has endless energy and in that sense he has devotion. But he's not so well-endowed with religious intelligence. So much for Peter.

Finally, we come to John. John is the best runner, which the Fathers of the Church sometimes explained by pointing out he was unmarried. As I said, he gets to the tomb first. But it's no use just being there unless you know what to look for. The eyes of the heart have to be open to find the Resurrection amid the paraphernalia of the grave. John is not only the athlete among the disciples. He is, in the evangelist's pregnant phrase, the 'beloved disciple'. And everything we know about the Fourth Gospel reinforces the impression that this is how he and, at the beginning, he alone both saw and believed.

There are some things that cannot be known without love, some dimensions of reality that are a closed book without it. By love two persons are opened to each other's mystery. Love in this sense is not Mary Magdalen's clinging to the physical remains. Nor is it Peter's violent enthusiasm. It is larger and deeper than either of these. It goes by signs: by hints and allusions. It doesn't need to be bombarded with evidence. Straightaway it sees the pattern in the little evidence it has.

The faith of John is the faith of the contemplative, the mystic, the saint. It is a faith that springs from a response of total intellectual-spiritual love, love with the mind and the spirit, and not simply with the emotions, the passions, the body. Faith that issues in this way is the only kind of faith that can discern finding in losing, presence in absence, communion in separation. This is the start of the Easter faith, though, to be sure, further encounters will follow. But it begins here. 'Why seek you the living among the dead? He is not here, he is risen.'

Easter Day (2)

At first sight it may seem off-putting that the heart of traditional faith, and the centre of the celebration of that faith by the Church in her liturgical year, is the question of what happened to a corpse: the empty tomb in the garden; the fate of a bundle of muscle and bone; the mystery, almost like detective fiction, about what happened to the body of Jesus.

Wouldn't it better, some people say, to confine ourselves to the purely spiritual dimensions of his life and teaching? Wouldn't it be more credible—and indeed more truly religious come to that? Never flinching from what fidelity to his mission demanded, divine inspiration sustained him to the end—and convinced the first disciples that his work was ratified by God, was valid.

That austere message, or cold comfort, is all that theological liberalism can offer us, because it can't credit that divine action, divine agency, is at work in the world. It is not, however, the message of the apostolic teaching. Though we can sense how the apostolic writers are struggling to press into play all the resources of an old language so as to speak of an utterly new and unique event, one thing about the texts of the New Testament is very plain indeed. As far back as you can get in tracing the tradition of the proclamation, 'He is risen!', we encounter the claim that a woman, or some women, early on the day after the Sabbath that followed Good Friday, found the tomb of Jesus emptied of its contents. The absence, interpreted by a whole set of experiences that followed, persuaded them that the body of Jesus was no longer part of the world we take for granted.

And so we come back to my opening question: why is a body that significant? In general, bodies are significant because it is in and by our bodies that we belong to the world we do. That the world is a very different world for you and for your dog is intimately bound up with the fact that the organs by which a dog orders and experiences its world—as a great stock of interesting and attractive sights, smells, and sounds—are very different from the organism by which, as human beings, we experience the world. It is the humanness of the human body, with its specific configu-ration—its 'soul'—that makes the world the kind of world it is for us. To a large extent, it is by the body that we share our experience of that world and make it a common world. It is by the body that we are in communication with each other. The human body is the medium of our mutual presence.

The Creed ends with the words, 'I believe in the resurrection of the body and the life everlasting'. Those two articles are in a sense just one. I believe in life everlasting through the resurrection of the body. At Easter, the body of Jesus became the medium of a new quality of divine communication. His risen body became the organism which now orders a new world, a world filled with divine joy and peace, because God was in Christ reconciling the world to himself, and doing so through the Resurrection of his crucified Son. It was through the body that God has made available life everlasting. In the words of the Church Father St John Damascene, 'I do not worship matter but I worship the God of matter who for my sake stooped to become material and through matter effected my salvation'.

So matter matters. And what sort of matter matters. The unique example of human matter that was joined to the uncreated person of the Word matters. And so too, and supremely—this is why Easter is the heart of the faith, the centre of the year—the transformation matter underwent matters when by divine power, in the glorious risen body of our Lord, it was made the nucleus of a new God-communicating world.

Easter Monday

'You would not let your Holy One see corruption.' These words remind us how the Resurrection of Christ is, not least, a transfiguration of biology, a sort of supernatural flowering. One of the mediaeval doctors, the Franciscan St Bonaventure, had this to say: 'The beautiful flower of the root of Jesse, who had blossomed in the Incarnation, and withered in the Passion, has now blossomed anew in the Resurrection, so as to become our crown of beauty'.

As the 'Art of the Almighty', the eternal Word is the archetype of all possible beauty. Through him all the beauty we know on earth was made. God had intended man to be the supreme image of his own loveliness, but sin by making the soul ugly turned whatever beauty the body has into a lie. Bodily death and the collapse of the body into corruption symbolize this deformity of soul and are its naturally unavoidable conclusion.

This is the situation which the One sprung from 'the root of Jesse' must enter, inhabit and change from within: that is the programme, we might say, of the Incarnation. At Easter, having gone deeper than any merely human being could into the disfigurement of suffering and death, Christ rose again to bring to perfection God's sin-interrupted creative work.

Bonaventure's contemporary, and fellow-Franciscan, the poet Jacopone da Todi underlined the contrast. It seemed that the radiance of the incarnate Word was extinguished. 'Splendour lightening every shadow/ darkened in fierce grief and sorrow,/ Light of light in death's dark furrow,/ Closed in the tomb, in the garden of flowers.' But the flowers and candles with which the Church surrounds the Liturgy of the Easter Octave tell a different story. 'The Flower placed there lay a-slumbering,/ rose again, to life a-leaping,/ blessed body, pure re-flowering,/ aglow with brightness made his appearing.' Jesus was raised as the Head of a new humanity, so that we, who are by Baptism his members, might throw off the beastliness of sin and decay, and come one day to share his glory.

Easter Tuesday

Mary Magdalen, meeting with the risen Christ and mistaking him at first for a gardener, was not being wholly irrational. She was after all, in a garden and in the early morning, when perhaps Jerusalem gardeners, like gardeners in some other parts of the world do the rounds, checking for plants that may have been damaged by frost or animals.

The Fathers of the Church, moreover, saw her mistake as highly suggestive—suggestive, that is, of an entirely appropriate symbolism. The risen Christ *is* a gardener, he is the New Adam preparing his new creation in the soil of his own humanity. To them, this was not reading something back into the data, 'projecting' as we call it. Providence itself had arranged things so as to make available this symbol. All these things, including even cases of mistaken identity, happened for our instruction.

But as we heard, the New Adam cannot begin his work until he has ascended to his Father. Whatever distance still remains between his human condition and the Father has to be done away with; his humanity has to be totally penetrated by the Father's glory before it can act as the nucleus of a new creation.

As Eastertide proceeds, the Church's mind will turn increasingly to consider not just the Ascension but Pentecost, when the power of the risen Christ to re-make the whole creation is first released into the world.

Easter Wednesday

In today's Gospel, the risen Lord tells the disciples that the Law and the prophets—the Old Testament, then—only make sense in terms of him. Israel's history points to what has just happened, the Resurrection of the Crucified, and doesn't add up otherwise.

But how much does the Old Testament matter to us? It matters a great deal. From the Old Testament, especially the Psalms, we learn the ABC of our religious attitude: how to express the praise and the fear of the Lord. We also learn—gradually, like the Israelites themselves, much about what God is like and how his plan for creation will be taken forward.

In another sense, though, the Old Testament is the national history of the Jews and it can't have the same importance for other people as it has for them.

Perhaps that is why St Luke goes on to give us a second climax to his story. It's not just that the risen Lord made his hearers' hearts burn within them when he explained to them the Scriptures. It's also true that when he stepped out of the light, out of the visible, he left with them the elements of a meal. A meal is a universal thing, as familiar to Gentiles as to Jews. The guest, the risen Lord, turned out to have managed this meal. He was the real host, and a host who gave himself to them in the food he blessed. For Jews, too, surely, it must be more important that the living Lord is still available in the food of the sacrament than that he is the key to ancient texts. And as blind people of any racial origin could tell us, more important than that he was once visible is the fact that he remains present.

Easter Thursday

We are sometimes told that we mustn't confuse resurrection with resuscitation. In principle, this is true, but there is a certain ambiguity in the remark. Does resurrection differ from resuscitation by excluding it, or does it differ by including it? Today's Gospel plumps definitively for the second of these options. 'A spirit has not flesh and bones as you see that I have.'

We might put it like this. In the first place, the Resurrection of Christ is a new relationship of the incarnate Son to the Father. His humanity is brought—by way of the total self-offering of his sacrificial Death—to that condition of perfect communion with the Father which the eternal Son not just has but *is*. And because his humanity is solidary with ours (he is our Representative), we too are all potential inheritors of this new life, and receive indeed the first instalment of it here and now by faith and the sacraments of faith.

But where is this new relationship of Christ's humanity to the Father located? Where does it take place? What is its medium? And here the answer of the New Testament is that the risen Lord's life of glory is enacted *in his flesh*. As if to counter the tendency of religion to flee the finite and the natural, God chose as the locus of the new life the biology of his Son made man. The resuscitated and transfigured body of the Lord has become the nucleus of a new creation drawing all men to itself.

No doubt, Christ draws people to himself by his spiritual beauty, but that beauty which shines through the sacred images and the faces of the saints is inclusive of a beauty belonging to his flesh. According to St Thomas, Christ was always beautiful with the beauty of the divine nature which he shared. But now in the Resurrection his beauty has shone out in a special way from the place of the wounds. Everything that is beautiful is beautiful in a certain respect. The marks of Christ's wounds are beautiful because they are expressly proportioned to his sacrificial love. The glorified wounds are the biological location of the victory of love, and so they are the sign of our future transforming.

Easter Friday

St John's Gospel invites its readers to approach it not only on the literal but also on the symbolic level. Everything both means what it says and means more than what it says.

The miraculous haul of fish is a case in point. The fish are attracted by the presence of their Creator, the giver of their instincts and behaviour patterns, present by the Lake in his human nature now filled with risen glory. So the amazing fullness of the catch is no fiction. The story is not less than literally true. And yet its reference isn't confined to its literal truth. Earlier, when his public ministry started, our Lord had told Peter, James and John: 'From now on you will be fishers of men'. So the Fathers of the Church, like the modern scholars, see in the miraculous haul of fish a symbol of the Church. There's reason to think that the crucial number, one hundred and fifty three, represents the total number of different kinds of fish recognized in the ancient world. In other words, it is a prophecy of the Church's catholicity—all races, all nations, all sorts and conditions of men, are to be caught up together in the supernatural haul.

And whereas in secular life, throwing everyone together into a great melting-pot generally produces severe tensions and even violence, with the Church it will be different. Within this great brotherhood-sisterhood, no nation, no class, rules. Like divine Wisdom, she stretches mightily yet sweetly from one end of the earth to the other. As the Psalm puts it, 'All peoples will call her mother, for all shall be her children'.

Easter Saturday

In today's Gospel, the disciples are told to preach the Gospel not to all human beings only but to the whole creation.

In the years between the First and Second World Wars there was an interesting debate among Catholic theologians about whether non-human rational species, were any such discovered by science, should be evangelized and baptized.

The case for evangelization was felt to be stronger than that for Baptism. Baptism, and the whole redemptive economy which it applies to the individual, is, not least, a remedy for sin, and sin here means the kind of action which renews or confirms Adam's fall: the moral disaster that overtook the first human beings. Other rational species may be unfallen, or not fallen in the way we are—certainly not by descent from Adam, at any rate. To this extent the human Redeemer is irrelevant to them

But redemption is not all there is to the Trinitarian action in history. There is also revelation, the sheer self-disclosure of the Triune God for the manifesting of his inmost life and love. And the good news that the Creator became one of his own creatures, to die from charity and so to show forth his glory, expressed in the Resurrection: this Gospel seems as relevant to Martians or inhabitants of distant nebulae as to ourselves. In one of C. S. Lewis' science fantasies, this is how things are portrayed when other species lower their voices in awe to speak of the condescension the Holy One showed once upon a time on the dark planet.

THE SECOND WEEK OF EASTER

Low Sunday

When in the Liturgy the celebrant recites the Roman Canon he says on behalf of those assisting at Mass—and indeed of the whole Church—that the faith which these mysteries express is the 'apostolic' faith, the faith transmitted from the apostles. In the Gospel today we have two examples of what that means: two of the situations when the risen Christ showed himself to the apostles: on the first day, Easter Day, and then on the eighth day, the Octave of Easter, today, when the Eleven were gathered in the Cenacle, the Upper Room of the Last Supper. Our faith turns on the reliability of these narratives, on the trustworthiness of the apostles, on those who, to their joy and amazement, saw the risen Lord.

And this may seem strange because when we say 'I believe in' and give those words their full Christian force, the only possible way to end that phrase is by naming a divine person. 'Believing in' means giving assent to God through trust in the truthfulness of his word. Yet—this is the message of today's Gospel—that truth of God to which faith responds is brought to us via the frail fabric of human testimony. 'Go and tell his disciples and Peter.' 'The Lord has arisen and has appeared to Simon.' 'Their eyes were opened and they knew him in the breaking of the bread.' 'We have seen the Lord.' These are the claims they made.

The people who said or wrote these words had at least one thing in common. They were changed overnight. From defeat and disillusion they became men and women utterly convinced of God's victory over sin and death in Jesus Christ. And this is just as well, because there is indeed a sense in which our faith, though it is in God alone, depends *for its acquisition* on the authority of the eye-witnesses. The word 'authority' comes from the same root as does the word 'author'. It means being the start of something, the source of it. And here in our context it means that the apostles, who began the chain of transmission of the faith, were trustworthy at source, reliable from the moment—the Easter moment—when Christianity began.

The Catholic understanding of the Church takes this for granted. Faith involves us in Tradition—witness to the Gospel of God handed down from the original authorities, from one generation to the next. This witness to the Resurrection is present first of all in the New Testament Scripture, the apostolic writings, which contain divine revelation in written form. It is expressed, further, in a variety of ways in the life of the Church the apostles founded: in the teaching of the Fathers who succeeded the apostles, in the holiness of the saints who drew strength from the Resurrection, in the Liturgies and the sacred art that celebrate the Church's grasp of the apostolic message. Finally, that witness is guarded and interpreted by the living voice of the Church's magisterium—the pope, and the bishops when the latter are united with the pope throughout the world. Faithfulness to what has in this way been received from the apostolic past is vital for us: we call it 'passing on the deposit', the faith once delivered to the saints: meaning here, *the apostles*.

The importance of passing on a precious witness is such that it could, unless one is careful, rather swamp the sense that we too—the ordinary members of the contemporary Church—are to be witnesses to the 'event' of Jesus Christ. Not that we can time-travel back to Galilee or Jerusalem in the year 30 or thereabouts. But nevertheless, we are meant to experience something of the realities the Gospels describe. Faith involves us in some way in personal experience. Perhaps when we think of our own individual case, we wonder whether this is so. We may never have had some striking religious experience, not the sort the mystics claim like, for instance, to mention but one the twentieth century Polish nun St Faustina Kowalska. I mention her since of course this is the day, the Octave of Easter, when she asked for special attention to be paid in the Church to the mercy of God, following her vision of Christ with streams of life issuing from his heart, described as the gushing out onto the world of the fountain of mercy. You and I are not visionaries—at least I don't suppose so. But we can at least agree, surely, that the world of the believer and the world of the unbeliever are not the same world. And in that difference between 'us' and 'them'—that not tiny crack but real cleavage—our own faith experience has its home. It entails a contact, however discreet and usually unspoken, with God, with Christ, with the Holy Spirit, with all the realities of which the New Testament speaks. Prayer, frequenting the sacraments, making use of a Christian imagination impacted by grace: these are modes of experiential contact with the risen Lord.

The peace, joy, reconciliation, forgiveness, the risen Christ brought with him—and *as* him—to the first disciples, these are brought within our reach too, in the places where we worship liturgically and in the inner room of our own hearts. Thanks to the apostolic witness, the revelation the Church carries makes it possible for us to enjoy an experience that is distinctively Christian and, above all, Paschal: filled with Easter. May we all have a touch of it this Eastertide.

Monday of the Second Week of Easter

The night-time visit of Nicodemus to Jesus to talk about (so it turns out) the Holy Spirit is a rather prophetic event. The meeting under cover of darkness (the concern, amid mounting opposition to the Gospel-bearer, was, evidently, security) anticipates the night in the Garden when the Saviour was apprehended and his Passion began. The topic to which the discussion turns, the Holy Spirit, looks ahead to the Pentecostal outflow in which the Paschal consummation of Jesus' ministry is going to issue. So in a way the entire scenario of Passiontide and Paschaltide is encapsulated here.

To what purpose? Surely so that we should have the advantage of the revelation of the Spirit's work, his collaboration with the element of water in the great sacrament of Christian initiation which opens the Kingdom of heaven to all believers.

Tuesday of the Second Week of Easter

'Unless you are born again... you will not enter the Kingdom of God.' Today's Gospel is the charter of 'born-again' Christians.

For Catholics being born is rather less dramatic than it is for Protestant Evangelicals. It means being dowsed in the waters of the font, typically at 3 o'clock on a Sunday afternoon. In Baptism, our faith—my act of faith if I am an adult convert, or the faith of the Church for the candidate if I am too young to have faith of my own — is joined to Christ's dying and rising again.

But eventually, if, like most members of the Church, I underwent infant Baptism, I have to make my own what was done for me at the font. I have to appropriate it, to take it over for myself. And this may be, as with the born-again Christians of American legend, by a faith that is sudden and spectacular in its coming, or, alternatively, it may be by a faith that comes slowly, fitfully, and in a way that is easily overlooked.

We shouldn't then, write off, the dramatically born-again, but neither should we envy them. What we should be doing is to co-operate with the grace that *we* have received, not looking wistfully over our shoulders at somebody else's.

St Paul was the archetypal born-again Christian if ever there was one. His conversion, as the poet Hopkins says, was 'once at a crash'. St Augustine's conversion is also highly celebrated, but it could hardly have been more different. Hopkins calls it 'a lingering-out sweet skill'. In either case it is the gift of faith joining them to the Easter Lord that counts. It is exactly the same with us. Just how it comes about is much less important.

Wednesday of the Second Week of Easter

The opening saying of our Lord to Nicodemus in this short discourse is a high point in St John's Gospel. Someone may ask you, Supposing there was such a thing as an Incarnation, what could possibly be the point of it, what purpose could it serve? With this text in your pocket you could never be short of a reply. The sending of the Son in our flesh manifests the love of the Father for his creation, and notably his human creation. And that love has as its aim to bring people into relation with the Son so that they can have a share in the divine life itself, or, as St Thomas would say, become the friends of God because sharing a life is the hallmark of friendship.

It bears repeating, then: 'God loved the world so much that he gave his only Son, that whoever believes in him should not perish but have eternal life'. Obviously enough, no one who has been caught up by God into friendship with him, into a share in the

uncreated life of the Trinity, could possibly perish—perish spiritually or indeed, since the life of the human soul has its proper locus
in the body, perish physically for ever. So this isn't just a handy
quick explanation of Incarnational believing. In this text, the whole
Christian hope rises up before our eyes: the vision of God, life in
the divine friendship, immortality for the soul, resurrection for the
body.

This makes all the more important that we should weigh the
words that follow which have as their subject the very real possibility of missing the boat. An initial act of recoil when faced with the
Gospel of the Incarnation (not for me, thank you) can harden into
an attitude of determined rejection. Why all the negativity, when
revelation is so beautiful? Jesus replies, 'Men loved darkness more
than light, because their deeds were evil'. Harsh words but true
ones. So often there is a moral difficulty behind opposition to the
grace of God. The gift doesn't reach us because a wall of pride
intervenes. Walls defend the embattled self which insists on its side
of the story, just as they also shut out from view deeds we prefer to
keep unknown. The Saviour invites us to knock down our defences,
and let the good light come in.

Thursday of the Second Week of Easter

Today's Gospel is a very ambitious statement of the claims of Jesus:
his origins are divine, from the side of the Creator—not human,
from the side of the creation; anyone who does not accept his
message is making God out to be a liar; his words are the words
of God; the Spirit has been given him in a total, unqualified sense;
God in his love for the Son has made him the agent of his
providential rule in history; belief in the Son means eternal life,
rejection of him means undergoing the wrath of God.

We stand by these claims, or the doctrines that they lead to it,
because we believe that in Jesus Christ God has intervened in the
very structure of the cosmos, and the very unfolding of history—
intervened so as to change the world's relation to himself. He has
put his own Word, now humanized in Jesus Christ, at the heart of
the world, so that human beings can no longer reach their destiny
without going via Christ.

Are these claims credible? The French philosopher Blaise Pascal, whose most famous work, the *Pensées*, is about this very thing, concluded: 'There is enough light'. In other words, there is not overwhelming light, but neither is there insufficient light. There are enough reasons for this Christ-centred faith to justify the believer in his belief and convict the unbeliever in his unbelief.

More coolly, the 1992 *Catechism of the Catholic Church* mentions various causes of unbelief. At the end of its list it mentions the cause which the author of this Gospel would surely have put at the head of any list, and that is the tendency of sinful man to hide himself from God and to evade God's call. At the deepest level, that perhaps is explanation enough for the Cross; the persistence of God is shown in the Resurrection.

Friday of the Second Week of Easter

This Gospel recounts the miracle of the Multiplication of the Loaves and Fishes in the version given by the evangelist John.

We could ask ourselves, what is the 'sign' which Jesus did that made people think of him as a prophet to end all prophets, to sum up all the hopes and dreams of the Old Testament: what they called '*the* prophet who was to come into the world'? Was it simply the miracle that made people think that? I would suggest not.

Of course the miracle was wonderful in its demonstration of divine power to feed the hungry, power that was indisputably at work before the onlookers' eyes. But by itself does it explain the far-reachingness of the claim? The sign, I think, was the sheer lavishness of what the miracle provided; all those baskets of extra food left over, over and above what anyone could manage to eat. For St John who, of all the evangelists, is the most sensitive to the symbolic resonances of what our Lord said and did, that would have been a key point. That sheer abundance, extravagance, you could almost say *wastefulness* of the Multiplication—compare all those gallons of wine at the first of his signs, at Cana—points to the way the Son of God will lavish the divine life on us. That will happen in the Atonement—yes, of course. But it will also happen under signs of bread and wine, in the Blessed Sacrament of the altar where week by week, or even day by day, we come to be nourished by his in his real Presence, as he gives himself through the hands of the apostles' successors, the priests of the Church.

Saturday of the Second Week of Easter

It is in the Church a long-standing tradition to read the Acts of the Apostles in Eastertide. What we are seeing in the period from Easter to Pentecost is how stage by stage, with first the Resurrection appearances to the disciples, then the Ascension, and finally Pentecost itself, the Gospel of Christ becomes the Gospel of the Church. It's not just that the Church *carries* the Gospel, bears it out into the world (though that's obviously true), but that in a sense, and to a certain degree, the Gospel is now actually *about* the Church — about this unique community, the Mystical Body of Jesus Christ, the Soul of which is the Holy Spirit.

So the Eastertide readings from Acts about how the early Church got going are not ecclesiastical distractions from the real business of Easter. On the contrary, they show how the risen Lord and his Spirit inspired the apostolic community to do things that serve the purposes for which the Saviour died.

That is the perspective in which we should see today's event, the institution of the Seven, the first deacons of the Church. To provide practical charitable assistance for the hungry is one of the things God wants the Church to do, but even more important is the ministry of the Word: the call to give the truth that satisfies that hunger more deeply still, in the human soul.

THE THIRD WEEK OF EASTER

The Third Sunday of Easter (Year A)

If today you set out to walk from Jerusalem to Emmaus, you will soon find yourself rather confused. The Franciscans, who have the custody of the Latin shrines in the Holy Land, will point you to a site about eight miles from the City, and this corresponds to the distance given in most manuscripts of St Luke's Gospel: sixty *stadia*. There the Crusaders rebuilt a Byzantine church which may have enclosed the original home of Cleopas, one of the disciples the risen Lord sought out on the road.

Yet the name 'Emmaus' means, it would seem, 'place of the warm well', and there aren't any of these, which may divert your attention to another site, almost three times the distance, corresponding to the one hundred and sixty *stadia* of one of the oldest New Testament manuscripts, the Codex Sinaiticus, and confirmed by the testimony of the early Church historian Eusebius. Local Arabs still call this place 'Amwas', which sounds pretty much like 'Emmaus', and its cisterns of naturally occurring tepid water bear out the name. Fit travellers could just about do the walk to Jerusalem and back in a day, if you count the day as stretching on to midnight when at least at Passovertide, with its full moon, there would still be some light in the sky.

The distance is a bit of a difficulty, however, so one might wish to try a third contender, a village beautifully situated among olive trees only four miles from Jerusalem and named by the Jewish historian Josephus, a contemporary of Our Lord, as 'Ammaus'.

Does it matter? At one level, it does. Though the risen Christ does not belong to empirical history in the same way in which the Crucified did, he belongs to such history *in a certain sense*. St Luke, whose Gospel opens with an appeal to his own credentials as an historian, bases himself on interviews and evidence-gathering from what he calls 'eye-witnesses and ministers of the Word'. He offers no health-warning that, in the chapters that deal with the Resurrection, he is going to switch to another method and appeal instead to spiritual experience, symbolically expressed, rather than to what transpired in the public domain. Our Resurrection faith depends, at one level, on the veracity of eye-witnesses among whom Cleopas and his friend must be numbered. The credibility of their claims belongs with that of the Easter witnesses as a whole. Those claims, which in all probability are rooted in one of the three places I described, tells us little, perhaps, about the *meaning* of the Resurrection but they tell us a lot about the *fact*—and the meaning without the fact hasn't got a leg to stand on.

I said, however, that the risen Lord belonged only *in a certain sense* with that empirical history. The glorified embodied existence of the Saviour differs from what he was before, not through being immaterial but through being perfectly transparent to, and exclusively the instrument of, his deepest reality as the eternal uncreated Word whose obedience to the Father when time was not is now translated into his mission to heal humankind and raise it up to grace and glory. The appearances of the risen Christ belong to empirical history only insofar as his glorified body there and then *intersected with* the time and space of his disciples as the visible manifestation of his enhanced life and love.

But the activity of the risen Christ is not confined to such occasional intersection with our time and space. More fundamentally and characteristically, he now acts to bring us into *his* time and space, the universe of his own renewed being to which the faith and sacraments of the Church, his Mystical Body, give access, so that we can be raised up with him into the heavenly places. On the road to Emmaus the risen One eventually withdraws his visibility but he leaves behind the elements of a meal, a breaking of bread, which in St Luke's other work, the Acts of the Apostles, is a sobriquet for the Holy Eucharist.

In the Mass the risen Lord provides, and more than provides, for any deficiencies in the eye-witness accounts as the nourishment of faith we need. Here he makes himself ever accessible to us in his posture of sacrifice for us—the Sacrifice the Father accepted for our salvation in raising his Son. Here he is present, as the sufficient cause of the Paschal alleluias of the Church.

The Third Sunday of Eastertide (Year B)

This Sunday's Gospel shows the first disciples having difficulties and doubts about the Resurrection. Is it real? Did it really happen? Or are we somehow misinterpreting the evidence?

Traditionally, the Church has distinguished between difficulties and doubts. According to Blessed John Henry Newman, 'Ten thousand difficulties do not make one doubt'. As reasoning people, we naturally apply our minds to our religion, including to what happened in the aftermath of the Crucifixion. There are difficulties here — about the sources, about the agreement of the witnesses, about the possibility of miracle, and, in the larger picture, about how the Resurrection of the Messiah can be said to fulfil the hope of Israel and consummate the creation. We face up to these difficulties, none of which is insuperable, and through our handling of them we grow into a more informed and intelligent faith.

Doubt is something more radical. Doubt is wondering whether key religious terms have any reference to reality at all. 'God', 'Christ', 'the Holy Spirit': are these words mere counters? Is it all a game? Curiously enough, this sort of radical doubt is mentioned by both St Luke and St Matthew in connexion with the Resurrection appearances. With the risen Christ before their very eyes, some doubted. In today's Gospel, our Lord gives his own analysis of why this could be. His explanation runs: the cause is fear or anxiety. 'Why are you so agitated?' 'Why are these doubts arising in your hearts?' *Your hearts*, we notice, not 'your intellects'. Something is affecting their sensibility: their passions, their emotions, and is doing damage to their judgment — causing, in fact, radical doubt.

Stepping back a little from the Gospel narrative, we can reflect on a general datum of human experience at large. If we are in some way fearful of reality in some respect, we tend to clam up in its regard. We shut out from our minds the unknown, the unexpected, the unsought for. By and large, we like to have things taped, so that we can feel secure and unchallenged. Predictability is a comfort zone. The routine even of a hard life becomes dear to people. T. S. Eliot wrote, 'Human kind cannot bear too much reality' — or, come to that, too varied a diet of it.

Applying that generalization to the present case: to accept the risen Christ—which must mean, among other things, accepting that we shall be in some manner altered by such acceptance—may be more than we want to bear, at any rate at some particular time in our lives. The closed-in self must be opened out before it can reciprocate the offered Easter contact. 'Why are you troubled?' 'Peace be with you!.' It brings to a climax a theme already sounded during the public ministry. 'Why are you afraid?' 'You believe in God, believe also in me.'

Christian faith requires us to receive this mystery: to let it flow over us and shape our life. There is a parallel here with the philosophical realism we are taught in the school of St Thomas Aquinas. As knowing agents, we are not to seek to dictate to reality, to force it into the shape we prefer. Instead, we are to let ourselves be moulded by it in all its glorious objectivity. If that is how we ought to approach creation, then the new creation—the world of the Resurrection—surely has its realism as well. So in Paschaltide we hold out our hands to the Living One, the risen and exalted Lord, and taste in some fashion the joy of his victory over death. He is truly risen, alleluia.

The Third Sunday of Easter (Year C)

In the Gospels of Mark and Matthew, the women at the tomb bring back the message that the risen Lord will show himself to his disciples back home in Galilee. 'You must go and tell his disciples and Peter, "He is going before you to Galilee; it is there you will see him".' And here in the Gospel of John, in today's Gospel, we see that promise fulfilled. The Christ keeps the promise made on his behalf. He will meet up with Peter and the others.

Evidently, the disciples have gone back to their own haunts, their old business, almost as though the three years spent with Jesus had never been. Fishing through the night—in early summer in the Middle East nights are pleasanter to work in than are days. In the first light of morning, the silhouette of a figure begins to stand out on the shore. The evangelist hints that Jesus' appearance has been transformed. At first they didn't realize it was he. As usual, it is the beloved disciple who first cottons on to what is happening. 'The disciple Jesus loved, said, "It is the Lord".'

All of this is setting the scene for the main point of the Gospel reading, the rehabilitation of Peter. Peter had always been the most impressive of the disciples, for good and for ill. It was Peter whom Jesus had made the leader of his disciples—the Rock-man, the foundation-figure of the group. It was Peter who lifted his sword to defend Jesus in the Garden and volunteered to die for him. It was also Peter, unfortunately, who denied him three times. Here in the last chapter of the Fourth Gospel, the evangelist describes how Peter was forgiven, reconciled, restored to his charge as the primate of the apostolic fellowship, and allowed at last (in prophecy) to die for his Master as once he had said he would.

Three times our Lord asks him, 'Do you love me?' Three times that echo the three denials of Peter in the courtyard of the house of the High Priest. Three times he answers, 'I do', and three times Jesus affirms Peter's pastoral authority over the flock: the many brethren of the Church that will soon be, prefigured in the catch of fish they have just made.

The time-phase of Jesus's ministry is ending; the time-phase of the Church is dawning. There is not much time left, and this is how the risen Lord spends it—in the first place by forgiving people, and in the second place by taking steps to order or arrange the mission of his Church. How does the Gospel deal with these two themes, forgiveness and mission?

First, forgiveness. A formula used in the confessional runs, 'By my sins I have crucified my loving Saviour, Jesus Christ'. Sometimes it is easier to believe that my life has contributed to the sin of the world, which took the Word to Calvary, than it is to believe in the possibility of forgiveness. So many live in a state of semi-acknowledged despair about themselves, and about whether their existence is worthwhile. That must have occurred to Peter during the Passion. It must underlie his bitter tears. To such as these, to such as Peter, Jesus devotes the little time of the Resurrection appearances. He invites Peter to eat with him, he draws him into the intimacy of a meal he himself has prepared—an echo there of the Holy Eucharist. And, as so often, actions speak louder than words and set up reverberations that stay with us a whole life long.

In the second place, mission. We are not here just to learn how as sinners to accept forgiveness directly and simply from our Lord. We are also here as disciples to carry on his work, his ministry, his proclamation, and to build up by our actions and our prayer the divine humanity of the Church. After Peter's forgiveness comes his installation as chief shepherd of the Church.

We are 'Roman' Catholics,—a better phrase would be 'Petrine' Catholics—for we are interested in Rome only inasmuch as the bishop of Rome is Peter's successor. But today's Gospel makes clear that it is Christ, not Peter, who is the centre of Catholicism. The pope is the chief ministerial pastor of the flock, but the flock does not belong to Peter. The flock belongs to Jesus. 'Feed my lambs', he says, not 'your lambs'. 'Feed my sheep', not 'your sheep'.

What the Church asks of the pope is nothing more—but also nothing less—than faithfully to transmit the words and work of Christ in the spirit indicated by the last recorded words of Peter in the Gospels: 'Lord, you know everything; you know that I love you'.

Monday of the Third Week of Easter

The Book of the Acts of Apostles is the fifth book in our New Testament, coming straight after the four Gospels. Some have seen it as a fifth Gospel, giving the Good News of the coming of the Holy Spirit on the Church, to take further the work of Christ as described in the other four. The Fourth Eucharistic Prayer of the Roman rite says of Christ that he sent the Holy Spirit from the Father to complete his work on earth, bringing us thereby the fullness of grace. This fits in rather neatly with that wide claim about the Book of Acts.

More particularly, we have today the first instalment of a three-part account of the death of St Stephen, the Church's first martyr. Here the Acts of the Apostles is establishing martyrdom as a recognised fruit of the Spirit in the Church. Stephen stands at the head of an enormously long line of witnesses summoned up by the Holy Spirit from a multitude of cultures—from third century Rome, and Elizabethan England, and twentieth century China—as one major way in which the third divine Person carries out the task our Lord ascribes to him. When the Advocate comes, he 'will bear witness to me, and will convict the world of sin, of righteousness, and of judgment'.

To the world considered as a fallen reality, and to the thinking that reflects that reality, the martyrs are fanatics or fools. They gave up the only certain good, which is life, for a remote metaphysical possibility. But to the martyrs themselves, with their firm grasp of the good things that are eternal, the situation looks rather different. To them, people who can't see the point of martyrdom are like those immature personalities who can't defer satisfaction—impulse buyers in the supermarket, or people who never learn to control their adolescent sexual strivings. The good which will fulfil human nature with all its capacities and desires eludes them.

It is because this good is not apparent here and now that in today's Gospel Jesus can single out faith as the most important human act we can perform. 'This is the work of God, that you believe in him whom he has sent.' To believe what God reveals about human destiny is the only way to achieve a correct overall perspective on human life, and only within such a perspective do all other human acts find their proper place.

Tuesday of the Third Week of Easter

Moses gave them manna, nourishment so unexpected in the desert that it seemed to have dropped from the sky. But the Father gives the true Bread from Heaven, and it is the wisdom and the life—the very substance—of the Only-begotten Son. Side by side with the Ark of God in the Temple sanctuary of Zion were the relics of the Exodus and the desert wanderings: the tablets of the Law, Aaron's rod, and a jar of the fabled manna. Or at any rate these objects were there until the Babylonians came and cleared its furnishings away. By contrast, in every Catholic church the Ark in the midst of the sanctuary contains the Eucharistic Bread which is imperishable and inexhaustible.

What do we mean in saying so? Not of course that the form of this particular bread—the bread of the Blessed Sacrament—is resistant to decay or decomposition. Nor do we mean that it cannot run out when distributed. But in this new Ark of the Christian dispensation, the real being of what is presented to our senses is nothing other the immortal life of the Son of God, who is consubstantial with the Father and the Holy Spirit. Here lies hidden uncreated life, and it is uncreated life forever coursing through the human channels God made his own in the Incarnation. All this is now made available to us under the form of bread in the holy Sign.

St Thomas Aquinas, in his theology of the real Presence, points out that the New Covenant must have something more than the Old if its newness, its innovatory character, is to be justified. And what could be more in keeping with the Incarnation than for this 'something more' to be *intimacy*—the new intimacy of a presence of Emmanuel so close that by this sacramental feeding we bring it into our very selves. Only to find, of course, that it is, rather, we who are being brought into him.

Wednesday of the Third Week of Easter

Today's Gospel gives us in a nutshell what the work of Christ was all about. The first thing to note comes in the words, 'I am the Bread of Life'. Here he presents himself as our essential nourishment— what we need to take in order to flourish, truly to live. Christ can be this because, as he says, he has come not to do his own will but the will of him who sent him—the Father. As God, the Son has no other will than the Father. As man, his will was perfectly aligned with the divine will—not without moments of struggle and anxiety owing to the natural shrinking of the flesh from the sacrifice involved. We saw as much in Holy Week, in the agony in the Garden. But thanks to that perfect alignment of will, the saving energy of the Triune God could pour out through him, and so it did at Easter and Pentecost, to make the Creator's purpose really effective in the world.

We read, 'The will of him who sent me is that I should lose nothing of all that he has given to me, but that I should raise it up on the Last Day'. In other words, God's plan is through Christ to incorporate us into his own immortality—to make us live for ever with his own divine life. Though this particular Gospel doesn't say as much, we know God wills this for us on the basis of his abundant generosity, for the better manifestation of his glory, his sovereign love.

Thursday of the Third Week of Easter

This Gospel raises—at least for me—the question of the ultimate destiny of non-believers and, indeed, of the adherents of other religions. Jesus tells his hearers that all who have really grasped divine truth come to him, the incarnate Son of God, the living Bread of man's spiritual life. Just so, earlier in St John's Gospel, he had told Nicodemus that without Baptism, without initiation into his life by water and the Spirit, there is no new birth, no entry into the fullness of salvation. That is why tradition speaks of the baptismal waters as the element in which we must live like fish or else perish, and as the sea that keeps afloat the true Ark, the Church, outside of which there is, except for the invincibly ignorant, no salvation.

Of course, as is shown by that modifying phrase 'except for the invincibly ignorant', the Church's doctrine has sought to interpret Christ's teaching mercifully and intelligently. There is, after all, in the Letter to the Hebrews a much invoked statement of the two general conditions of entry into God's presence: one must believe that he is and that he is a rewarder of those who seek him. There are many who seek him who are not Christians, though many who are not Christians do not, it would appear, seek him: either because, like Buddhists, they reject the notion of God or at any rate of a personal God, or because they are confirmed in their agnosticism or atheism.

In recent times, theologians have speculated that values such as peace, truth, brotherhood may act as surrogates for God in non-Christian aspiration. Admittedly, once removed from their ordering to God and set up as ends-in-themselves, these values are, objectively speaking, idols. Yet subjectively, it is possible that God may allow people tacitly to approach him by means of them. But we are by now, as Evangelicals will remind us, very far indeed from the message of the Bible.

Two other possibilities remain. In the experience of death, unbelievers may be confronted with God and his saving grace for the first time and be able, under grace, to make their response.

Alternatively, they may be regarded, on concluding their time of probation in this world, as spiritually unformed beings, and come to God only by some faint echo of the music of the beatific vision (itself once memorably described as like eating pâté de foie gras to the sound of trumpets) in a kind of supernatural version of Limbo.

These are speculations. Our task, the task of the Church, is to be true to the faith and sacraments of Jesus Christ which give us entry into the Covenant of salvation, and leave the rest to the Holy Spirit. We leave it to him not so much in *faith* (since in these questions revelation is virtually silent) as, rather, in *hope* for the full extent of his marvellous work.

Friday of the Third Week of Easter

We hear today one of the great set-pieces of the Acts of the Apostles, the conversion of St Paul. The Acts of the Apostles has been called the Gospel of the Holy Spirit. It shows how the Holy Spirit ran like wildfire through the Church after the events of the Resurrection and Ascension of Christ. The conversion of Saul to become Paul takes its place here.

We read this account for its own sake when we keep the feast of St Paul's Conversion and thank God for the career of the apostle of the Gentiles. When we read it in Eastertide, it puts somewhat different thoughts into our minds. What was it Paul saw on the Damascus Road? Was it just a vision, as with many later saints and mystics? Or was this an actual encounter with the risen Christ like Mary Magdalen or Doubting Thomas had?

In his own writings, St Paul makes it clear that he held it to have been the latter, though he recognized it was highly anomalous. The Easter Lord had appeared to him as to 'one untimely born'. Paul didn't just see our Lord in a mental image as when St Margaret Mary saw the Sacred Heart. Our Lord left heaven for him. That is perhaps a rather brutal way of putting it. Let us say, rather, that the conditions of the space and time occupied by the risen Lord were modified so as to enable Paul to experience what the other apostles experienced. We might also put it in yet another way and say: in judgment and grace, our Lord brought heaven onto earth for one last time before his coming in glory.

And if we ask why he should want to do that, we can look around us for the answer. It was so that there could be a Church of the Gentiles, a universal Church. It was so that there could be us.

Saturday of the Third Week of Easter

The opening prayer of today's Mass asks that we may resist not just evil in general but false beliefs. Modern religion rather tends to shy at the notion that evil could include false beliefs, as distinct from spiritual or moral deficiency. Religion is to do with making people better, spiritually or morally, more than it is with doctrine. But when Christianity came into the world it struck people as a wonderful truth—about God and themselves, about past, present and future—and so inevitably it struck them as doctrine too.

That doesn't mean that the apostolic Church was like a University seminar in permanent session. As we can see from today's reading from the Acts of the Apostles, the life of that Church was made up of practical charity, prayer, and mutual concern, punctuated by the occasional miracle. Yet all this flowed from the acceptance of a truth which changed people's perspective on reality and so their norms of behaviour.

That is what we see in the Gospel. During the public ministry, becoming a disciple turned on whether one accepted that Christ had the 'words of eternal life'—whether he really had a capacity to communicate a truth coming from God himself, a truth that, if accepted, would change one's life.

That is why to develop an anti-intellectual mind-set as a Catholic Christian is a very mistaken strategy indeed.

The Fourth Sunday of Eastertide (Year A)

In Old Testament times, people had often pictured life with God
under the image of a sheepfold with its shepherd. 'The Lord is my
shepherd', sings the Psalmist, 'there us nothing I shall want.' And
the prophet Isaiah describes how God will 'feed his flock like a
shepherd, he will gather the lambs in his arms and gently feed
those that are with young'. A sheep with its shepherd: a clear and
striking image of what virtually anybody and everybody hopes to
get from religion: a basic, primordial security and sense of wellbeing, an assurance that the risks in life are not the last word, since
underlying everything is the good God who will make everything
right in the end. The sense that ultimately things are 'all right', that
there is a good and friendly order at the bottom of reality: this is
surely the heart of religion for most individuals and most cultures.

But in the discourse from which today's Gospel is taken our
Lord doesn't simply reiterate the poetry of the Old Testament
about God shepherding Israel. He applies this language directly
to himself. He is himself the shepherd of the sheep, the Good
Shepherd. Often during the night a Palestinian shepherd would
guard his sheep by lying across the entrance to the fold as a sort
of human gate, and so Jesus claims to be the very gate of the
sheepfold as well. And since this is St John's Gospel we are
speaking about, which tells us in its Prologue that the One who
was made flesh as Jesus is the universal Logos through whom all
things were made, this will be a universal claim. He is claiming to
be the place where human sheep generally (and not simply Israelite
sheep) encounter their divine Shepherd, and are protected and
secured for time and eternity,

As rehearsed in the Scriptures and continued in the Church
which reads those Scriptures at the Liturgy, this claim is a truly
extraordinary business. Man's share in divine life stands or falls
with one particular religious Founder who died twenty centuries
ago. Does that mean, then, that all the other teachers and found-
ers—Gautama, Zoroaster, Muhammad—are to be lumped together

as 'thieves and robbers'? In one sense, yes, it does. Jesus and he alone is the personal embodiment of the Godhead, really one with God, consubstantial with him, in his deepest being. 'I am in the Father and the Father is in me.' What Jesus is like shows us definitively what the Father is like. You cannot be a Christian if you simply regard Jesus as one revelation among many. If you did, you could not regard what Jesus is like as the key to what God is like, and so could not say with St John, 'God is love': that breathtakingly simple credo it will take all of us more than the rest of our lives to understand. God is not just, as Jews think, holiness. He is not just, as Muslims think, an all-demanding yet merciful will. He is not just, as Buddhists think, a nameless indescribable ocean of being. The Christian thinks of God first and last as Love, and more specifically the sacrificial Love shown in the Crucified on God's Friday, Good Friday, and if anyone denies that God is such love we must not mince our words. To steal such costly knowledge of God from people is to be no better than a thief or a robber.

This does not mean, however, that other descriptions of God have no truth in them at all. There are hints, echoes, suggestions, of God's truth scattered throughout culture. A number of the early Fathers held this view. There were, they said, those among the pagans who had lived with the Logos: those who had been attuned, up to a point, to the divinity behind the universe and had been able to give it halting and fragmentary yet not totally misleading expression. We have to be open, then, to this possible presence of divine truth in human culture, and be ready to welcome these rays of light wherever they are found. As Catholic Christians we are not, though, wishy-washy liberals whose hearts are in the right place but whose minds are unlocatable. We recognize what is good and true in other religions and philosophies *in the light of Jesus Christ*: of his teaching, his Death and Resurrection, and the revelation of God he brought: the revelation of the Good Shepherd, that God is love.

The Fourth Sunday of Eastertide (B)

Being compared with sheep is not generally regarded as highly complimentary. Sheep have a reputation for being silly, over-docile, following each other snout-to-tail in an uncritical fashion. But are these the qualities of sheep, real or alleged, that Jesus had in mind? Almost certainly not. In a largely pastoral society there would be a great deal more respect for, and understanding of, what sheep are and the kind of relation they have to their shepherd. What aspects of that relation, may we ask, are important for this Gospel?

First and foremost, the shepherd enjoys a kind of instinctive communication with his sheep. It's actually an acquired capacity to read little signals or symptoms, so that the shepherd has a sense for what the sheep are wanting or feeling. They are transparent to him, so that whether the sheep's preoccupation is hunger or thirst, predators or better grass on the other side of the mountain, the shepherd can pick it up and act on it. There's a network of stimulus and response which creates a mutual knowledge. 'I know my sheep and they know me.'

We all have a desire to be known: to be perfectly, intimately, known. One of our great needs is to share our sense of ourselves with what our contemporaries call a 'significant other'. We want someone else to understand our fears and anxieties, and to witness and share our joys and happiness. But—and this is a very large 'but' indeed—we want this someone never to abuse this knowledge. We need to be known in this intimate way by someone who will never disparage or humiliate us, never use or manipulate us. We require a well-grounded absolute trust in this perfect confidant or we might be seriously damaged by him or her. And, unfortunately, this is to ask for the moon. If these are the non-negotiable criteria, human beings are virtually *bound* to be sheep without a shepherd. Yet precisely this is the quality of relationship offered by Christ since, in his divine-human perfection, he really *is* the Good Shepherd.

What he says is, 'I know my sheep and mine know me, just as the Father knows me and I know the Father'. The second part of this statement—the part about the Son's knowledge of the Father— is obviously vital to understanding the first part, the inter-relation of the shepherd and the sheep. Friendship with the Good Shepherd is not simply a crutch to help us hobble a little better through life. No, it's an invitation to mysticism: to an experiential journey into the life of God himself. He says that the knowledge he will have of us will be like the very knowledge the Father has of the Son. So we need to ask, And what is *that* knowledge like, pray?

It is an extraordinary knowledge. The Father's loving knowledge of Son is the act whereby the Son exists—generated from before all worlds. For Jesus to promise he will know us in the way the Father knows him is for him to say he wants our existence to blossom with that same generative love, the love that has been going on in God before the world was made.

The Fourth Sunday of Eastertide (C)

The image of Christ as the Good Shepherd is one of the most ancient in Christian art, and it has never lost its appeal to subsequent generations in the Church. But why, we might ask, is the Sunday devoted to the Good (it can also be translated the 'Beautiful') Shepherd always kept in Eastertide, and not some other season? What is the special connexion?

The Good Shepherd could only show his mettle by, in his own words in the Gospel of St John, laying down his life for his sheep. Or to put it in terms of the parable recorded elsewhere in the Gospels, he could only bring back to the Father the lost sheep of fallen humanity when he had gone the full distance of his saving work to find them. The Easter proclamation runs: in his Resurrection and Ascension the Shepherd returned triumphant from the search. Never again shall any power on earth or the underworld snatch his sheep from his hand.

Our Lord's discourse on the Good Shepherd occupies a large chunk of the tenth chapter of St John's Gospel. It is leisurely enough for themes to recur and be orchestrated in different ways. Earlier on in the chapter the reader has already heard about the distinctive communion of knowledge and love which unites the Good Shepherd with his own. That is repeated in the Gospel we are given today but now it is brought together with an emphasis we have not come across before.

What is new is the stress on how invulnerable this communion is. Nothing outside it can destroy it, ravage it, even damage it. The love of Christ for us is more powerful than any other agency in the cosmos. How is that so? It is owing to the unity of being of the Son with the Father. As we say in the Creed, he is 'consubstantial with the Father'. And that means that all the Father has — and this must include, then, his almightiness — he shares everlastingly with the Son. 'I and the Father are one.'

Nothing outside the communion of knowledge and love between the Good Shepherd and his sheep can undermine it. But what about factors *within* that communion? From inside the Covenant relationship, we, the sheep, can let the communion with our Lord corrode. That is the only way it can deteriorate, disintegrate. It is a relation of persons, and therefore a relation exercised in freedom. His freedom is set for ever in one direction — our salvation, but our freedom is not so set. It takes two to tango. It also takes two to retain this communion. That is why keeping up the habit of prayer is a spiritual life-saver for us. That is where we must be alert to the way our life is taking us, where we must be, for the sake of our place in his Covenant, on our guard.

Monday of the Fourth Week of Easter

Today's readings present us with a very sharp contrast: on the one hand, the inclusiveness of St Peter's vision in Acts, which is a vision of the whole creation as 'cleansed', clean, because made by the good God, and on the other hand, the exclusiveness of our Lord's words in St John's Gospel where he tells the disciples that he is the only entrance to the sheepfold of salvation, all other claimants being thieves and robbers.

Nowadays we are more likely to warm to St Peter here than to St John — even though in other respects we would probably prefer John since in the New Testament Peter stands for Church authority while John stands for Christ-centred love. So anyway the Russian philosopher Vladimir Solovyev thought, and there is certainly something in this. And yet — so we can remind ourselves — Peter represents pastoral authority and indeed repentant pastoral authority, authority which, because it has been humbled, is the more considerate of other people — whereas the love represented by John can all too easily be a narrow love, constricted by its very zeal to be ultra-faithful to the one it loves.

However, what if this contrast—which so easily gives comfort to our lack of enthusiasm for mission, for evangelization, and indeed to our own incipient religious indifferentism—is really one not between Peter and John but between Peter and Christ? Then it would be much more embarrassing to vote for Peter and his universalism over against the incarnate God who alone, obviously, can provide for the true unity of his creation.

And so we look again at the context of Peter's speech. When we do so, we find that the practical conclusion Peter draws from his vision is not that since all the world is 'clean'—is fundamentally worthwhile—it has no need of the Gospel and the Church. On the contrary, the conclusion Peter draws is that being clean, being fundamentally worthwhile, all the world *may be received into the Church*—there to undergo first, healing of the wound of sin, and then, secondly, transfiguration by raising up into the life of the Kingdom, which is to say the life of love the Blessed Trinity both offers and is, and all that through the only Mediator, Christ our Lord.

Tuesday of the Fourth Week of Easter

Today's reading from the Acts of the Apostles is a good example of how God writes straight with crooked lines. The dispersal of the Jerusalem church in the wake of the persecution that made of St Stephen the proto-martyr of the universal Church had beneficial consequences for the growth of that Church on the Palestinian coast (Phoenicia), in the largest Greek-speaking island of the Mediterranean (Cyprus), and at the capital of Roman Syria (Antioch), which may well have been after Rome, the second most populous city of the empire.

This is not an isolated phenomenon in Church history. To take a reasonably modern parallel: it was only through the flight or expulsion of so many Russian Orthodox—including theologians—in between the Bolshevik Revolution and 1922, that the twentieth century renaissance of Orthodoxy in Western Europe, notably in France, was made possible, and could influence—very much to the good, in my opinion—Western Christian thought, worship, and life.

What Luke the historian is describing here in Acts is the *original diaspora*. We notice that he rubs in the sheer scale of the conversions at Antioch in particular. This, he tells us, is where the disciples were first called 'Christians', and perhaps that innovation is related to the issue of scale. To have an impact, such that a new name for what you represent enters into common currency, a certain mass is required.

The Church needs quantity, as at Antioch, and not just quality, as with the Russian thinkers in Paris. We are sometimes told that we must choose between being a large 'popular' Church, what the Germans call a *Volkskirche*, and being a small confessing Church of the deeply engaged. But actually we need both scale and quality if we are to imitate the achievements of the Church of the original apostles.

Wednesday of the Fourth Week of Easter

In the Acts of the Apostles we hear today and tomorrow about St Paul's apostolic journey to Cyprus. The Roman Lectionary is not, however, terribly satisfactory in its coverage of the Pauline visit. Today we hear of Paul's arrival for the beginning of the visit: 'Paul set sail for the island and arrived at Salamis': that's the ancient Greek port situated in the south-east corner of Cyprus. Looking ahead to tomorrow's reading, we get news of the end of the visit: 'So they sailed from Paphos', now a major resort in the south-west of the island. In so doing 'they' — that is, St Paul and St Barnabas — 'left Cyprus behind'. Could any visit be so uneventful? Check this out and you will find from the Book of Acts that a dramatic, not to say melodramatic, episode has been elided by the Lectionary's compilers.

Paul, struggling to convert Sergius Paulus, the proconsul of Cyprus, is frustrated by the counter-influence of a magician whom the apostle curses and renders temporarily blind. In the words of the author of Acts: 'Mist and darkness came down upon him and he sought the aid of another to lead him by the hand'. That is, I think, a very powerful description of someone whom a frightening experience confronts with the possible error of their ways.

And yet, theologically speaking, the Lectionary is right to think the most important thing about this visit is captured by Luke when he reports how on Cyprus Paul preached 'in the synagogues of the Jews': it was all part of the apostle's attempt to proclaim the Gospel representatively to the diaspora of Israel and indeed to the known world.

Moving on to the Gospel reading for today: we find our Lord fervently insisting that he must not be separated from the God of Old Testament revelation, the One he calls his Father. The Son acts only so that the Father may be seen acting, and heard speaking. He is only a medium—a go-between—for the Father's saving work.

This isn't to put himself down. Someone who is the vehicle of everything the Father wants to be for the world is more than human. Indeed, such a person is, by implication, staking out a claim to share the Godhead. To share the Godhead—but only by receiving it. As we say in the Creed, the Son is God *from* God. The Son is pure receptivity to the Father, sheer transparency to him, like a window letting through light. To reject that window, once having seen it, is to wander indeed in mist and darkness.

Thursday of the Fourth Week of Easter

The opening prayer of today's Mass reminds us of a truth which ought never to be far from our life and thinking. Today's collect thanks God for giving human nature an even greater dignity than that in which it was created. An even greater dignity because, thanks to the Incarnation, the Atonement, and the sending of the Spirit of the risen Christ, our nature is now being drawn into communion with God himself. It is being divinized.

And this means that there is something particularly unfitting—something, in the original sense of the word, 'indecent'—about the sins of Christians. When the Fathers and the mediaeval moralists want to make us pull up what they say is, 'Recognise your dignity!' We would not be so petty, so mean-minded and self-indulgent and back-biting if we really did recognize our dignity: not just notionally but with real assent, in our bones, in our blood.

And what turns on this is not just the quality or ethos of the society we move in, but our own final salvation as well. In today's

Gospel our Lord says, 'I know whom I have chosen'. In the Roman Canon the Church asks that God may count us—those praying at the Liturgy—among those he has chosen. It's not enough that our nature is now on the way of redemption. We who are in that nature but as persons—as free subjects—have to lay hold of redemption by our own act and make it our own. God will not save us without some co-operation on the part of our freedom, and he gives the grace of final perseverance to those whom he sees so co-operating.

So: first, we are by faith to come to some understanding of the new dignity that is ours, but then, by hope and charity, we are to let awareness of that dignity soak through us so that with the help of God it can change our lives.

Friday of the Fourth Week of Easter

Today's reading from the Acts of the Apostles makes it plain that the Gospel is directed in the first place toward the Jews. Christians who want as a matter of priority to include Jews among the baptized are not, as some maintain nowadays, insulting Jews. On the contrary, they are drawing attention to the privilege of Israel—a privilege she can never lose. All the treasures of the New Covenant are meant first and foremost for her.

In the Letter to the Romans St Paul will tell the Roman church that it is the Gentiles who are the wild olive that has been grafted onto the cultivated stock of Israel. We are the Johnnie-come-latelys, the ones whose standing in the Church really has to be argued for. The Church is primarily 'from the Circumcision', a Church of Hebrew Christians, and only secondarily a Church 'from the peoples', a Church of Gentile Christians.

In his speech to the Jewish community at Pisidian Antioch Paul gives the reason why. The promises were made to the Jewish ancestors: the prophecies emerged from the Jewish people, and that same people were the instrument of God in fulfilling the promises and prophecies even when their role was a negative one—namely, when they brought the Messiah to his Sacrifice. In a word, only the Jews have the whole story. Only they can experience it at all points from the inside.

Fortunately, as today's Gospel tells us, in the Father's house there are many mansions. There are many ways in which each of us (if we are Gentiles, not Jews) can make our own the story of how God had mercy on the human race, and focussed that mercy: first on one people (Israel); next, on one woman among that people (Mary), and then—not as mercy but as infinite condescension—brought his electing grace to bear on the fruit of that mother's womb by the Incarnation as her Child of his own eternal Word. Thus it was that from this highly focussed point the mercy could spread and spread until it became as wide as the world.

Saturday of the Fourth Week of Easter

In today's Gospel our Lord tells St Philip that 'he who has seen me has seen the Father'. But when we recall that Christ is the divine person of the Word now living in two natures, divine and human, we might feel an objection here. Surely, he who has seen Jesus has seen the humanity assumed by the Word and not the divine Word himself, much less the Father?

But this is not in fact how the Church has argued, notably at the seventh of the Ecumenical Councils, Nicaea II, in 787, when the doctrinal basis of the cult of the icon was laid down. The humanity of Jesus is the concrete disclosure of the divine person of the Word. It is marked or characterized—made characteristically itself—by the person of the eternal Word whose humanity it is. Jesus's humanity, without being in any way confused with the divine nature, *is* the manifestation of his divine person. So, in seeing Jesus, we see God incarnate.

But then the objection might resume. What we see, as you rightly say, is the Word, the Son—but surely that means that what we see is precisely *not* the Source of the Word, the *Father of the Son*. Here is where our Trinitarian doctrine steps in to save the day. Everything in the Trinity is one, except for the manner of origin of the persons. Everything the Father is, that the Word is, except for the fact of being the Source, the absolute Origin. So all that the Son shows us, that he has by reflection of his Father. The humanity of Jesus *does* show Philip—and show us too—what the Father is like.

That is why, meditating on the ministry and the Paschal Mystery which was the ministry's climax, St John could come to his great affirmations: God is love, and God is light and in him there is no darkness at all.

THE FIFTH WEEK OF EASTER

The Fifth Sunday of Easter (Year A)

After leaving school and before going to University I worked for six months in a hostel for tramps in Dublin. Some of the older tramps who came for the night had spent the day wandering about art-galleries. Not, generally, because they were devoted to the early Flemish masters but because it was dry, warm and cost nothing. But, so one of them told me, he found more in it than that. Living with the paintings on a daily basis, he found that some canvases stood out and spoke to him, came to life, while others faded back. Some paintings became interlocutors, even friends. Maybe it sounds bizarre, but is it really so surprising? Here, after all, were objects into which others had expressed themselves—expressed themselves onto canvas and into paint and in that way had created things that were full of meaning, with human and spiritual significance built into them. Is it so surprising that lonely and derelict old men should find themselves drawn into a sort of conversation with the paintings they looked at each weekday from 9 to 5? Would it be going too far to say that they *loved* them? Perhaps it would not be excessive to say even that.

If you really look at a great painting, what you see is the spirit of the artist who made it. So the New Testament calls Jesus the artwork, the icon, the visual image of God because in him you will find God expressed.

> Philip said, 'Lord, let us see the Father and we shall be satisfied'. 'Have I been with you all this time, Philip', Jesus said to him, 'and you still do not know me. To have seen me is to have seen the Father'.

Jesus was inviting Philip to look at him with greater engagement, like the tramp did in the city gallery. In conversion to Jesus Christ, his humanity takes on new depth for us, like a painting that comes alive and begins to speak of the vision of its artist. But in Jesus's case what that iconic humanity speaks of is the Father. The Son sees the Father eternally and as man he moulds his human expression in accordance with that blessed vision.

So one looks at Jesus and finds he is not as other men. He is the icon in which we can discern the ultimate Artist, the Father, the Source of all: the Source even of the Son. Christ is what God looks like when he expresses himself in our world. He is the visibility of God.

Does it make sense to claim that the infinite God expressed his own being into a finite object? If that worries us, we have to go back to the original comparison, the painting. A little rectangle of canvas can contain a depth of significance that is endless, that can't be exhausted, that can continue to feed us even if someone looks at it for a lifetime.

The Fifth Sunday of Easter (Year B)

In the opening words of today's epistle, St John warns us against too facile an understanding, in the Christian context, of the word 'love'. One American religious educator has noted wryly how, starting in the 1960s, the correct answer to every question put in high school theology classes has been 'love'. St Augustine had written, 'Love and do as you will'. The Beatles declared 'All you need is love'. Was there a difference between them, or were they all saying the same thing?

Of course there was a difference between them! The Beatles thought of love in carnal and/or sentimental terms, and unlike Augustine they had no doctrine that could teach them how to incarnate love amid the tedium or grind of daily life. By contrast, the kind of love St John is talking about is a love for God and for our neighbour for God's sake. It is a love that is given divinely, by grace, but comes to be rooted humanly in our own powers of understanding and will. It is nurtured by prayer and the sacraments, and especially the Holy Eucharist. It is inconceivable without a spiritual commitment to the teaching of Christ and his Church.

The love St John is talking about is rewarding but hard. How rewarding our Lord himself tells us in the parable of the Vine and the Branches. The Vine is the source of the wine that makes glad the heart of man. But we cannot be wine for others or indeed for ourselves — we cannot be fruitful — unless we allow the Vinedresser to prune us. Without being cut about, without the hardship the Way of the Cross brings in our lives, we are likely to remain spiritually unproductive. A vine that just grows wildly and is never pruned soon ceases to produce grapes worth having. It stops being of much use to anyone. The alternative to accepting the Vinedresser's discipline is to be cut away from the vine, and wood cut away from vines was notoriously useless.

There is a saying I heard when I worked as a priest in Scotland, The Catholic religion is a hard one to live in but an easy one to die in. We do have to be careful, as a Church, not to turn that saying round. We can fail the Gospel by making the practice of our religion too easy, by inculcating a message of love that is not sufficiently distinguished from the message of the Beatles to approximate to that of the saints and doctors of the Church.

The Fifth Sunday of Easter (Year C)

What is our aim as Catholic Christians? What is the Church for? This is always a reasonable sort of question. The English legal philosopher Jeremy Bentham advised not to ask how old something is but to ask what use it is. That is fine so long as we don't take the word 'use' too literally and end up like Dickens' Mr Gradgrind: a narrow, calculating, materialistic Philistine. To ask what use something is to ask what good it serves. What good, then, does the Church serve?

The three readings of today's Mass suggest, or can be made to suggest, three answers to this question. In the first reading, from Acts, St Luke exults over the unexpected breakthrough of the apostles Paul and Barnabas in bringing the Gospel to the interior of Asia Minor, an area with almost no Jewish settlement and therefore much harder terrain. God, we read, opened a door for them to the Gentiles. Though St Luke couldn't know this, the area would become outstanding for the writing of Christian philosophy and theology, for the monastic life, for spirituality, for the visual arts. It will produce some of the greatest of the Fathers of the Church. This gives us our first answer to the question, What is the Church for? It is for shaping civilizations that give the world great thought and great art and call the world to a God-centred way of life.

As we move onto the second reading, we can take with us the thought that, for Paul and Barnabas, it was *God* who opened this door, not they themselves, opening it by their own efforts. That is pertinent to the second reading which makes it plain that, as a Church, we are waiting for God to do something marvellous—or, rather, to do something marvellous *again*. We are waiting for the new heavens and the new earth which already exist in the world of the Resurrection where our Lord lives in glory with his blessed Mother Mary, where happiness and holiness are unified, where physical nature and the life of the soul have been brought alike to their completion. It's not just that God has got the whole world in his hands. It's that he's going to do something wonderful with and within the whole world, something of which Easter and Pentecost are simply the first-fruits.

And this gives us a second answer to the question, What is the Church for? The Church exists so as to keep alive the divine promise that history and human life are going somewhere, and the somewhere is so wonderful it make it all worthwhile. 'He will wipe away all tears from their eyes.'

That future already exists in the glorified Lamb, Jesus Christ, and by dependence on him in the Mother of the Lord whose flesh the Holy One took to himself when he entered our world. In today's Gospel St John speaks of the mutual glorifying of the Father and the Son. It is because Jesus made his whole being a sacrificial love-offering to the Father—and in that sense 'glorified' the Father—that the Father in a different (but related) sense 'glorifies' the Son by giving him as man a permanent share in the bliss the Son had as God with the Father before time began.

And in the rest of this Gospel passage, the evangelist shows what happens when that mutual glorifying of the Father and the Son begins to spill over to us. It begins to spill over to us when we start to live by charity—and charity is ultimately to be identified with the Holy Spirit, the Ground of the union of Father and the Son, the living love that binds them together.

So what is the Church for now? It is to be a communion of charity, both in heroic undertakings and in the details of everyday life. To be a communion of charity: that means to put God and others first, glorifying the Father and being glorified by him. It means becoming saints.

Monday of the Fifth Week of Easter

We could easily be very snooty about the Lycaonians. Honestly, it was so crude and superstitious of them to try to worship Paul and Barnabas.

But before rushing to condemn them, we should remember the strength of their position. There was something wonderful about that Hellenic morning of our civilization when earth and sky, gods and humans, seemed woven together into one web — when at any moment a god could epiphanise in a sanctuary or in nature, in a beast or in a man. The Jewish horror of confusing the created with the Uncreated, what is not God with what is God — the same horror with which Paul and Barnabas react to their projected apotheosis — this has meant (it might be thought) loss as well as gain. One could say that the logical — or, better, the psychological — conclusion of such horror is deism, where God is pushed out of the universe altogether and leaves culture to its own devices: the sort of thing we see round us in the West today.

Of course we know that is not the right conclusion to draw. Good philosophy tells us that the infinite Cause has to energise all finite causes, that unless God were ceaselessly giving being to the smallest thing it would cease to be. And that is already a presence of God to his world — not an episodic presence, which is how the Hellenes saw divine epiphany, but a systemic presence, an abiding and comprehensive presence. The Schoolmen called it the 'presence by immensity'.

Today's Gospel tells us more even than this: tells us more inasmuch as it is part of the great meditation on the Triune relationships with which, according to St John, Jesus celebrates the last evening of his earthly life. Thanks to the missions of the Son and the Spirit, the Father is present to the world more intimately, more personally, more cordially, than either Zeus or the God of the philosophers could ever be.

That is what the great post-Ascension feasts—Pentecost, Corpus Christi, the Sacred Heart—will soon be telling us too.

Tuesday of the Fifth Week of Easter

During my adult lifetime, we have heard a great deal in Western countries about so-called Peace Movements: organizations which feed people with information, more or less accurate, about the possibilities of conflict, and encourage them to apply pressure on governments with a view to reducing the threat of war. The late Father Herbert McCabe once refused to join one of these movements on the ground that he already belonged to a peace movement. It was called, he explained, the Catholic Church.

And indeed in today's Gospel, our Lord implicitly proclaims the Church to be a peace movement, but the kind of peace involved is not a peace that the world can give, nor a peace that the world—when defined as unbelieving human beings in their totality—can even understand.

This more mysterious peace has to do with the relation of the Son to the Father. It concerns the manner in which the Father and the Son enjoy their being. In terms of the Church's later reflection on this text, it is the Holy Spirit who is personally the communion of the Father and the Son and the fruit of their love. Not till the world lives by the Holy Spirit—by faith, hope, and love, rather than by natural principles of action—will it be able to understand such peace, never mind be in a position to give it.

Only then will the world have the capacity to achieve the peace in which competing egos are not simply restrained by fear of what might befall if war breaks out, but re-made in the image of the perfect reciprocal self-giving that is the Blessed Trinity.

Wednesday of the Fifth Week of Easter

When we read the story of the great circumcision debate in the early Church, we naturally tend to take the side of St Paul and liberty. We have, after all, no desire to be circumcised ourselves: that is understandable. Nor as Gentiles do we have a hankering after the ceremonial Law of Judaism. But we should be careful not to say, or think, or feel, that, after the great circumcision debate, the Church now really belongs to Gentiles, and that Jews in the Church, if not exactly here on sufferance, are at least an oddity.

That is the opposite of what the liberty party, including St Paul, their chief spokesman, believed. We, the Gentiles, are the wild olive grafted onto the cultivated stock of Israel, and so the Church of the Circumcised, the Church of baptized Jews, is not only as important in the plan of God as is the Church of the Gentiles: it is *more* important, or more fundamental, anyway. The liberty party took that for granted.

That realization has led in our day to a movement, still small and relatively unknown, to bring together Hebrew Catholics, Catholics of Jewish origin, not only for common fellowship but also with a view to keeping those festivals which the Church at large in her historic Liturgies has never taken up and Christianised.

What would be the point of that? Delight in the gift of the Law is a keynote of the Old Testament and that means for an observant Jew delight in carrying out all its ritual practices. A Christian Jew will naturally wish to celebrate in their Church-form those festivals which have become part and parcel of the Church year and now speak eloquently of the fulfillment of Judaism in the Messiah, Jesus Christ, and his saving work. But that leaves out of the count other festivals which are landmarks in the Old Testament story and as such important for Jewish identity.

In today's Gospel our Lord lays down the criterion that should be used to test all movements in the Church. By their fruits you shall know them. Fruitfulness in bearing witness to the rest of Israel; fruitfulness in a God-centred life, in a good life. Fruitfulness like his own on the Cross. So it all depends, as with ourselves, the Church of the Gentiles, on whether we are in him and he in us.

Thursday of the Fifth Week of Easter

Today's Gospel is a miniature summary of the faith. It opens, unremarkably enough you may think, with the words, 'Jesus said to his disciples'. Those words are added by the Church but they are not just a rubric. They place us within the context of a privileged relationship. To be a Christian is to be taken up into the dialogue between the incarnate Word and those who listened to him. It is to be incorporated into the fellowship of the original disciples.

So what does Jesus have to say? He begins by referring to the Father. The Father comes first and last in the message of Jesus. Not just as a name for God the Creator, but as a way of referring to that unfathomable Source of love from whom the Son eternally proceeds. That is made clear by what follows: 'As the Father has loved me, so I have loved you'. In other words, the love which the disciples experienced in Jesus is not just some vaguely uplifting kind of benevolence. It is the same uncreated Love by which the Father brought forth the Son when time was not. It is a goodness more powerful, more generative, than even the goodness which created the world. That's the love in comparison with which all other loves are only shadows, and this is what Christ has extended to the disciples, letting it pour out over them.

However, this doesn't mean that the disciples are only recipients of something. They also have something to do. What is that? It is, as Jesus now says, 'to abide in my love'. How will they do so? He explains. 'If you keep my commandments you will abide in my love.' Keeping his commandments: the law of Christ. Our Lord took up the ethical teachings of the Old Testament, and behind that the natural law, the wisdom of the nations when it really was wisdom, and these he crowned and clarified by issuing his 'new commandment', the commandment of charity. This 'law' is not just a matter of duty, of moral obligation. By keeping this law we participate in the communion of the Father and the Son. By conforming our lives to God's goodness as revealed in Christ we begin to share the inner life of God—the love-exchange of Father and Son.

And then finally, we hear: 'These things I have spoken to you that my joy may be in you, and that your joy may be full'. The New Testament calls joy one of the fruits of the Holy Spirit, a give-away sign of his presence. In St John's Gospel, the Holy Spirit is never far from our Lord's thoughts on the eve of his Passion when these words were spoken. He speaks explicitly of the Spirit as the Comforter or Advocate, but more allusively as peace, glory, truth, to be shared with the disciples through Christ's Sacrifice.

The gift of the Holy Spirit seals our participation in the love-exchange of Father and Son, just as in the Godhead the Spirit is the living bond of their union. The Father sends the Son to create the conditions in which human persons can receive the Holy Spirit and so be one with each other in him everlastingly. To facilitate that is what, in the final analysis, the Church is for.

Friday of the Fifth Week of Easter

Today's first reading sounds rather strange. The apostles agree on a code of practice for Gentile converts—pagans, non-Jews who become Christians. The code turns out to consist in four rather bizarre-sounding, or any rate strangely assorted, points: abstaining from what has been sacrificed to idols and from blood, and from what has been strangled, and from unchastity. What on earth can be going on?

What this Council in Jerusalem set out to do was to satisfy the strong feelings of Jewish Christians that Gentile Christians should offer some sign of solidarity with those who followed the ritual law of the Old Testament. Not the whole caboodle, necessarily but something at least. So the decision is that Gentile Christians will not offend Jewish-Christian sensibilities by eating foodstuffs that in Jewish eyes are ritually unclean—whether because they are leftovers from pagan banquets or meats prepared for the table in a non-kosher way. To this is added the requirement that Gentile Christians will not marry within those close degrees of kindred which the Jewish Law regarded as disabling people from marriage. The boundaries between kinship based on descent and the unique relationship of the marriage-bond should be preserved.

Had the Jewish-Christian church survived, or if a Jewish Catholic rite existed in the Church today to set an example to others, we as Gentile Catholics might well have continued to keep this code, eating kosher-wise like the Jews and refraining from marriage with a wider range of blood-relatives than is the case now. But given that it didn't and we don't, what use is this Conciliar decision to us?

It tells us of the importance of the right sort of deferring to other people's strongly felt sensibilities or passionately held convictions.

Where the truth is at stake, that would not be justified, especially when what is involved is revealed truth—religious and moral truths stemming from God. But in other cases, and there are many of them, we should be ready to sacrifice our preferences for the common good. It is an example of charity in act, a deployment of the new commandment, to love one another, given by Christ in the Gospel.

Saturday of the Fifth Week of Easter

So in today's Gospel our Lord tells his disciples that the world will hate them—or, at any rate, it will hate them if they have made it clear that they do not belong to the world: to society as organized apart from his revelation and the community that carries it, the Church. The world will hate them if they challenge the world.

This I suppose is why monks and nuns attracted so much hostility in nineteenth century England. The monastic way of life and what it represented was just not understood. Or rather it *was* to some extent understood—as a challenge to what Mrs Thatcher called 'Victorian values': thrift, self-help, progress and Gladstonian Liberalism.

In one sense of course it's a good thing that Catholics are now more or less accepted as part and parcel of English society and public life. Mutual acceptance, peace, reconciliation: these are evident goods. Admittedly, patriotic anti-Catholicism was always impudent when one considers how the pre-Reformation Catholic Church had made England what it was. But we are not likely to hear much again about the Catholic menace so long as militant Islam is around, which is likely to be for a very long time. So we can breathe a sigh of relief.

Or can we? If Catholic Christians cease altogether to be suspect in the eyes of the world, or cold-shouldered by the world (in the strong words of our Lord, 'hated'), could this be in part because we are not doing our job? The world will hate us if we do not belong to it. If it stops hating us, is this because we are too much like it? Is it because we have come to terms with it, accommodated ourselves to it?

The Church is in a healthy condition when she attracts at one and the same time both hostility and fascination. Hostility — because that points to the way the Ark of salvation differs from the floods of the world around that Ark; fascination — because that points to the power of the truth, goodness and beauty the Ark has taken on board.

Can you be fascinated by something to which you feel hostility? Of course: that is the cocktail of emotions the grace of conversion usually sets up. We resent the disturbance of this alien intrusion, but we also have the wonderful feeling: it is calling us home.

THE SIXTH WEEK OF EASTER

The Sixth Sunday of Eastertide (Year A)

Today's Gospel raises the question, Why should we keep his commandments? Why should we keep those precepts that bind us, morally speaking?

The common view of the man in the street is or was that a decent human being doesn't do certain things, most of which are in any case against the law in a civilized society. Theft, perjury, adultery, all go against important values—the right to one's own property, the importance of truth-telling, fidelity in the marriage relationship. Unless penalized, at least in the first two cases, these practices would create anarchy in the social world. Adultery creates anarchy in the world of the home, but the disadvantages of criminalizing it have usually been held to outweigh the advantages. The objectivity of this answer is admirable so far as it goes: the good is to be respected whether it suits my personal convenience or not.

Unfortunately, it is difficult to do wholeheartedly that which is good unless we actually *love* the good: unless our emotions and inward dispositions are moving towards the good spontaneously and with a sense of delight. That was well understood by the ancient philosopher Plato. Ideally, we love the good because we find it beautiful. Otherwise, if we manage to respect the rule and do the right thing, we may find ourselves doing so in a frigid and resentful manner, or in a calculating manner, asking what is the minimum that can count as duty performed.

These disadvantages emerge by contrast in the light of today's Gospel. On the eve of his Passion when he would demonstrate the love for humankind of the Triune God, our Lord tells the disciples, 'If you love me, you will keep my commandments'. If they respond to him by love, if they match what the Greek Fathers call his *philanthropia*, his divine love for man, then they will find themselves keeping his commandments. How? 'Automatically' would create the wrong impression; 'spontaneously' would not.

We all know how for someone we love romantically some task that in any other context would be a chore becomes mysteriously a pleasure. In the transience of romance that is fated not to endure. But it is a formative life-experience nonetheless. When the bloom of romance has faded, in the case of spouses or of very close friends, we continue to find, in an enduring way, that there is something satisfying about doing things for them and we know from our taste of the romantic experience that this is thanks to—in some sense of the word—love. Applying this more widely, then: If behind the commandments, the rules, there stands not only an objective something, the Good, but in and through the Good, a Someone with whom we are caught up in reciprocal affection, then striving to do the objective good changes its character. The rules are no longer rules, they are invitations to do the Beloved's willing.

St Thomas Aquinas asks, What is the law of the New Testament? By which he meant, What is the distinctive moral practice of Christians? And his answer is that *principally* the law of the New Testament is the grace of the Holy Spirit. The Spirit of Christ, poured by the Father into human hearts, to be among other things the dynamo of the moral life, gives us not only a fuller discernment of what is right and good but also the energy with which to pursue it. It is for that Spirit of love we shall be praying in Ascensiontide.

The Sixth Sunday of Easter (Year B)

A Cambridge clergyman, a study of whose work is entitled 'Atheist Priest', warns us in one of his many books that while the idea of God is a beautiful idea, it is important for us that—objectively speaking—God does not exist.

The reason he gives underlies a great deal of modern atheism, so it seems important to ask why, even prescinding from the useful fact that an answer will take us into today's Gospel.

The idea of God, so it is said, is that of a good and loving Lord and Master, but a good Master is still a master, so if God existed we would be his slaves. To be authentically human—as the modern West has discovered—is to be our own masters, to work out our own lives, to decide our own set of values: what things we shall count as important and which rules we shall live by. You cannot be both a real person and a slave: not even a slave to an all-good master. God is incompatible with moral autonomy, with proper liberty.

In today's Gospel, our Lord tells his disciples, 'I shall not call you servants any more, because a servant does not know his master's business; I call you friends....' By this point in St John's text, we are supposed to realize that Jesus is no ordinary man. He is not simply a man at all, though he is altogether a man, fully one of us. He is not simply on our side of the gulf between the infinite and the finite. He bridges the gulf because he is the very Word of God made flesh. He is not God full stop, for only the Father is the Source and Origin of all that is divine. He is, as we say in the Creed, 'God *from* God': the Father's uncreated self-expression. So this Jesus who is the divine-human expression of the Father says to his disciples, 'I shall not call you servants any more'.

The divine purpose is not to enslave mankind, not even to make us happy, comfortable servants looked after by a kind master who will provide every amenity. The aim of the Incarnation was to make us friends: to take us into the divine friendship. Friendship is a very important kind of love because it is based on our need for a *sort of loving that is not itself based on need*, if that doesn't sound too paradoxical. A loving that reaches out to another for his or her own sake, not for any service or satisfaction they can give.

This is the love which has been going on for all eternity in God where Father, Son and Holy Spirit share one co-equal majesty. God *is* friendship, he is perfect friendship, in his own tripersonal life. He does not need human beings to be his friends, but he chooses to love us with the love of friendship. Friendship is freely elected, although once it is both given and received it carries great and inescapable responsibilities. There is high nobility in being a friend and never more so, for human beings, than in being the friend of God.

The Sixth Sunday of Easter (Year C)

The easiest place to begin an account of this Gospel is half-way through, when our Lord quotes from an earlier conversation with his disciples: 'I go away, and I will come to you'.

This sounds fairly straightforward. 'I go away' refers to Good Friday, the Passion and Death of Christ. 'I will come to you' refers to Easter, his Resurrection. The language is so low-key, almost dead-pan, that we could miss its real force. 'I go away': each Holy Week we set ourselves to recall what that 'going away' entailed. The abandonment of Jesus by his disciples: a going away into a condition of personal isolation, an extreme instance of the bereavement we feel when a friend packs it in and leave us. Secondly, the humiliation of Jesus by all sorts of people from the civil and religious top brass to private soldiers: a going away from selfhood into the condition of a thing, being treated as an object, all rights of subjective action stripped from him. The physical pain of Jesus: a going away from all the pleasure this world holds since the body has become one enormous pain. The death of Jesus: a radical going away from this world which, though we may not like it, is the only world we have. Lastly, the descent into Hell: a going away into confrontation with the accumulated evil of angels and men which kept them from God.

What about the other part? 'I will come to you'. The most obvious thing to think of would be the Resurrection appearances as the Gospels describe them: the encounters in a garden, or by the lakeside, or in the Upper Room. Beautiful moments in the Gospel story—but precisely because they are beautiful moments, now long past, only to be shared by an exercise of historical imagination. And probably this is why today's Gospel does not mention the Resurrection appearances but speaks of how Jesus will come again to his disciples in terms of a mode of presence available to all disciples as long as the world lasts.

To anyone who 'keeps his words', he will come and 'take up his dwelling' in them. Though the language is strange it is not impenetrable. In human relationships two persons don't exist side by side in the way that two books lie side by side on a shelf or two glasses on a bar counter. Unlike things, persons can become interior to each other. Give me someone who loves, says St Augustine, and he will know what I mean.

When Christ is present to us by indwelling, two further dimensions open up. First, the Father also comes to inhabit us. The being of Christ as Son of God is not thinkable without the Father, his existence is nothing other than relation with the Father. And then there is a second further dimension, to do with the Holy Spirit. With the Father comes the Spirit whom the Father sends in Christ's name, and the Spirit will resuscitate all the encounters that have taken place between Jesus and the original disciples and bring out their implications for the rest of the Church. 'He will teach you all things, and bring to your remembrance all that I have said to you.'

The indwelling of God the Trinity in our souls. That is what we are asked to think about at this time of year. It is the charter of Christian mysticism. It is also what makes the saints who they are.

Monday of the Sixth Week of Easter

Does it matter where we worship? Today's readings concern the relation of religion to buildings or at any rate to locations. In the Gospel, the apostles are warned that they will be put out of the synagogues, and in the Acts of the Apostles we see that starting to happen. And so the apostolic fellowship has to regroup in houses, like the house of Lydia. Where we house our religion may be partly a matter of chance, but it can also say something about what we consider our religion essentially to be.

Synagogues seem to have arisen partly by chance, owing to the circumstances of the Exile when people could no longer worship in the Temple. But as a type of building they soon took off and spread to Palestine in the time of the Second Temple. The reason was that in stone and marble they summed up a key tenet of Judaism. They were buildings suited to those who gathered round to listen to the Torah, the book of the Law.

What about the buildings the apostles transferred to? House churches didn't have staying power. Soon they would be replaced by hall-like basilicas, rotundas over the remains over the martyrs, and, eventually, parish churches with, in the West, towers and spires, or, in the East, domes and lanterns. And this seems to follow from the words of our Lord in this Gospel where he describes the apostles as taking part in a public trial of the truth or rightness of the Gospel. Our religion is not for private coteries, it is a public religion which makes a statement about what public doctrine in society ought to be.

We can be grateful for what holy women like Lydia did to nurture the infant Church. But we are not meant to go back to the womb: warm, safe, and above all private.

Tuesday of the Sixth Week of Easter

The reading from Acts today describes the miraculous escape of Paul and Silas from prison at Philippi. Miracles tell us that the order of the world is, in the last analysis, a divine order, an order expressive of God's purpose for history. In that purpose, St Paul, as it happens, was an extremely important player. At the time of his arrest, most of his missionary journeys as apostle of the Gentiles lay ahead of him—not to mention his martyrdom for the faith at Rome, where the Roman church was sealed in its faith by the shedding of his blood. It would have been profoundly disorderly had Paul's apostolate to the nations and his foundational role in the church of the universal primacy been frustrated by a trumped-up charge in a one-horse town that was scarcely more than a glorified barracks somewhere in the middle of Macedonia. It was because God's plan for the world is orderly that Paul had to be freed to preach the Gospel to the Gentiles and eventually in the place to which all roads in the Empire led and from which, in the mission of the later Church, many roads led out as well.

Can we prove that? We can forward persuasive considerations which the Holy Spirit can render convictions in our hearers. This is what our Lord tells us in today's Gospel. When the Advocate comes, he will show the world how wrong it was about who was in the right in the trial to which Christ and his message were subjected. How will he show the world? At the Mass of Pentecost the Sequence—the *Veni Creator Spiritus*—will tell us how. It will be by softening hearts, moving wills, and thus changing minds. The Holy Spirit clears away the inner obstacles to wholehearted and clear-sighted acceptance of God's order, the order God is bringing out of the world or, if you prefer, the order he is drawing the world into. The Holy Spirit enables us to see among other things how miracles fit in to the order of God. Physical miracles, yes—but also the moral miracles that are the making of the saints.

Wednesday of the Sixth Week of Easter

In today's first reading, from the Acts of the Apostles, a tragedy unfolds. St Paul finds himself in the heart of Athens, just as Athens was at the heart of Hellas, of ancient Greece. He is in the Areopagus, the forum where issues were debated and the philosophical acuity of the Greek mind brought to bear on topics great and small. St Paul's theme is the divine. And he takes the opportunity of the existence on the Areopagus of an altar inscribed 'to an unknown God' (presumably, it was a statue of an unidentified god) to give his hearers the true doctrine of divine transcendence as found in biblical revelation.

It is because God is the absolute Source of everything, and thereby utterly different from anything in the world, that he can be at the same time so intimately close to everything. 'In him we live and move and have our being.' But just at the moment when the key to the nature of the divine is in the grasp of the Athenians, Paul mentions the Resurrection. Shocked at the apparent irrationality of this supra-rational claim (which in fact was not against reason but went beyond it), the pagan philosophers draw back and let the key fall from their hands.

'When the Spirit of truth comes he will guide you into all the truth.' Yes, we need the Holy Spirit as a new principle of intellectual enlightenment. It is the Spirit who opens the eyes of our minds to see how resurrection is the climax of creation and Providence, so that we can say with the Creed, 'I believe in the resurrection of the dead and the life of the world to come'.

The Ascension of the Lord

In 1977, by sheer accident it fell to me to represent the French Dominican priory of St Stephen in Jerusalem at the Silver Jubilee celebration of Elizabeth II at St George's Anglican Cathedral there. I'd gone to lunch at the priory where the French saw in my visit the perfect opportunity of getting out of devoting the rest of the afternoon to the Queen of England. One of the canons of St George's, an aged Englishman, acted as my host. He told me his job was to take visitors round the Holy Places and other archaeological sites associated with the Gospel story. He'd just taken a party of theological students up Mount Olivet, and, so he reported, said to them when they reached the modest summit, 'This then is the place from where our Lord returned to his Father by ascending into heaven'. They looked at each other, he told me, and their looks could mean only one thing. He has read nothing since 1935. And of course, he said, they were wrong.

If pressed, they would probably have said that early Christians lived in a 'triple decker' universe (hell below, heaven above) where if you went high enough you would be in severe danger of bumping into God, whereas we know that, really, space is a receptacle for bodies and forces (see Sir Isaac Newton) which wouldn't have let Christ disappear from the cosmos behind a convenient cloud.

Actually, the biblical writers knew quite well that the space that belongs to God is different in kind from the space that belongs to us. 'The heaven of heavens cannot contain him.' But in any case, are we so sure that we understand what we mean by 'space' — so sure as to be confident that talk of the Ascension of Christ can only survive now as a 'way of speaking', and not as a way of truly speaking about an authentic and perhaps vitally significant event?

Insofar as I understand it: in the wake of Einstein, contemporary science treats time and space as functions of events in the universe. It regards them as forms of the sequence and structure of those events. If that's so, we can never abstract the notion of space from what is going on in space. More widely, then, we have to see location and chronology, place and time, in terms for that for which they exist, that for which they function,

Our space is defined by the pattern of structures in the physical world where we live out our life. God's 'space' (the term can only be used by analogy) is defined by the structure of his eternal life and activity.

So when we celebrate the Ascension of Christ we celebrate something with two poles or ends. At one end the Ascension is bounded by humanity and our space. At the other end it is 'bounded' only by the boundless nature of God, 'limited' only by the limitless room God makes for himself in his eternal life and activity.

To return to that 1970s conversation on the hill-top, Canon Every might have replied, You think that space as modern science knows it to be wouldn't have let Christ disappear from the surrounding universe. But modern science 'knows' no such thing. The idea of the space-time tracks of very different realities intersecting is not alien to modern science. That is not why the Ascension is a mystery.

Why the Ascension is a mystery isn't so much a matter of astrophysics which already theorises about black holes, so why not a radiant hole? With its talk of possible 'parallel universes' modern cosmology has become entirely speculative anyway. Why the Ascension is a mystery is, rather, a matter of morals, or perhaps we should say it is a matter of the metaphysic of morals. What is mysterious about the Ascension is that in Jesus Christ, the New Adam, our humanity has broken through by means of this event into the space of the life and holiness of God. It has broken through because, although Jesus Christ identified himself totally with us in our flawed and sinful condition, in his own flawless goodness he made the perfect Offering for us. That atoning Sacrifice which he made on the Cross has now been taken up into God. There it remains not only valid but effective—empowered to touch and affect you and me.

So the Ascension, for all its special metaphysics, is a moral mystery of love and acceptance—the mystery that, despite the shoddiness of so much in our lives, we can, thanks to our relation with Jesus Christ, enter into the transforming presence of God.

Friday of the Sixth Week of Easter

We all know that children who ask questions in class are showing much more real engagement with the subject than those who just sit there like puddings. Putting questions to Scripture was one of the ways in which the Church Fathers liked to set out their understanding of the biblical text, and no doubt they advanced their understanding by that way as well.

That is one of the main senses in which the Fathers stand at the fountainhead of Christian Scholasticism. The Scholastic 'method', as we see from St Thomas, consisted in putting questions: setting and, if possible resolving, disputed questions. Where would life be without questions? The philosopher Kant held there were three that ran through everything we think about: What can I know? What ought I to do? What can I hope for? When I was young, a very popular radio programme was called 'Any Questions'.

But in today's Gospel our Lord says, 'When that day comes you will not ask me any questions'. This question-posing business is all meant eventually to come to its fulfillment. We are given the instinct to ask questions, to press questions, because we're made for truth, made to know and delight in the reality which the questions, in one way or another, are actually about. Some people get so wrapped up in the pleasure of asking questions they forget that the point of opening the mind is to close it on something solid (thus Chesterton).

As today's Gospel also shows, it might be better to say that question-putting comes not so much to a fulfillment but to a 'head': to our Head, our divine-human Head, the God-man Jesus Christ. When he and we see each other in the vision of God, a definitive joy will steal over our intelligence as our minds are sated with reality. We shall have no more questions, because when we see our Head we shall see how all the ways of God with man in creation and redemption pass through him, and take on in him a pattern more fulfilling than any we can imagine.

Saturday of the Sixth Week of Easter

Shall we really receive whatever we ask of the Father if we ask it in the name of the Son? We shall if what we ask for are the Paschal gifts, the fruit of the Son's Sacrifice and thus the consummation of the deepest longings of Israel and—whether they know it or not—of all the world.

After his Passover to the Father, the Son will enter again the lives of his own, this time as power and spirit and life. He will not only be *with* them, as he was in the historic ministry; he will be *in* them.

Throughout Eastertide we have been reading the Acts of the Apostles, and this is exactly what that particular New Testament book is all about. It is about the invisible yet real life of Christ in his own, in his Church. And it begins here, with Jesus' going to the Father—with his Ascension, in fact, when he became in fullness the exalted Lord. That is where the holy Gospels need to stop so that the Book of Acts can take over. From now on the story will be the story of the saints, the story of the Christ-life in the baptized.

What we are to 'ask for' is what will take this story forward: faith and love, patience and fidelity, courage and steadfastness in trials, strength in suffering, and growth in self-surrender to God.

THE SEVENTH WEEK OF EASTER

The Seventh Sunday of Easter (Year A)

On the Seventh Sunday of Eastertide, the last Sunday before Pentecost, the Church reads to us at Mass some part of the High Priestly Prayer of Jesus at the Last Supper: a prayer that was to be superlatively answered in the descent of the Spirit on the infant Church. It's a prayer that throws us into the depths of what our religion is about. 'Eternal life', says Jesus at its opening, 'is to know you, the only true God, and Jesus Christ whom you have sent'.

The High Priestly Prayer is also a prayer that cuts across all optimistic humanism. Jesus tells the disciples horribly plainly: 'I am not praying for the world'. His mission is a divine one, in which the disciples are to be prepared for the true goal of human life, and that goal is not inner-worldly, it is life with the Father. '[I] am praying for these you have given me, because they belong to you.' He is not praying for the world inasmuch as, ignorant of the Father as it is, 'the world' simply can't be the vehicle for this going beyond into God. Rather later in the Prayer, behind the verses set for today, he declares: 'O righteous Father, the world has not known you, but I have known you, and these know that you have sent me'.

For many Christians today, anxious to co-operate with their fellow-citizens of all religions or, more probably, none, in the common cause of improving the quality of life for themselves and others, words like this are found to be embarrassing. Yet in the High Priestly Prayer nothing is said against the legitimacy of ordinary good works of the sort that, whether mediated by the State or not, are a kindness to our neighbour. What the Prayer *does* say — what it resoundingly affirms — is that the excellence of our faith lies in the way that, by means of that same faith, we are taken up into the very life of the Godhead. Eternal life is 'knowing God' — not just knowing about him — and it is knowing God 'through Jesus Christ whom you have sent'.

St Thomas calls faith 'the seed of glory', and this seed is already planted in our hearts. The life of the seed derives from the energy released in the Cross and Resurrection of our Lord. That was the

moment when the Father glorified the Son so that the Son could
glorify him—glorify him in us, and in those who have been before
us and those who will come after us in the Church. That same
energy—which is the power of God for salvation—whether it be
active or dormant lies deep within us, because if the Father and
the Son are God then the Son's prayer that we might have eternal
life 'in' God just had to be heard.

The Seventh Sunday of Easter (Year B)

In what sense are the disciples of Jesus 'not in the world'—which
is how our Lord describes them in the section of his High Priestly
Prayer, made on the eve of his Passion, which we read as the
Gospel for today? The question is relevant to ourselves, because
the disciples here are not simply the holy apostles, a restricted
group of future leaders of the Church; they stand for all the
disciples who will ever be, whatever their condition in life.

We can think of this 'not being in the world' in three ways. We
can think of it in terms of our beliefs; in terms of our values; and
in terms of our priorities.

First of all, then, we can think of it in terms of our beliefs. As
Catholic Christians, many of our beliefs differ from those of other
people because they are based not on observation or reasoning but
on revelation: divine disclosure. That revelation comes to us
through history as the greatest truth there is: better—more glad-
dening, more beautiful—as well as more comprehensive. Living
with revelation, as we do, changes our mind, by giving us a
different perspective on nature, on history, on human life.

And as a consequence, then, and secondly, many of our values
are not the same as those of other people either. They are Gospel
values that stem directly from the ethos conveyed by our Lord and
his Spirit. Think of the character sketch St Paul gives of the
Christian when he lists the fruits of the Holy Spirit, or think of the
passion with which Catholics defend the human embryo, mankind's weakest members. Think too of the lives of the saints, so
different from each other but they have it in common that their
values do not reflect the way of the world.

And thirdly, our priorities are not those of this world. Our hearts are set on heaven where Christ lives in glory in the transformed condition of his Resurrection. Our care for this world is important, it is our stewardship of the original creation which was God's first gift to us, and yet it takes a subordinate place when compared with concern for the new creation, the life of grace and glory, the second gift, which alone gives the world its ultimate point and purpose.

That is rather a tall order, you may say. How on earth did I get committed to all that? You were committed at Holy Baptism when you ceased to belong to this world as the Spirit of God renewed your being at its very root. On the basis of baptismal grace we are free to love whatever is good into the world without being sucked into its false claim to self-sufficiency, to being the be-all and end-all of everything. Only God is that be-all and end-all. In the font we received in a sacramental sign the first-fruits of the Holy Spirit so that we might begin to develop a feel for the new and definitive life God has in store for those who love him. In the Holy Eucharist we take that re-orientation further, by receiving the emblems of the heavenly Banquet and in and though them the One who made all this possible, the uncreated Person of the Saviour himself.

The Seventh Sunday of Easter (Year C)

'The glory which thou hast given me I have given to them, that they may be one even as we are one.' Words of our Lord from the section of the High Priestly Prayer set as the Gospel for today. It holds out a wonderful prospect of unity for the disciples—not just for the little group of the holy apostles gathered in the Cenacle on the eve of Christ's Passion but for the countless millions the Lord sees in his mind's eye, looking far into the future with the gifts of supernatural insight that are his. 'I do not pray for these only, but also for those who will believe in me through their word.' The unity of the Church—the one, holy, catholic, and apostolic Church we profess in the Creed—is exceedingly important to Catholics because it was exceedingly important to their Lord and Master, preoccupying him, as the High Priestly Prayer shows, the night before he died.

Note how our Lord does not speak of the unity of the disciples as though it will be simply something sociological. Their unity turns on the 'glory' the Son is passing onto them, the 'glory' he has received as man from the Father. The Church father St Gregory of Nyssa, followed by others, identifies the 'glory' Christ is speaking about with the Holy Spirit, whom the Saviour will pour out on the disciples in fulfillment of the Messianic prophecies.

So the unity of the disciples will be a fruit of the descent of the Holy Spirit at Pentecost. It is, then, a divine gift, indestructible, irrevocable: part and parcel of the consummation of time through the Paschal Mystery. That is how it comes about that the Church, which is the community of Christ's disciples, can never cease to possess the unity for which the Son asked the Father. That is so even though many people will, alas, fall away from that unity, into the separation we call 'schism'.

How will the unity of the disciples show itself? For classical Catholic theology, that unity shows itself in three ways. The unity of the Church manifested at Pentecost will be a unity in obedient listening to the apostolic preaching, and therefore a unity in faith. Catholics are united by doctrine, by the contents of the Catechism which reflect the overall mind of the Church.

That unity will also be manifest as a unity in the offering of prayers, especially of the Holy Eucharist: a unity in cult and the celebration of the sacraments. Catholics are united by sharing in the same liturgical life in the different Western and Eastern traditions of worship in the Church.

Lastly, the unity of the disciples will show itself as a unity in fraternal communion and therefore a unity in social life, with charity as its regulating principle and goal. Catholics are united in the great causes they seek to further by practising the works of mercy for the assistance of human bodies and human souls.

This is exactly what we read in the account of the mother church, the church of Jerusalem, in the Book of the Acts—and the Acts of the Apostles is the continuation of the holy Gospels, it is the Gospel of the Spirit in the Spirit's continuation of the work of the Son. This is how St Luke will describe the life of the first church, the church of Jerusalem: 'They devoted themselves to the apostles' teaching and fellowship, to the breaking of bread and the prayers'.

'Teaching', 'prayer', and 'fellowship' for which a better translation of the Greek might be 'communion in charity'. Unity in these is how the 'Glory', the Holy Spirit, binds the disciples together with a unity like that of the Father and the Son. May we never be tempted to disfigure the face of the Church by departing from it.

Monday of the Seventh Week of Easter

Today's epistle finds St Paul at Ephesus with converts who have some catching up to do.

First of all, they are extremely ignorant of the doctrine of the Church in her opening yet constitutive New Testament phase (they had never heard of the Holy Spirit). But equally bad, they have never been properly initiated sacramentally: never entered through the sacramental signs into the community of the Church, the Church which at that time was in the course of receiving the climactic revelation from the apostles and so had already become the divinely appointed way of salvation for all peoples.

Fundamentally, then, these people are Jews or converts to Judaism who have seen the need for a new start, a new expression of the divine Covenant—hence their submission to the baptism practised by John the Forerunner. They are people who know, furthermore, that 'Jesus' is the name of Israel's Messiah in whom the New Covenant has been created. But that's about as far as it goes. So St Paul gives them the sacraments of initiation: Baptism and Confirmation, and the result is to us distinctly unexpected—a great outburst of glossolalia, speaking in tongues, and also what the author of Acts calls 'prophecy'.

So what is happening? Speaking in tongues, in the sense of producing sounds that have all the appearance of proper words without being such, is in itself a natural capacity. We all had it to a limited degree as babies. Here, however, it takes the stronger form of continuous ecstatic speech. We can reasonably suppose that the content of that speech was prayer and praise. A meaning too great to take in fully has been apprehended or at least surmised, and it has overloaded the system which short-circuits and produces the linguistic version of electric sparks—glossolalia.

This is done on the basis of the grace of God: it's a testimony, given by the Holy Spirit, for the good of the Church; a testimony to the fact that with Christian salvation the End of the ages has come upon the human race. This is the transcendent fulfillment for which the heart of man was made.

And that in turn gives us the key to the prophesying also: inspired interpretation of the Old Testament, witnessing to how it has all come to its intended climax in Jesus Christ, in the fire of the Holy Spirit, and the vision of the Father.

So the message sent us in such at first sight strange and off-putting form from the church at Ephesus is really the same as the message of today's Gospel: 'Be of good cheer, I have overcome the world'.

Tuesday of the Seventh Week of Easter

The Son is returning to the Father and that means he must leave behind a world which, for all its elements of natural goodness, is not transparent to the Father—not itself a sacrament of God, not an effective sign of his presence. But he is leaving behind something even more wonderful than the world: the seed of eternal life, which, as he says, is knowing God—knowing him, being in communion with him, not just knowing about him, and that 'through Jesus Christ' whom God has sent. And in today's Gospel the disciples tell him that, yes, they've got it, the penny has dropped, and they really are becoming his apostles.

How *do* we know God through Christ? Of course we cannot know him without also knowing about him, and indeed knowing about him normally comes first—chronologically, that is. How then, as a preliminary to knowing him, do we know about him? When I was an Anglican, people used to say, through the 'three C's': Canon, Creed and Crozier. The Bible found in the Canon of Scripture, the Creed which sums up the Bible, and the crozier of the bishops who teach—or ought to teach—the traditional understanding of the Creed and hence of the Bible which gives us access to God's truth. There is nothing in that formula which a Catholic would object to, except perhaps to say it is incomplete. There are truths about God that we know from Tradition as well as Scripture, and bishops, under and with the pope, teach more than what is in the Creed since doctrine continues to develop—though always in the line of the Creed and never against it. A Catholic version of how we know about God would be, then, the '4 C's': Canon, Creed, Crozier, and Catechism.

But knowing about God is only a preliminary to knowing God. The disclosure of divine truth is not only doctrine, it is also an invitation to enter into the depths of the New Covenant: the life and love of the Father as the Son shares them with us by the Holy Spirit in the sacramental living of the Church. When we really live the sacramental life—the liturgical life—doctrine comes alive for us. We incorporate it into the pattern of our lives, just as by the New Covenant we are ourselves being incorporated into the life of God.

For this to happen we don't need to be great mystics. We don't need moments of rapturous experimental awareness of God though no doubt these are very wonderful if they happen. Our faith is already knowledge, knowledge of God—and not just in the sense of knowing about God (though certainly that!) but in the further sense of enjoying a communion with him which underlines and animates all that we are.

Wednesday of the Seventh Week of Easter

Living with divine revelation changes your minds. Naturally, because it's the greatest truth ever known. We say to the world, your truth is too small. We don't identify with the world. That was St Paul's main preoccupation in his moving farewell speech to the priests of the church of Ephesus, and it fits well with what he says in his surviving letters. Don't let your thinking be conformed to that of the world; have that mind in you which was in Christ Jesus.

And because our values follow from our beliefs, our values don't correspond to the way of the world either. Paul never found a pithier way to sum it up than when addressing the Ephesian presbyterate: 'It is a more blessed thing to give than to receive'. All his moral teaching about the fruits of the Holy Spirit is there in those few little words.

And, furthermore, our priorities are not those of the world since our hearts are set on heaven where Christ lives in the glory of his Resurrection which is God's answer to all that is wrong with his world. I would connect that to the tears and embraces when the apostle left them at Ephesus. Our Lord had said of his apostles that to receive them was to receive him, so presumably to take leave of the apostles was in some sense to take leave of him too — but for the sake, since the mission of the Church required it, of a deeper communion, a more intimate fellowship, which Christ can make possible in the Holy Spirit. The people at Ephesus knew they'd been with a saint, someone who had already begun to live in the heavenly places, and not just any saint but one of those who were to guide the Church from heaven. We confess as much in the Roman Liturgy in the Preface for the feasts of the apostles. The apostles draw the Church towards the heavenly Jerusalem. They are the ones who sit there on the thrones of judgment, those whose names are inscribed on the foundation stones of the heavenly City.

As Christians we don't just look to the past, to where Jesus came from. We look to the future as the grace of God draws us towards the marriage supper of the Lamb, which is the wedding of heaven and earth. Then for the first time we shall be able to belong to the world without ceasing to belong to God because there will only be the world of God, the world in God.

Thursday of the Seventh Week of Easter

In today's reading from the Acts of the Apostles St Paul shows himself to be a smooth operator. Brought before a mixed panel of judges, part Sadducee, part Pharisee, he adopts a strategy of divine and conquer. The aspect of his message about the risen Christ which will appeal to the Pharisees — the idea of the resurrection of the body — can enable him to set them against the Sadducees, who denied that there was any form of life after death, either for the body or for the soul, and for good measure rejected the idea of pure minds — angels — as well.

The Sadducees' worldliness and materialist outlook on the human person might make us forget that they were in other respects deeply religious people, because these particular views align them with those of our atheist contemporaries who think that the brain is the mind and, consequently, that with biological death the entire person becomes extinct.

Such views were uncommon in antiquity. The later Greek philosophers regarded the immortality of the soul almost as a truism, and the Catholic Church has accepted their arguments about the impossibility of reducing things like self-reflection and conceptual thought merely to the status of bodily processes. It is part of our doctrine that the existence and immortality of the human soul can be known with certainty by the light of human reason. And if that wasn't so, if people couldn't work out for themselves that they need to prepare for a life beyond this world as well as a life within it, why should they interest themselves in a religion that centres on the post-mortem existence of someone who was crucified?

What distinguished Paul from educated pagans and placed him on the side of the Pharisees was the further belief that the human soul is essentially incomplete without the body, and so, if God is to give life and true happiness to the human being as a whole, this must involve an intention, in some unimaginable way, to reconstitute the soul-body unity of man—except that for Paul and the other apostles it wasn't unimaginable any longer: they had seen the risen Lord.

Both these beliefs—the immortality of the soul and the resurrection of the body—have, or should have, far-reaching consequences. A civilization that believes that every man and woman is, in the poet Hopkins' words, 'immortal diamond', is likely to have a higher view of humanity that one that treats them as advanced animals or sub-standard computers. And similarly there is likely to be more reverence for the human body in a culture that holds, with Christendom, that the human body is destined not for the ash-heap but for glory.

Friday of the Seventh Week of Easter

The dialogue between Christ and St Peter in today's Gospel links love of Christ to responsibility for other people.

The idea of being responsible for one's own life, though alarming, is straightforward. The idea of being responsible for someone else's life (being their shepherd, in the language of the Bible) is more difficult. Since I can't live someone else's life, how can I be responsible for it? (I leave aside the case of the profoundly mentally handicapped or the comatose and those who have—as we put it—lost their minds, who cannot exercise personal responsibility.)

We can think of it like this. Providence is constantly giving people some sort of role in the lives of others. We have a duty to see to it that in carrying out that role we tend to bring others closer to goodness and truth, because goodness and truth are the aims of all responsible action. In that sense, I can be responsible for others; I can have sheep to feed.

But this kind of creative interventionism in other peoples' lives is a delicate business. It can so easily become attempted domination or manipulation. And this is surely why our Lord makes Peter's love for him the necessary condition for the shepherding role he and his successors are to fulfil vis-à-vis the members of the universal Church.

The effect of looking to Christ with the desire to obey him, to emulate him—the desire to share, then, his sacrificial love of the Father and the Father's adopted sons and daughters—will surely, if it is authentic, curb the relentless ego of the ambitious or the self-willed. Such a person can be a rock for others; such a person can be a supreme pastor for many sheep. What we know of the rest of Peter's life and the manner of his death, which here is prophesied by Jesus, confirms that this was so.

As Catholic Christians, we look to the bishops of Rome for a sign of this selfless, creative, enabling pastoral care for the Church. The popes who have failed to give such a sign—the so-called 'bad popes'—must find a defence before the judgment-seat of Christ. For ourselves, we also need sometimes a touch of the Petrine charism if we are to be a blessing to others and not a curse. Through the intercession of the glorious apostle and martyr Peter may we be purified by a non-sentimental love for Jesus Christ and so be able to help purify others in our turn.

Saturday of the Seventh Week of Easter

'The time is coming when I shall not speak to you in figures but tell you plainly of the Father.' The disciples gathered in the Cenacle were inclined to think that this plain speaking had started already in the course of the High Priestly Prayer of Jesus of which these words formed part. That the Church of the Roman rite gives us this Gospel to listen to on the eve of Pentecost suggests that the 'plainness' became far more marked when the Spirit of truth came and launched onto the world the life of the Church.

How might that be? The apostles' preaching of the message given them by our Lord, warmed and also steadied by the gift of the Holy Spirit at Pentecost, passed over in due time into the teaching of the Church. The great images Christ used for God, for himself, and for human relations with God ('speaking in figures'), became distilled into the doctrine of the Church. And doctrine certainly is plain speaking: plain speaking about the truths of the faith where everything comes from and goes back to the Father whose revelation it is. Generally speaking, we don't go to catechisms to find inspired expression. We go to find greater clarity about who and what God is and what his plan for us entails.

There is also another point. In the Gospel according to St John it is rare to have speaking of any sort, whether in figures or plainly, without at the same time some sort of *showing*. John's is a very visual Gospel which works by means of dramatic episodes that embed the teaching given and in some way illustrate it. So we are not surprised, in the course of John's Gospel, to hear our Lord say to St Philip, 'He who has seen me has seen the Father'. Can we think, then, of a dramatic scene where Jesus 'speaks plainly' about the Father by showing us plainly who the Father is? Yes, we can. His Death and Resurrection do just that. These events speak plainly of the Father as the all-demanding but also all-giving One who inspires the Son to make his perfect Sacrifice for sin and then gives the Son back to us as the means of our raising up to grace and glory. This is what the Liturgy of Eastertide, for seven weeks that end tomorrow, has sought to tell us.

Pentecost

So today it all comes to a climax—an end but a fresh beginning as well. The whole story of the Incarnation of the Word—his birth in a manger, his Baptism, the things he said, did and suffered, his Cross, Descent to the dead, Resurrection and Ascension. Today at Pentecost we see the issue of it, the upshot of it, what it was all for: the coming of the Holy Spirit and the birth of the Church.

And what does *that* mean? Just as we have to get Pentecost into the perspective of the life of Christ, so we have to get the Incarnation into the right perspective too.

To do so, may we go back to basics? Our Creator is concerned for our dignity and our salvation. God created us as free spirits. It was because we enjoyed the dignity of freedom that he permitted evil. If we chose to commit evil, we should be allowed to. We did, and we were. But in that same moment when God willed to allow evil, he also willed for us a way of salvation that would fit our humanity, would be in accord with our nature as social animals who belong to a single family, the family of man. This is what we see happening in the Incarnation and the way of salvation opened out by it.

It was because he respected our nature as inter-acting, inter-dependent beings, joined in the single spiritual community that is humanity, that God permitted the sin of one man—the sin of Adam—to affect all other people. And by a brilliant master-stroke, so to say, God used those very same features of our human nature to restore our nature—and more than restore it, to bring it through complete fulfilment to super-fulfilment, to the life of glory.

This is what we see happening at Pentecost. The life of the Holy Spirit who, stage by stage, had filled the humanity of Christ in all its powers, from the Annunciation through the Baptism to the Resurrection, was at Pentecost extended to Jesus's disciples, his Church, which from now on was to be his Mystical Body. It is a Body where all the members are joined to their Head and animated (if they allow it) by the Holy Spirit, and take up all kinds of tasks, roles and missions that complement each other—as you might expect when people are bonded in an inter-active, inter-dependent unity.

And so we come to the really amazing part. The same act which makes us sons and daughters of God—the pouring out of the sanctifying Spirit who forgives, reconciles, restores and makes us surpass our original humanity, this act which covered us in a robe of righteousness and made us beloved children of the Father, making us sit with Christ in the heavenly places: this very same act and no other did all of that by making us members of a single, visible, social community which any sociologist could study—the Catholic Church.

But that was the right way to save people endowed with the dignity of free spirits who were also a social species. God did not choose to save us, sanctify us, as individuals, purely, for that would not respect our nature.

So he did this instead, and it makes the Church an extraordinary thing. The Church is as tangible to historians or sociologists as is Albania or the British Labour Party. But it's also so mysterious that on the day it came into being all the dead who were ready for salvation were joined to it, all those ever since who have been worthy are invisibly connected with it even if they've never heard of it, and those Christians who, mistakenly, reject it, albeit in good faith, are members of it, though not perfectly. This is the Church, founded in Mary, founded on Peter and the apostles, so as to be the sign of unity and the means of unity for the human race.

Why is this—the Church—the sign and means of uniting the whole human race and not, say the United Nations Organisation or the worldwide caliphate of Islam? The answer is given by today's Solemnity. This sign and means for unity was set up by God in the same action whereby he poured out the whole fruitfulness of his Son's Incarnation onto the world: the Spirit of love, who in eternity joins the Father and the Son. That is why the global future is not a world government or submission to Allah but the reign of charity, the love of God and neighbour through Jesus Christ our Lord.

Lightning Source UK Ltd.
Milton Keynes UK
UKOW04f0521161114

241667UK00002B/33/P